Themes in United States History

Themes in United States History

James F. Wickens

Chabot College
Hayward, California

GLENCOE PRESS
A Division of The Macmillan Company
Beverly Hills, California
Collier-Macmillan Ltd., London

Printed in the United States of America

GLENCOE PRESS
A Division of The Macmillan Company
8701 Wilshire Boulevard
Beverly Hills, California 90211
Collier-Macmillan Canada, Ltd., Toronto, Canada

Library of Congress catalog card number: 70-107043

First printing, 1970
Second printing, 1970
Third printing, 1971

FOR MY PRECIOUS CHILDREN

Timothy, Andrew & Kristina

Contents

Note to Instructors

The purpose of *Themes in United States History* is to provide the student with stimulating reading material which will facilitate his learning of American history. Hopefully he will gain a deeper insight into the meanings of such questions as, who am I?, why am I studying history? and, how can history help me to understand present day events?

To accomplish this purpose, I have combined elements of several types of history texts. *Themes in United States History* incorporates formats found in textbooks, collections of readings, and workbooks, but it is not any one of these. Unlike textbooks, which provide a chronological survey of events, this book is topical and selective. Compared to standard collections of readings, which are often detailed in content, this book offers abbreviated coverage of specific topics. I call each topical assemblage a "theme." And, at the conclusion of each of these themes is a page similar to that found in a workbook.

This combination of formats contributes to the purposeful structure of this book. The fact that it is a single volume embracing the entire span of American history eliminates the confusion facing college students who take survey courses in American history out of chronological order.

Furthermore, this book follows the academic calendar, making it virtually a ready-made lesson plan. Excluding initial classes, mid-terms, quizzes, reviews and holidays, a comfortable schedule is eight weeks per quarter and twelve weeks per semester, or twenty-four weeks per year. In accordance, *Themes in United States History* treats American history in twenty-four themes, each running about ten pages. This amount of supplemental reading does not appear to be overly demanding. (Instructors who split the course at 1877 may use Theme 10 as background material for post-Civil War industrialism, shifting Theme 13 to the first half of the book.)

Topics and problems common in American History courses provide the subjects for the themes. Current material introduces each theme to indicate a meaningful relationship between something in the present and something in the past. Then follow short and simply written pertinent excerpts, each preceded by an editorial introduction. The themes emphasize only a *few* basic ideas rather than attempting to be comprehensive.

Several specific features of this collection further facilitate the learning of American history. In order to entice the student's immediate interest, a cartoon introduces each theme. A subject definition puts the emphasis of the theme in a nutshell. A chronological outline provides quick references to correlate the time period of each theme with material in the textbook. In addition I have added very brief theme summations to consolidate student thinking on the topic. Concluding each theme is a removable workbook page for use as a classroom quiz or for student self-examination. I have designed the questions specifically to require the student to read the material thoughtfully and have allowed space for the instructor to add his own questions according to the emphasis which he desires. (For the instructor's use, a *Teacher's Manual* provides brief answers to these questions and objective questions and answers on the theme.)

I have constructed *Themes in United States History* to meet the needs of unskilled readers, particularly those in junior colleges. Generally, they have difficulty reading and comprehending material required in most college level courses of American history. There are few if any reading prerequisites for entrance into such a course, and there is little evidence to indicate their introduction in the future. To be sure, students can perform far beyond what their reading level might indicate with imaginative, inspiring and enthusiastic classroom instruction. Yet who can deny that the primary tool in the learning of college level history is an ability to read and understand the printed word?

The instructor of American history has difficulty finding reading material appropriate for his unskilled readers. Authors of present supplementary texts have geared their intellectually-oriented works to the needs of the highly motivated and skilled reader. Therefore these works, with their unexplained historical jargon, tend to lose the unskilled reader before they ever have a chance to stimulate him.

Themes in United States History offers a solution to this problem. It is an attempt to fulfill a need, to bridge the gap in the communication of ideas. In using it each instructor will maintain his own standards, and in doing so might consider the use of this collection of themes to accompany one of the fine short textbooks available. Certainly he will want to expand upon various word definitions, quoted materials and concepts. For the more aggressive student, each theme concludes with suggestions for additional work, either as outside reading or as term projects. I have intended each of these to be mutually exclusive of the other, although there is overlapping at times.

It is not possible for me to acknowledge every person who has contributed something to the writing and editing of this book. Certainly many of my students did. Nevertheless, for their major contributions to the manuscript, I wish to express my gratitude to several individuals. First, my colleagues, Robert T. Whalen and John E. Cleary of Chabot College, Hayward, offered valuable suggestions. Second, Peter F. Neumeyer, Associate Professor of English, New York State University at Stony Brook, went beyond the bounds of friendship to stimulate my thinking. Third, the librarians of Chabot College, California State College at Hayward and the University of California, Berkeley, rendered helpful guidance in the location of materials. And finally, my wife, Claire Louise Smith Wickens, encouraged me to develop ideas, offered constructive criticism of the manuscript, and endured many hardships during the creation of this book. All helped to turn a wish into a tenable reality.

Hayward, California — James F. Wickens
July 1, 1969

Themes in United States History

UNTITLED COMMENT from "Here It Comes,"
a cartoon collection by Lee Lorenz

1 Let Bygones Be Bygones?

HISTORY: A record of mankind which describes major events and attempts to explain why they took place and what resulted from them.

IT TOOK FROM	FOR THE EARTH'S POPULATION TO REACH
the beginning of man to the Neolithic age	7,990,000 years to reach 10 million
Neolithic to the Birth of Christ	10,000 years to reach 300 million
Birth of Christ to the days of Columbus	1,500 years to reach 500 million
Columbus to 1850 A.D.	350 years to reach 1 BILLION
1850 to 1925 A.D.	75 years to reach 2 BILLION
1925 to 1962 A.D.	37 years to reach 3 BILLION
and will take to 1975	13 years to reach 4 BILLION
and from there to 1985	10 years to reach 5 BILLION
and then to 1993	8 years to reach 6 BILLION
and thus by 2000	7 years to reach 7 BILLION

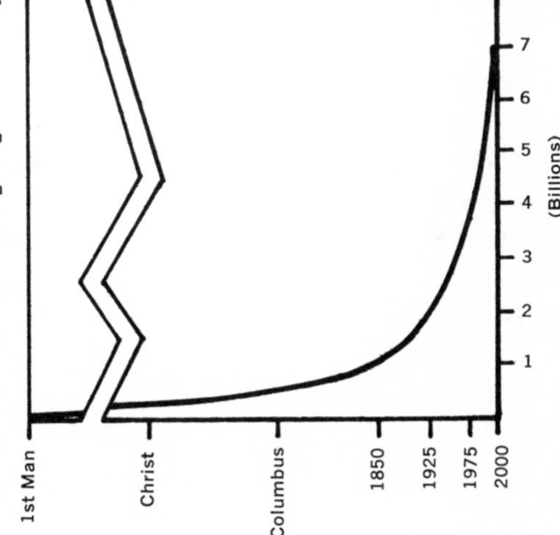

How Is History Useful?

Man bases his thinking upon past experience. Every day in practically every way all of us rely upon a past personal experience to guide us. Investment in the stock market provides an example. Among other things, investors consider past performance to determine the future prospects of the market. The following situation illustrates this point.

In April, 1968, the stock market soared to record volume on the hope of peace talks and a settlement in Vietnam. The thought that hostilities might end was enough to lift the stock market out of a decline. Foreseeing this change, Robert T. Allen used the past in his 1967 stock analysis to help predict the future.[1]

> . . . [T]he stock market has always greeted the end of a major war with enthusiasm. There were sizable rallies following both World War II and Korea, not to mention World War I and the Spanish-American War, plus probably the Civil War and the Revolutionary War, if records went back that far. There is considerable logic in this relationship. During any major war, the diversion of manpower, funds and productive capacity causes dislocations and strains, even on as large an economy as that of the U.S. Needed government programs must be deferred; there are often labor and material shortages, formal or informal price controls, and other interferences with the functioning of the free market. War also inflates corporate earnings to some extent. . . .
>
> War's end, on the other hand, not only restores the confidence factor [the people's confidence in the future] but also generally means expanded consumer markets, greater government fiscal inflexibility, and a more smoothly functioning economy. Thus, a cease-fire has been seized upon as an excuse for a lengthy rally by the stock market more than once in the past. . . .

Besides employing history as a tool for coping with the present, students may use it to prepare themselves for the future. History provides a valuable background knowledge for many walks of life. To mention a few, salesmen use past sales records to help determine their orders; journalists provide background material for current stories; lawyers refer to past cases; generals base strategy on past experience; and, even presidents consider past events as they guide the nation into the future.

---

[1]Robert T. Allen, *Business and Securities,* pamphlet (Shearson, Hammill and Co., March 1967), p. 2.

Why Study History Again?

"We've already had American history in high school. Why do we have to take it again?" college students complain. Perhaps Norman F. Cantor and Richard I. Schneider best answered that question.[2]

College freshmen in survey courses particularly need to be urged to anticipate a fundamental reshaping of their historical insights and attitudes. While it is true that history nowadays is coming to be well taught in secondary schools, in a great many high schools what passes for history is still merely a jejune miscellany of names and dates. The freshman is going to find that at the college level, chronology is merely the outer skeleton of historical study and that even total recall of every name and date in the textbook is very far from the kind of critical and imaginative thinking he will be required to undertake.

All American college freshmen will have had a high school survey course in United States history; consequently the college survey course in American history may appear at first sight to be largely a repetition of what has already been encountered. But the novice college students will be surprised to discover that even if the same textbook is used as in his senior year in high school, the level of conceptualization for the most part, and of insight into complex problems of historical change, is now much higher. Early in the term the freshman will learn that repetition of the well-known outline facts of American history is not adequate and that a much higher level of thought and communication is demanded of him.

Why Does The Study of History Not Offer Easy Solutions?

College students frequently find that the study of history offers them few simple explanations of American life. Robert V. Daniels presented reasoning behind the complexity of history.[3]

History never repeats itself exactly; no historical situation is the same as any other; even two like events differ in that the first has no precedent, while the second has. But even in this respect history can teach a lesson—namely, that nothing ever stays the same. "You cannot step twice into the same river," said the ancient Greek philosopher Heraclitus, "for fresh waters are ever

---

[2]Norman F. Cantor and Richard I. Schneider, *How to Study History* (New York: Thomas Y. Crowell, 1967), p. 7.

[3]Robert V. Daniels, *Studying History: How and Why* (Englewood Cliffs, New Jersey; Prentice-Hall, 1966), pp. 4-5. © 1966. Reprinted by permission.

flowing in upon you." The only unchanging thing in human affairs is the constancy of change itself.

The process of history is unique, but nonetheless intelligible. Each situation and event is distinct, but each is connected to all the foregoing and succeeding ones by a complex web of cause and effect, probability and accident. The present may be the consequence of accidents, or of irresistible forces, but in either case the present consequences of past events are real and irreversible. The unique present, just as each unique point in the past, is utterly unintelligible unless we understand the history of how it came to be.

While history is a record of unique happenings, it is something more than chaos. To perceive the elements of order in the chaotic record of past events is the great task of the historian. Events, people, groups, institutions fall into certain classes that exhibit at least partial regularities. We can use the words *France, king, war, caravan route* independently of particular times and people and still know more or less what we are talking about. On a broader scale the historian can conceive of historical "trends" or "processes," where one event leads to another in a more or less logical way. Thinking in such terms is very important when it comes to understanding how the present—which is really the immediate, perceivable past—has grown out of the more remote past. The same approach is the only way in which we can rationally anticipate the future—to observe the processes of change or development that appear to have been going on up to now and to project them into the future, i.e., to guess what will happen if they continue in the same way.

Why Do Historians Revise Written History?

Another reason why written history appears complex to students is because historians keep rewriting it. In fact writers have produced works on American history for over three hundred years, depicting fateful events and portraying the major characters involved in them. In the process, some historians have passed on the erroneous beliefs of one generation to the next. Sometimes historians uncover new evidence, such as a letter or diary, and the relevant facts lead to revisions of earlier historical works. At other times, the values of the historians' own societies change. Historians then adapt their interpretations to reflect these changes.

In both cases, new facts and reinterpretation, historians have challenged an accepted explanation to revise it in perspective and correct any known errors. They do so for the sake of truth. But "truth" is a difficult word to describe accurately, for it is relative. What seemed to be "true" for one era is not necessarily regarded as "true" for another.

Studying what historians believe to be true can be difficult. It requires the student to have an open mind and to use that mind to think critically about history, as Robert V. Daniels suggested.[4]

> Historical study teaches the recognition of legitimate differences of viewpoint and the difficulty of final judgments in human affairs. Historical thinking appreciates the mixture of motives and the balance of wisdom and error in any human situation. . . .
>
> Good historical study recognizes how rarely, if ever, clearcut conflicts occur between good and evil, black and white. It also recognizes the differences among the many distinct shades of gray. This is the most important lesson that history can offer its students for coping with their own world.

How Did Turner, Beard and Parrington Revise Written History?

These "shades of grey" which students must ponder also provide difficulty for the writers and teachers of history. The following review illustrated this point.[5]

> No nation ever began with a richer inheritance or more radiant prospects than the United States of America. But living up to the promise of a perfect childhood can be a terrible strain. . . . As the pioneer vanguard of the young Republic swept westward, Americans were gradually confronted by an embarrassing discrepancy between political dreams and everyday realities. There was on the one hand the agrarian, egalitarian Eden of their early (often mythical) memory, and on the other, the violent have-and-have-not realities of an incipient industrial state. . . . Where was America going? . . . Faith in progress was an essential American religion. How was it to be sustained?

Around the beginning of the twentieth century, the *Time* review noted, three historians, Frederick Jackson Turner, Charles A. Beard and Vernon L. Parrington, contributed much to the concept that American history was one of a people making steady progress toward the perfect society.

> As Turner grasped it, American democracy was neither a perfected political boon granted to the Founding Fathers by a Protestant Providence nor an inher-

---

[4]*Ibid,* pp. 9-10.

[5]"The Uses of Yesterday," review of *The Progressive Historians,* by Richard Hofstadter, in *Time,* 25 October 1968, pp. 103-104.

itance from European political theorists, but something else again. It was a unique, home-grown institution shaped on the American frontier. Free land, Turner argued, made Americans free and generous. Frontier hardship made them self-reliant and individualistic. Frontier challenges made them willing to cooperate democratically with one another. The absence of the trappings of privilege made them egalitarian.

It was in vain that later critics pointed out Turner's contradictions, observing that the frontier had also made Americans ruthless and violent and that many of the facts on which Turner based his theory did not check out. (For example, frontier settlers, who Turner insisted always wanted to broaden the vote, in fact often lagged behind their urban neighbors.) Turner's creative concept had caught the imagination, not merely of historians and students who revered him but of the people as well. It still does—witness Barry Goldwater's appeal in 1964 to the nostalgic hope of returning to the simple virtues of the American frontier.

Sharp-tongued and hard-hitting, Beard shattered the myth of America's perfect past by a frontal assault on the Founding Fathers. In *An Economic Interpretation of the Constitution,* he argued that the great document, far from promoting the general welfare, was the reactionary work of wealthy men who in 1787 stood to profit from the creation of a strong, central and, above all, solvent government (nearly half the signers had lent the Government money). By suggesting that economic interests play a strong role in human events, Beard helped bring American history closer to the bitter realities of contemporary life. By implying that businessmen had betrayed the radical spirit of the American Revolution, he made U.S. history not a long fall from grace but an enduring crusade to restore lost revolutionary rights. . . .

. . . In a series of interlocking biographical sketches—marked by Anglophobia and a gift for rhetoric—Parrington, in *Main Currents in American Thoughts,* reconstructed the U.S. cultural evolution. His notion, deeply ingrained in the American character, was that art should have a social purpose; realism, it followed, was better than fantasy. The great republic, he said, had evolved through a struggle between the ideas of Good Guy liberals, dissenters, democrats and humanitarians, like Roger Williams, Ben Franklin, and naturally, Thomas Jefferson, and Bad Guy conservatives like Jonathan Edwards, Increase Mather and Alexander Hamilton.

This kind of partisan polarity is as familiar to Americans as Sears Roebuck and peanut butter. But since World War II, modern scholarship has nit-picked Turner to death—on grounds of detailed inaccuracy and cloudy thinking. Parrington has been buried by the New Criticism [recent critics] as a prejudiced bore and a square to boot—both of which he most emphatically was. Beard has not so much been demolished as deplored for his slighting of the non-economic complexities of history.

How Do Modern Interpretations Illustrate the Complexity of History?

Writers stressing a new interpretation have recently criticized the progressive historians. John Higham identified this new viewpoint.[6]

> By reducing the importance of these turning points, the newer interpretations have enabled us to rediscover the continuity of American history, the stability of basic institutions, the toughness of the social fabric. The same result is also being attained by dissolving the persistent dualisms, which Parrington and Beard emphasized, and substituting a monistic pattern. Instead of two traditions or sections or classes deployed against one another all along the line of national development, we are told that America in the largest sense has had one unified culture. Classes have turned into myths, sections have lost their solidarity, ideologies have vaporized into climates of opinion. The phrase "the American experience" has become an incantation [ritual].

Richard Hofstadter has attacked this consensus interpretation in *The Progressive Historians,*[7] as Robert Sklar summarized.[8]

> Hofstadter . . . saves his interpretative framework for a brief final chapter, "Conflict and Consensus in American History," in which the contemporary message of his book becomes unmistakably clear—he is preaching a gentle jeremiad against the simple-minded history of his Progressive predecessors and of his New Left heirs.
>
> The argument of Hofstadter's final chapter may be summarized like this: The historians of the 1950s, in their reaction against the mistakes of the Progressive historians, obviously carried the theme of consensus in American history too far. Who would still argue that Americans basically agree on their political views and that sweet agreement has dominated our political life—when foreign war and domestic conflict threaten to tear the nation apart? Of course you young historians are right to stress conflict, only recognize what the consensus school achieved—a new sophistication about complexity of motive, interest and behavior. I have written this immense book to show you the dangers of simple-minded history. By all means write about conflicts, but do

---

[6]John Higham, "The Cult of the 'American Consensus'; Homogenizing Our History," *Commentary*, February 1959, p. 94.

[7]Richard Hofstadter, *The Progressive Historians* (New York: Alfred A. Knopf, 1968).

[8]Robert Sklar, "Historians: Simple-Minded and Complex," *The Nation,* 18 November 1968, p. 533.

so with a sense of complexity. Thereby may history contribute to holding our endangered republic together.

Refuting Hofstadter, Sklar defended those consensus historians who attacked the progressive historians.[9]

This is a very fine sermon, but it does not precisely reflect the actual issues of disagreement. The issues are more political than historical, and in ways that Hofstadter does not choose to stress. . . . He suggests that the idea of consensus in the American past is intrinsically neither conservative nor radical. He implores us, most of all, to remember the importance of comity in social life—humanity, civility, community, regard for the rights and values of others. But he leaves unstated the actual political views, implied and expressed, of his own works and the works of other historians identified with the consensus school.

. . . .

The fact of the matter is that young scholars have attacked Hofstadter's view of history not because he is in some way identified with a consensus school of history but because of the overt political views he has expressed in his historical works. Hofstadter has been a leading exponent not of a consensus view of history but of an elitist view of history. His influential historical works have concentrated on finding fault with the motives, style and perspective of political movements for social change and social justice, stressing such factors as anti-intellectualism, status-consciousness, and anti-Semitism to the neglect of specific political proposals and concrete social circumstances.

What Study Techniques Will Lead To Success?

The complexities of history have caused students to seek easier ways to succeed. While no secret formulas exist, though some students wish for one, there are specific aids to make learning easier and more meaningful. Generally, most successful students will incorporate the following six steps:

(1) *Have the Tools:* Every student of history must have and use reference works if he expects to be successful. Just as a carpenter must use his tools to build something, so the history student should have the following: (a) a collegiate dictionary to consult for word meanings and spellings; (b) a recently published atlas to check place names. He also needs a quiet place to study, uninterrupted by outside disturbances.

---

[9] *Ibid*, pp. 533-534.

(2) *Study Systematically:* Systematic study is more effective than haphazard cramming. Plan to study a little American history at a specific time each day. Spend two to three hours per week in study for each hour of class.

(3) *Learn Ideas First:* Read each chapter in the textbook in a telescopic manner. Get acquainted with the general ideas first. Skim the chapter in a few minutes and then try to answer the following questions. What does the chapter title mean? What does each subtitle mean? Do the pictures, charts, and maps illustrate any points? After scanning, page through the chapter asking and answering the same questions once again.

(4) *Study Facts Next:* Then read carefully for the details. When and why did an event occur? Who played the major roles in the event? What resulted? How do you evaluate the event?

(5) *Relate All Material:* Turn to your class notes. Try to relate your text to your class notes as well as other material.

(6) *Take Your Own Test:* Pretend you are the instructor. Make up a test, and then take it. Try to outguess the instructor.

Summary

History has many uses. Not only does it explain our past, but it assists us in understanding the present and coping with the future. Students find the learning of American history in college more complex than that in high school. The complexity is due in part to changes in historical interpretation. For example, historians such as Turner, Beard and Parrington emphasized conflict in events whereas recent historians stress consensus. Specific aids in the study of historical writings should make learning easier.

Selected References:

Note: The following material will help students further their knowledge of the subject discussed in each chapter. The asterisk (*) indicates that the work is available in paperback.

Norman E. Cantor and Richard I. Schneider, *How To Study History* (New York: Thomas Y. Crowell Company, 1967).*

A comprehensive guide which covers every aspect of the subject for undergraduates.

Robert V. Daniels, *Studying History, How and Why* (Englewood Cliffs, New Jersey: Prentice-Hall Inc., 1966).*
Similar to the above work but abbreviated.

Allan Nevins, *The Gateway To History,* revised edition (Chicago: Quadrangle Books, 1963).*
A philosophical approach of how history helps mankind.

Walter T. K. Nugent, *Creative History, An Introduction To Historical Study* (New York: J. B. Lippincott, 1967).*
An easy-to-read guide book with exercises on studying history.

TERM PROJECTS:

Note: Consult with your instructor about the possibility of working on one of the term projects listed below. He can provide you with guideposts and suggested references in their development.

A. Prepare a pro or con script for T.V. debate over the issue "Should National History Be Taught in Newly Emerging Nations?"

B. Write a history of your college from the sources available in your library and local newspaper files.

CHECKUP FOR STUDY

Name: ______________________________

(*Note:* After reading Theme 1, briefly answer the following questions. Numbers 9 and 10 are left blank for the student's or instructor's own questions.)

1. How does the chapter title relate to the subject discussed?

2. Define "history" in your own words.

3. Explain the meaning of "You cannot step twice into the same river."

4. Comment on the following title: *A True History of the Civil War.*

To remove this page: Open the book as widely as possible several times to loosen this page from the binding. Lay the book flat on your desk and gently but firmly pull this page *straight up* and away from the binding from top to bottom.

5. What major point does the review of *The Progressive Historians* reveal?

6. Explain the meaning of "the continuity of history."

7. How can you improve your study skills?

8. List and define all new words you learned in this Theme.

9.

10.

"Eighty more white men in your boat? How do we know you won't send over four or five hundred before you're finished?"

Burr Shafer, *Through More History with J. Wesley Smith,* New York: The Vanguard Press, 1958

2 The Grass Is Greener

MIGRATION: The movement of people from one country or place to another locality. Add "e" to "migration" and another word emerges: "emigration," or the process of leaving a country for permanent residence elsewhere. Add "im" to "migration" and a different word appears: "immigration," the process of entering another country for permanent residence.

REFERENCE DATES:

1492-1504 Four voyages of Columbus to America, initiating European colonization

1607	First successful British colonization, Jamestown (Va.)
1619	English introduced captured Africans.
1620	Separatists (Pilgrims) began Plymouth (Mass.)
1630	Puritans made "Great Migration" to Salem (Mass.)
1732	Georgia founded, the last of the original thirteen colonies

Where Were You Born?

Many students of today do not go to college in the locality of their birth because their families have moved. Americans seem to be in constant movement. For generations that movement has been westward, and, as Eugene Burdick suggested for California, it is still going on.[1]

> Even today, after a century of prodigious growth, California's chief source of population increase is "outsiders" who migrate to the state. . . .
>
> Why do they come? What do they seek? What are they like? Are they in flight from something dreaded or in search of something desired? Are they mostly men or mostly women? Are they the rejects of older communities, or the more aggressive and more brainy of Americans? No one knows the full answers. . . . The state grows by 1,600 persons a day (New York grows by 600 a day) and will have 5,000,000 more citizens than New York by 1975. . . .

What Caused Immigration to America?

Long before the founding of California, "outsiders" engaged in a movement to America. Explorers and conquerers like Columbus, Cortez and Pizarro before the seventeeth century opened up an entire new area for migration. In the four centuries which followed, tens of millions of people left Europe, Africa and Asia to journey to the New World. For these immigrants, America acquired the image of utopia. It represented a chance to turn hopes and goals into reality.

[1]Eugene Burdick, "From Gold Rush to Sun Rush," *The New York Times Magazine*, 14 April 1963, p. 37.

Beginning in the early seventeenth century, the English set the pace of colonization in North America. Specific reasons why individual Englishmen migrated are complex, varied and uniquely personal. Yet, for the sake of study, these motives fall into three general categories. The greatest incentive to immigration was economic improvement. Religious freedom was second and political liberty served as the third motive. Most frequently, immigration was a result of a subtle combination of all three.

What Were the Economic Motives?

Three major economic motives contributed to the peopling of the thirteen American colonies. The first of these was to find precious metals, as Charles A. Beard and Mary R. Beard vividly portrayed.[2]

> . . . The air of England was still charged with vain imaginings awakened by Spanish luck. "Why, man," ran the lines of a play written in 1605 to laud the glories of America, "all their dripping pans are pure golde, and all the chaines with which they chaine up their streets are massive golde; all the prisoners they take are fettered in golde; and for rubies and diamonds, they goes forth in holy dayes and gather 'hem by the sea-shore, to hang on their children's coates and stick in their children's caps. . . ."
>
> . . . It was naturally the soldier of fortune who first grasped at the opportunity of migrating to Virginia.

When the gold mania faded away because of the lack of success of the migrants in finding riches, the expectation of wealth from exotic crops such as tobacco created a second economic motive which stimulated immigration. Land hungry Englishmen looked with favor at the unsettled lands of America. To explain this lust for land, Marcus Lee Hansen made the following observations.[3]

> Private property and family life influenced the attitude of individuals, but it was tobacco that gave the principal impulse to the extension of settlement. Virginia had discovered a staple richer than gold. . . . In order to replenish the

---

[2]Charles A. and Mary R. Beard, *The Rise of American Civilization* (New York: The Macmillan Co., 1930), p. 38.

[3]Marcus Lee Hansen, *The Atlantic Migration, 1607-1860* (New York: Harper and Brothers, 1961 ed.), pp. 29-30.

[Virginia] company's treasury . . . a definite tract of land was granted to organized groups of Englishmen who agreed to settle servants . . . at their own expense. . . . The company itself continued to assist migrants as its means allowed. . . . A broadside issued in 1620 promised anyone who would transport a person before 1625 a grant of fifty acres on a "first division" and fifty more of a second. (footnote excluded)

This last method, known as the head-right system, became the standard technique of immigration into seventeenth century Virginia. . . . No longer was immigration financed from the Old World; that obligation had been assumed by the New.

To find financially secure individuals in England for settlement in America proved difficult. The majority of Englishmen were destitute and unable to pay for their own passage. Therefore, profit-seeking shippers, acting as brokers, proposed to prospective immigrants that they go into debt to finance their voyage.

The debtors fell into two categories. First there were "indentured servants," people who legally bound themselves to work from four to seven years. In return, their owners paid for their transportation to America and their keep during their service. The second kind of debtors were the "redemptioners." These people could pay for part of their trip. The remaining debt they agreed to repay by indenturing themselves for a set time period. Frequently whole families bound themselves to service. Abbot Emerson Smith asserted that regardless of what caused the servants to leave Europe, they would not have had the opportunity to leave if shippers had not made a profit from human cargo. Below, Smith elaborated on this third economic influence on immigration.[4]

It was profitable for English merchants trading to the colonies to load their outgoing ships with a cargo of servants, for the labor of these servants could be transferred to colonial planters at a price well above the cost of transporting them. It was profitable to the colonial planter to buy them, for he could rise from mere subsistence to prosperity only by commanding the labor of others besides himself. Hence there was a constantly active stimulant to the emigration of servants. . . .

. . . .

More than half of all persons who came to the colonies south of New Eng-

---

[4]Abbot Emerson Smith, *Colonists in Bondage: White Servitude and Convict Labor in America, 1607-1776* (Chapel Hill: University of North Carolina Press, 1947), pp. 3-5.

land were servants. . . . They formed the principal labor supply of the earlier settlement. Not until the eighteenth century were they superseded in this respect by Negroes [in slavery], and not until the nineteenth did an influx of free white workers wholly remove the need for indentured labor.

Did Immigration Ever Involve Forced Entry?

Not all persons came to America of their own free will. Shippers also profited from forced migration. Abbot Smith (pp. 67-68) described the importance of "spiriting," or the kidnapping of people, who numbered in the tens of thousands.[5]

> Vessels were constantly leaving for the colonies, and their owners or captains, anxious to get a load of servants, would pay a pound or two for each candidate produced and ask no questions. There were plenty of unsavory characters around London and the seaport towns who would not scruple to collect a few wandering children, or simple-minded adults, or drunkards asleep in the gutter, and convey them on board the ship. Once aboard, the unfortunate victim never saw the light of day until the ship was at sea. . . . This business rapidly grew in proportion and organization, and by the fifth decade of the [seventeeth] century had ceased to be a casual occupation.

Besides transporting the abducted, English shippers exported convicts to America before independence. These included felons, vagabonds, and paupers. In addition, numerous unsuccessful revolts against the crown by Scotch, Irish and English groups during this age provided plenty of military and political prisoners for colonization. Despite American colonial objections, the British government permitted an estimated fifty thousand convicts to people the colonies. Most of them went to Virginia and Maryland, as James D. Butler suggested.[6]

> If fewer transports were imported into New England than into more southern colonies, the reason was that they sold at higher rates in the Southern markets, which also by their staple, tobacco, furnished better return freight to English vessels. Virginia and Maryland were held of more commercial value than all the other United States colonies.

---

[5]*Ibid,* pp. 67-68.

[6]James D. Butler, "British Convicts Shipped to American Colonies," *American Historical Review,* 2 (1896), p. 22.

Slavery provided a third profitable source of forced migration. The twenty "Negars" left at Jamestown in 1619 by a Dutch captain began another chapter in American immigration. After the mid-seventeenth century, when British colonists created slavery in America, a brisk slave trade developed which enriched an unknown number of entrepreneurs. The following eyewitness account tells how captive Africans—coastal natives naively enticed onto ships and prisoners of tribal wars—journeyed to America. John Newton, a British slave captain who later became a Methodist minister, a hymn-writer, and an abolitionist, testified to the treatment slaves received.[7]

> . . . Accordingly, as we dare not trust them, we receive them on board, from the first as enemies; and before their number exceeds, perhaps, ten or fifteen, they are all put in irons; in most ships, two and two together. And frequently, they are not thus confined, as they most conveniently stand or move, the right hand and one foot of one to the left of the other, but across. . . . Thus they must sit, walk, or lie, for many months (sometimes for nine or ten), without any migration or relief, unless they are sick.
>
> . . . .
>
> . . . Their lodgingrooms below the deck, which are three (for the men, the boys, and the women), besides a place for the sick, are sometimes more than five feet high, and sometimes less; and this height is divided towards the middle, for slaves to line in two rows, one above the other . . . like books upon a shelf. . . .
>
> . . . The heat and smell of these rooms, when the weather will not admit of the slaves being brought upon deck . . . would be almost insupportable to a person not accustomed to them. . . .
>
> Epidemical fevers and fluxes [dysentry] . . . often break out, and infect the seamen likewise. . . . I believe nearly one-half of the slaves on board, have, sometimes, died; and the loss of a third part, in these circumstances, is not unusual [during the normal six to sixteen week trip to America].

Slave resistance to such harsh treatment was an ever-present fact of the trade. Individually slaves attempted starvation in order to hasten death. Discovery of this behavior led to whippings and forced feedings. As a group, on the other hand, the captives used ingenuity in their attempt to escape. Captain Newton recounted the results of such ventures.[8]

---

[7]Bernard Martin and Mark Spurrell (eds.), *The Journal of a Slave Trader (John Newton), 1750-1754* (London: The Epworth Press, 1962), pp. 103, 110.
[8]*Ibid,* p. 104.

. . . An attempt to rise upon [rebel against] the ship's company [crew], brings on instantaneous and horrid war; for . . . they are desperate; and where they do not conquer, they are seldom quelled without much mischief and bloodshed on both sides.

. . . Punishments, in their nature and degree, depend upon the sovereign will of the captain. . . .

I have seen them sentenced to unmerciful whippings, continued till the poor creatures have not had power to groan under their misery. . . . I have seen them agonizing for hours, I believe for days together, under the torture of the thumbscrews. . . .

In the early nineteenth century, decades before the United States freed its slaves, England abolished slavery in its empire. Thus contraband slaving developed, and the British navy attempted to control it. C. M. MacInnes described what frequently happened when a slave ship captain spotted a patrol boat.[9]

When capture by a British cruiser was imminent, it was common for the captain to throw his cargo, as well as the ship's papers, overboard. Sometimes the negroes were dropped into the ocean in irons, sometimes with weights attached to their feet, sometimes in casks. The latter method was resorted to in order that the pursuing cruiser would be delayed while the negroes were picked up, which in turn would give the slaver an opportunity to escape.

What Was the Effect of the Slave Trade on Africa?

The slave trade had a marked effect on Africa. Robert I. Rotberg calculated the results.[10]

. . . It appears that white entrepreneurs probably transferred—conservatively speaking—at least twenty-five million slaves from western Africa to America before 1888, when Brazil officially abolished slavery. (footnote excluded) But this figure does not include about ten million Africans who lost their lives during the voyages to America. It also excluded about ten million slaves who may have been exported from eastern Africa to Arabia and Asia. Tropical

---

[9]C. M. MacInnes, *England and Slavery* (Bristol, Great Britain: J. W. Arrowsmith Ltd., 1934), p. 180.

[10]Robert I. Rotberg, *A Political History of Tropical Africa* (New York: Harcourt, Brace and World, 1965), p. 152.

Africa was therefore deprived of about fifty million inhabitants because of the traffic in slaves.

WHAT WERE THE RELIGIOUS MOTIVES BEHIND MIGRATION?

Besides the enticement and constraint involved in settling people in America, the opportunity to practice one's religion without interference encouraged immigration. The story of the Pilgrims, the Mayflower and the creation of the Plymouth Colony in 1620 is well known. After the Council for New England granted the Pilgrims this right, the Council discouraged any further settlement, desiring to retain all fishing and fur trapping rights. However, financial depression in the late 1620's caused the Council to cede its choicest territory to the Massachusetts Bay Colony. The so-called "Great Migration" of the Puritans followed.

What caused the Puritan migration is a matter of debate among historians. Was it purely religious–a result of Archbishop Laud's demands for Puritan conformity to Church of England rituals? Or was it also economic–a desire for land and profit? Franklin D. Scott synthesized the interwoven subtleties of these questions.[11]

While Jamestown and the Carolinas were founded for economic reasons, religious motivations blended strongly with economic in the founding and settlement of the early New England colonies. [Richard] Hakluyt also stated that England could "provide a safe and sure place to receive people from all parts of the world that are forced to flee for the truth of God's word." This fit the requirements of Pilgrim, Puritan and Quaker leaders exactly; dissenters and Catholics both used the opportunity to colonize to escape the Church of England. Even among these groups both religious and economic motivations blended. The familiar story of the Pilgrims tells only the religious side, and of all religious groups they were one of the most sincere. But the majority of the group was not Pilgrim, and the colony was financed by a company that sought not religious freedom, but profit. This dualism is more pronounced in the case of the Puritans. The first governor of the Massachusetts Bay Colony, John Winthrop, for instance, feared the judgment of God upon England, and thought it a great service to preserve a pure remnant in the New World. But he

---

[11]Franklin D. Scott, *Emigration and Immigration* (Washington, D.C., 1963), p. 8. Reprinted by permission of the Service Center for Teachers of History of the American Historical Association.

also thought that such a colony would be wrong unless it could be an economic success and he thought too a colony could alleviate economic depression in England. This mixture of religious and economic motives may also be seen in the Quaker settlement of Pennsylvania and in the settlement of Maryland. In the latter Lord Baltimore, the proprietor, wanted to build up a landed estate; he further wanted to find a place where his fellow-Catholics could worship freely. In Pennsylvania William Penn sincerely sought refuge for his fellow-Quakers and other Pietists, but he also wanted his quitrents paid.

Simultaneously, other nationalities were emigrating from Europe for religious reasons, as Franklin D. Scott described.[12]

. . . Among the most outstanding groups to flee the religious persecutions of Europe were the Huguenots. After the revocation of the Edict of Nantes in 1685 these Protestants had to flee France; they scattered widely, with one group going to South Africa, and some 15,000 coming to the United States. They were not as numerous, however, as the various German Pietist groups, whose reasons for emigrating were also primarily religious. The Thirty Years War and its horrors had helped to stimulate in Germany a more introspective religion, both in the Lutheran and Reformed Churches and in the new Pietist sects, such as the Mennonites and Moravians. These religious groups often found life uncomfortable in Germany, for they had notions of church and state, of pacifism, and oath-taking that were not welcomed by the petty German princes under whom they lived. They were attracted to the colonies in large part through the efforts of William Penn, who while visiting the continent in 1677 had met these Pietists, whose beliefs were similar to those of the Quakers.

How Did Political Conditions Stimulate Immigration?

Much related to the religious impetus for immigration were the political motives. Political systems persecuted certain religious persons and denied others the opportunity for economic gain. However, Franklin D. Scott pointed out the difficulty of separating this motive from the others.[13]

Political events brought other colonists. In several instances Scottish rebel prisoners were sent forcibly, notably after the Jacobite rebellions in 1715 and

[12]*Ibid*, pp. 9-10.
[13]*Ibid*, pp. 10-11.

1745, and many Scotch-Irish came because of the exclusion of dissenters from office by the Test Act of 1704. The religious factor produced an added impulse for, as Presbyterians, the Scotch-Irish had difficulties with the established Church of England. And the third great factor, economic difficulty, reinforced the other two. The Scotch-Irish were descendants of those Scots who had moved to Northern Ireland early in the seventeenth century. Though they became firmly established a century later large numbers moved again, not only to America, but also to England, Germany, France, Spain, the West Indies, and even back to Scotland. The big blow against their existence in Ireland came in 1699, when the Wool Act prohibited export of Irish woolens except to England or Wales. This deprived their basic industry of important markets and became the major reason for the second move, out of Ulster to new and scattered homes. . . .

Hope for economic gain and political power actuated both the Dutch in the founding of New Netherlands on the Hudson and the Swedes in the establishment of New Sweden on the Delaware. Both peoples and both hopes were disappointed.

Thus, by the time of the American Revolution, immigration to America had an established pattern. The nation's westward movement was under way because of a combination of economic, religious and political factors. A new society had emerged, comprised mainly of Europeans who were learning to conform to the Anglo-Saxon way of life, as Franklin D. Scott suggested.[14]

A striking feature of United States history is the stubborn and lasting persistence of the English impress, not exclusive but guiding even after other nationalities were added to the scene. The English language became a language of all. The fundamental political and social structure, even the basic ideals of the new society were well set in the founding period and to a considerable extent were codified in the Constitution and maintained in the almost universal use of the common law. To a large degree it was precisely those modified Anglo-Saxon institutions and ideals, created by the first wave of immigrants, that attracted later immigrants to American shores.

Summary

The migration of people is not a modern phenomenon. This nation formed as a result of people moving from the Old World to the New.

---

[14]*Ibid,* pp. 15-16.

Why they undertook such a venture is a question which historians still ponder. Undoubtedly economic incentives were the primary cause for immigration to America, followed by religious and economic motives, often intermixed. Regardless of the reason for migration, once the immigrant settled in colonial America, English customs eventually prevailed upon his way of life.

SELECTED REFERENCES:

Marcus Lee Hansen, *The Atlantic Migration, 1607-1860* (New York: Harper and Brothers, 1961 ed.).*
A readable and scholarly work emphasizing the 1815-1860 period.

Maldwyn Allen Jones, *American Immigration* (Chicago: The University of Chicago Press, 1960).*
A simply written survey which traces the interaction of inheritance and environment.

Franklin D. Scott, *Emigration and Immigration,* Service Center for Teachers of History, Publication Number 51 (Washington, D.C., American Historical Association, 1963).*
Current interpretations incorporated into an outline analysis of the subject.

Carl Wittke, *We Who Built America, The Saga of the Immigrant,* revised edition (Cleveland: The Press of Western Reserve University, 1964).
An analysis of various nationality groups who have peopled the United States.

TERM PROJECTS:

A. Choose a nationality or ethnic group and describe in outline form its migration to the United States in a given time period.

B. Compare the political pressures causing immigration to America today with those before Independence.

CHECKUP FOR STUDY

Name: ______________________________

1. Describe the main point of this Theme in one sentence.

2. What does the Theme title mean?

3. Illustrate the difference between "emigration" and "immigration."

4. Relate the importance of Columbus to the cartoon.

To remove this page: Open the book as wide as possible several times to loosen this page from the binding. Lay the book flat on your desk and gently but firmly pull this page *straight up* and away from the binding from top to bottom.

5. Explain the difficulty in separating immigration motives.

6. Compare indentured servitude to slavery.

7. How important was economics to the "Great Migration?"

8. List as many English influences as possible which have persisted to the present.

9.

10.

"Where I've been *isn't important. What* is *important is that I've finally made a dent in the Puritan ethic."*

The New Yorker, March 8, 1969, p. 41

3 Playing It Straight!

PURITANISM: A Protestant religious philosophy opposed to certain traditional ceremonies in the Church of England. In a larger sense, a way of life, often misunderstood as morally rigid.

REFERENCE DATES:

1536-1564	John Calvin preached in Geneva, Switzerland
1620	Mayflower brought Pilgrims to Plymouth
1630	Boston founded after the "Great Migration" of Puritans

1635-1638	Roger Williams and Anne Hutchinson expelled
1691	Upon consolidation, Massachusetts became a royal colony
1692	Salem witchcraft trials; 20 executed

Are Morals Changing?

"Changin', changin', things are changin'," chants the popular singer of this age. To the lament of some, life appears to be changing too rapidly, particularly in sexual morality. Many longingly remember when women always covered their bosoms, movie houses closed on Sundays and citizens' committees banned girly magazines. Yet, in urban America today, topless entertainment, films showing intimate exchanges of love, and periodicals exhibiting nudity are multiplying in spite of protests and raids.

A more far reaching aspect of this movement has been the new look in women's apparel. "Many Americans are changing dress habits in a form of silent protest . . ." reported the *New York Times* in 1968. Women's fashions now include peek-a-boo blouses, micro-mini skirts and the Anti-Underwear Look beneath.

In support of this so-called "new morality," *Playboy* Editor Hugh M. Hefner discussed this change.[1]

> America has come alive again. And with the social revolution has come a sexual revolution as well. Gone is much of the puritan prudishness and hypocrisy of the past. But far from being representatives of a moral decline, as some would like us to believe, we are in the process of acquiring a new moral maturity and honesty in which man's body, mind and soul are in harmony rather than in conflict.
>
> This revolution is nowhere more obvious than in the changing public taste in books, magazines, newspapers, movies, television and theater. A society's communications media offer an especially sensitive gauge to the changing manners and mores of any time and in this regard the contrast between the present generation and the one just past is remarkable.

---

[1]Hugh M. Hefner, *The Playboy Philosophy,* Part I (Chicago: HMH Publishing Co., 1962), p. 17.

When Did Sexual Standards Begin to Change?

What Hugh Hefner has implied is that only recently have Americans begun to reject older sexual mores, which he labels inaccurately as "puritan." Conflict over what comprises acceptable sexual behavior has raged in America for centuries. Robert R. Bell pointed out its importance in American history.[2]

> Conflict and confusion with regard to moral values and actual behavior have been characteristic of American society from its beginning. American moralists have historically lamented the "moral" breakdown of their time; as Max Lerner points out, "in few civilizations has there been the constant sense of moral crisis as found in the United States."

Bell also noted the origins of American morality.[3]

> Few scholars would quarrel with the assertion that "The culture of Puritan New England had more to do with the shaping of our national culture than did that of any other colonial region or that of any subsequent immigrant group." (footnote excluded)
>
> Many values basic to American society today have their origins with the New England Puritans. For example, the Puritan beliefs in thrift and hard work continue to be values highly respected in theory, if not always in practice. . . .

What Was a Puritan?

Before going further, we must define the term "Puritan" by placing it in its historical setting. In the late sixteenth century, a group of Englishmen desired to purify the newly created Church of England by eliminating many Roman Catholic ceremonies. A religious philosophy, called Puritanism, developed from this movement. It relied heavily, but not solely, upon Protestant concepts propounded by the French theologian, John Calvin.

---

[2]Robert R. Bell, *Premarital Sex in a Changing Society* (Englewood Cliffs, New Jersey: Prentice-Hall, 1966), p. 2.

[3]*Ibid*, p. 17.

Central to Puritan belief was the doctrine of original sin. This concept stressed that the fall of Adam had corrupted man's nature. Only by God's selection were the souls of a few mortals predestined to Heaven upon Christ's Atonement. These "elect" Puritans learned of their salvation directly from God through a religious experience. All other people were to receive eternal damnation. At least until the mid-seventeenth century, most Puritans believed that neither church attendance nor penance could change a man's eternal destiny.

By the time England settled Jamestown (1607), the English purifiers had divided into two groups. "Presbyterians" argued in favor of mass conversion and a central church authority. "Congregationalists," the second group, insisted upon small independently run churches whose members considered themselves the only ones selected for Heaven. This sect was itself split into two factions.

The "Separatists," or "Pilgrims," desired a complete separation from the Church of England. They left England to live first in Holland and then in Plymouth (Massachusetts). The other faction, the "Puritans," desired to remain in England and purify the Church. Eventually some left to create their own holy community at Massachusetts Bay, as noted in the previous Theme.

How Have Historians Interpreted Puritanism?

Puritans who migrated to America brought with them their Puritan beliefs. Interpretations of Puritanism vary greatly, as Gerald N. Grob and George Athan Billias described.[4]

> Puritanism occupies a crucial position in the mainstream of American thought. The term "Puritanism" is normally used to signify the religious philosophy and intellectual outlook which characterized the first settlers in New England. But as the descendants of New Englanders left the Northeast to pioneer in the West, they carried with them traits of the Puritan mind clear across the continent. Many historians, therefore, have postulated a direct connection between Puritanism and the subsequent evolution of American civilization. Indeed, one colonial scholar [Perry Miller] has gone so far as to remark, "Without some understanding of Puritanism . . . there is no understanding of America." (footnote excluded)

---

[4]Gerald N. Grob and George Athan Billias, *Interpretations of American History: Patterns and Perspectives* (New York: The Free Press, 1967), pp. 71-72.

Just what the understanding of Puritanism should be, however, is a matter of dispute. To one group of historians, the Puritans were a reactionary and theocratic people opposed to freedom of thought, religious liberty, and the idea of democratic government. For these historians, Massachusetts represents a perfect case study of the kind of undemocratic colony the Puritans founded. The colony, they claimed, was dominated by a Puritan oligarchy of ministers and magistrates who worked hand-in-hand to maintain a rigid religious orthodoxy and to keep themselves in political power. Resisting change and repressing all dissenting views, these Puritan oligarchs banished independent-minded persons like Anne Hutchinson and Roger Williams whose radical ideas represented a threat to the religious aims of the colony. The Puritan clergy in particular were intolerant in their narrow mental outlook. By rejecting the new ideas of Newtonian science and being indifferent to cultural matters, the ministers froze all freedom of thought in Massachusetts and imposed a "glacial period" on the intellectual life of the colony from the 1630's to the outbreak of the American Revolution.

A second group of historians took a much more sympathetic view of the Puritans and developments in Massachusetts. To them the Puritans represented the torchbearers of religious liberty and political freedom–brave pioneers who contributed significantly to the formulation of American democracy. The strict discipline and control exercised by the Puritan oligarchy in Massachusetts was necessitated by the rigors and demands of a frontier environment. Rather than being hostile to science and indifferent to culture, the Puritan clergy did everything possible to stimulate intellectual activity. In fact, it was largely through the efforts of the ministers that the Puritans founded the first college and public school system in the American colonies. These conflicting interpretations of the Puritans and the question of the influence of Puritanism on American life began with the founding of New England and are with us still.

Why Have Some Criticized the Puritan Philosophy?

The social values which Puritanism supposedly provided Americans, hard work, thrift, social responsibility and pre-marital chastity, among other things, comprise the Puritan ethic. This philosophy came under serious attack in the early twentieth century. Critics claimed that these traditional Puritan attitudes led to crass middle class hypocrisy, including alcoholic prohibition, book burning and sexual frigidity among women. According to this interpretation, Puritanism turned out to be a blight, not a blessing.

Representative of the criticism of the value of the Puritan philosophy, the brilliant intellect of the 1920's, H. L. Mencken attacked the Puritan ethic.[5]

> There is only one honest impulse at the bottom of Puritanism, and that is the impulse to punish man with a supreme capacity for happiness—to bury him down to the miserable level of "good" men, i.e., of stupid, cowardly, and chronically unhappy men.

How Austere Were the Puritans?

From the critical bombardments of Puritanism such as the above, there developed a separate and more modern usage of the word "puritan": one who abstains from or opposes social pleasures. These pleasures would include at least an appreciation of aesthetic beauty, an indulgence in alcoholic beverages, and a freedom of extra-marital sexual relations.

Historically speaking, of course, one must be wary of equating excessive moral rigidity with seventeenth century American Puritanism. In support of this point, Perry Miller and Thomas H. Johnson pointed out several modern misconceptions about the Puritans.[6]

> . . . It was the habit of proponents for the repeal of the Eighteenth Amendment during the 1920's to dub Prohibitionists "Puritans," and cartoonists made the nation familiar with an image of the Puritan: a gaunt, lank-haired killjoy, wearing a black steeple hat and compounding for sins he was inclined to by damning those to which he had no mind. Yet any acquaintance with the Puritans of the seventeenth century will reveal at once, not only that they did not wear such hats, but also that they attired themselves in all the hues of the rainbow, and furthermore that in their daily life they imbibed what seem to us prodigious quantities of alcoholic beverages, with never the slightest inkling that they were doing anything sinful. True, they opposed drinking to excess, and ministers preached lengthy sermons condemning intoxication, but at such pious ceremonies as the ordination of new ministers the bill for rum, wine, and beer consumed by the congregation was often staggering. . . .

Miller and Johnson also denied that Puritans lacked an appreciation of aesthetic beauty.

---

[5]H. L. Mencken, *The Vintage Mencken,* ed. Alistair Cooke. (New York: Alfred A. Knopf, 1955), p. 76.

[6]Perry Miller and Thomas H. Johnson, *The Puritans,* Vol. I, rev. ed. (New York: Harper and Row, 1963), p. 2.

. . . The Puritan has acquired the reputation of having been blind to all aesthetic enjoyment and starved of beauty; yet the architecture of the Puritan age grows in the esteem of critics and the household objects of Puritan manufacture, pewter and furniture, achieve prohibitive prices by their appeal to discriminating collectors. Examples of such discrepancies between the modern usage of the word and the historical fact could be multiplied indefinitely. . . . (footnote excluded)

Investigations of Puritan morality reveal the same general inaccuracy of definition. In the matter of sex relationships, Puritan actions were no match for their ideals, as Edmund S. Morgan explained.[7]

The Puritans became inured to sexual offenses, because there were so many. The impression which one gets from reading the records of seventeenth-century New England courts is that illicit sexual intercourse was fairly common. The testimony given in cases of fornication and adultery–by far the most numerous class of criminal cases in the records–suggests that many of the early New Englanders possessed a high degree of virility and very few inhibitions. . . .

The reasons for promiscuity among Puritans were twofold. First, men left their wives in England when coming to America, expecting to win a fortune and return home. Failing to attain their objectives, these men satisfied their sexual inclinations in the colonies. And second, because servants of both sexes rarely could marry, they engaged in sexual activities when they were able to escape their master's surveillance. The punishment for such offenses was light, as Morgan pointed out.[8]

. . . The Puritans could not maintain the severe penalties which their laws provided. Although cases of adultery occurred every year, the death penalty is not known to have been applied more than three times. The usual punishment was a whipping or a fine, or both, and perhaps a branding, combined with a symbolical execution in the form of standing on the gallows for an hour with a rope about the neck. Fornication met with a lighter whipping or a lighter fine, while rape was treated in the same way as adultery. Though the Puritans established a code of laws which demanded perfection–which demanded, in other words, strict obedience to the will of God, they nevertheless knew that frail human beings could never live up to the code. . . .

. . . .

[7]Edmund S. Morgan, "The Puritans and Sex," *The New England Quarterly,* Vol. XV (1942), pp. 595-596.

[8]*Ibid,* p. 602.

. . . The result was not a society in which most of us would care to live, for the methods of prevention often caused serious interference with personal liberty. It must nevertheless be admitted that in matters of sex the Puritans showed none of the blind zeal or narrow-minded bigotry which is too often supposed to have been characteristic of them. The more one learns about these people, the less do they appear to have resembled the sad and sour portraits which their modern critics have drawn of them.

If Not the Puritans, Then Who Enforced Rigid Morals?

During much of the century which followed American independence, Puritan ideals on sexual morality appear to have taken hold. Robert Bell contended that what emerged was a double standard of sexual behavior for men and a single standard for women.[9]

During this era it was commonly believed that for "good" women the sexual relations of marriage were an unspeakable and unpleasant duty necessary for reproduction and on some occasions to satisfy the "animal" sexual needs of their husbands. Women were not expected to experience sexual pleasure and to do so often led to suspicion by the husbands and guilt by the wives. . . .

The view that "good" women had no sexual interest was strongly supported by the males in the patriarchal society. . . . To meet the male sexual need, prostitution emerged as an important social institution. It was believed that only the prostitute as a woman felt any sexual desire and enjoyed sexual relations. The patriarchal male could turn to "bad" women not only to satisfy his "animal" needs, but also to protect his "good" women from his uncontrollable sexuality. . . .

The period between the Revolution and the Civil War was probably the most restrictive period in American history on the freedom of women. . . .

How Did Morals Change?

The impetus of the mid-century surge into heavy industrialization and the accompanying urbanization contributed much to the destruction of earlier rigid morality. Bell noted that this breakdown occurred in the late nineteenth century.[10] This change helps to explain why social critics

---

[9]Bell, *op cit.*, p. 27.

[10]Bell, *op cit.*, pp. 32-33.

of the 1920's such as H. L. Mencken criticized defenders of the old morality, calling them "puritans."

With the weakening of the patriarchal family system and its traditional support from religious and business institutions, the role of the woman was undergoing significant change in the period between the Civil War and World War I. It was during and immediately following the Civil War that the dress of women changed and allowed them far more bodily freedom. . . . As [Morton M.] Hunt writes, "The Industrial Revolution has spawned the Victorian family in one century, only to undo it in the next by giving the right to love priority over the act of begetting." Women were also slowly increasing their levels of formal education and beginning to enter more occupations in greater numbers.

The first World War may have served to trigger the emerging social forces resulting in the new social patterns in the 1920s. In sexual behavior a decrease in the "sinful" view of sex, along with the new arguments for sexual expression provided by science, was bringing about important changes. Also during this period the increasing knowledge and reliability of contraception led to an increasing view of sexual intercourse as an end in itself rather than a mere means to a procreative end.

World War I was the first American war to bring large numbers of young men into contact with other cultural values. Along with the internal social changes that occurred during the war, there also was a reduction in American provincialism and an increased questioning of traditional values. The period following the first World War was also one of new living patterns due to the new urban setting. Ira L. Reiss points out that the relative anonymity of the city "helped destroy many of the older sexual standards and made possible the growth of newer, more liberal and equalitarian standards."

What Puritan Attitudes Influence Us Today?

Although the Puritan society disappeared in the eighteenth century, the Puritan impact on American life is still with us. Alan Simpson outlined this influence.[11]

1. *His contribution to our system of limited government.*—The original Puritans had a genuine basis for their distrust of arbitrary power in addition to their experience of arbitrary government. They thought that man was too sinful to be trusted with too much power. . . .

---

[11]Alan Simpson, *Puritanism in Old and New England* (Chicago: University of Chicago Press, 1958), pp. 111-114.

2. *His contribution to self-government—to the development of initiative, and self-reliance in the body of the community.*—The Puritan pilgrimage has been a perpetual pilgrimage in self-help. The significance of the dissenting chapel as a training ground for working-class leadership in English history has often been emphasized, and much the same services have been performed by the free church tradition in America. Nor should we forget, in the nineteenth century as in the seventeenth, the direct transfer from church affairs to political affairs of certain techniques of action. . . .

3. *His contribution to education.*—The most anti-intellectual Puritan has been obliged to master at least one book—and that a great one. The most intellectual Puritans, in their desire to promote saving knowledge, have thrown up academy after academy, college after college, until their influence has been writ large over the history of education to England and America.

4. *His contribution to morality.*—The Puritan code has its repellent features, but it is no bad thing to have habits of honesty, sobriety, responsibility, and hard work impressed on the community. . . .

Summary

Each generation sets its own moral standards, often to the chagrin of its predecessor. It is a historical error to apply the label "puritan" to a person who upholds the older generation's morality. Puritan moral ideals were as pure as some believe, but their practices were not. The mundane actions of Puritans differed little from those of their contemporaries. What some twentieth century social critics call "puritanism" really stems from nineteenth century ethics which developed with the rise of industrialization and urbanization. Nevertheless, the Puritan philosophy still influences present-day Americans.

Selected References:

Perry Miller, *The New England Mind: the Seventeenth Century* (Cambridge, Mass.: Beacon Press, 1954).*
A topical analysis of New England thought.

Edmund S. Morgan, *The Puritan Family: Essays on Religion and Domestic Relations in Seventeenth-Century New England,* revised edition (New York: Harper & Row, 1966).*
Discussions of Puritan life.

Alan Simpson, *Puritanism in Old and New England* (Chicago: University of Chicago Press, 1958).*
A thorough treatment of Puritanism and its manifestations on both continents.

George M. Waller, ed., *Puritanism in Early America,* Problems in American Civilization (Boston: D. C. Heath & Co., 1950).*
A collection of excerpts from conflicting historical interpretations.

TERM PROJECTS:

A. Compare Puritan book censorship to McCarthy era book burning.

B. Citing all sources used, write a critical analysis of Arthur Miller's play, *The Crucible,* based upon reviews as well as your own reading of the play.

CHECKUP FOR STUDY

Name: ______________________________

1. What historical inaccuracy did the cartoonist draw?

2. Evaluate the following book title: *The Moral Breakdown In Present-Day America.*

3. Explain predestination.

4. List several social changes which have occurred in your lifetime.

To remove this page: Open the book as wide as possible several times to loosen this page from the binding. Lay the book flat on your desk and gently but firmly pull this page *straight up* and away from the binding from top to bottom.

5. What specific aspects of Puritanism have historians debated?

6. List several ways in which the Puritan ethic affects your life today.

7. How would you evaluate Puritan artisanship?

8. What heritage did Puritanism provide us?

9.

10.

"A fine Minute Man YOU are—we've been waiting half an hour!"

Burr Shafer, *The Wonderful World of J. Wesley Smith,* New York: The Vanguard Press, 1960

4 Down With The Establishment

REVOLUTION: A successful rebellion which produces a sudden and/or fundamental change in government.

REFERENCE DATES:

1756-1763	Seven Years War eliminated French power from North America
1775	Minute Men engaged English at Lexington and Concord
1776	The "United States of America" officially created

1778	Franco-American Alliance bolstered colonist war effort
1781	Cornwallis surrendered to Washington at Yorktown
1783	Peace of Paris recognized U.S. independence

How Do Present Revolutions Compare to the American Revolution?

Nearly every year during the past generation a story of colonial demands for autonomy has made news. Sometimes by peaceful withdrawal and sometimes after bloody warfare, new nations have won their independence. The growing membership of the United Nations illustrates this fact. At its founding in 1945, fifty nations were charter members; today, that membership has increased to more than 125. Most of these new countries are in Africa and Asia, and many fought revolutionary wars for independence. In this sense, Americans have much in common with these revolutionary fighters, for the American colonists of 1776 were the first to win such a colonial war for independence.

Any further comparison of these national movements for self-determination is a dangerous one. Carl N. Degler warned us of this pitfall.[1]

> Take the example of our colonial revolution from Great Britain. On the surface it was a simple war for independence against the greatest power of the day. Viewed as such it appears strikingly similar to the Indian movement for independence or the Indonesian revolt against the Dutch. But once we probe beneath the surface the analogy quickly evaporates.
>
> A salient feature of our Revolution was that its animating purpose was deeply conservative. The colonials revolted against British rule in order to keep things as they were, not to initiate a new era. The well-known argument of the colonists that they would not accept taxation without representation was not a demand for new liberties, but an appeal for the retention of rights long enjoyed and only recently taken away by a reinvigorated British government's efforts to impose a tax on stamps and later on tea. Indeed, the whole

[1]Carl N. Degler, "The American Past, An Unsuspected Obstacle in Foreign Affairs." Reprinted from *The American Scholar,* Vol. 22, Number 2, Spring 1963. Copyright © 1963 by the United Chapters of Phi Beta Kappa. By permission of the publishers. Pp. 193-194.

revolutionary decade from 1765 to 1776 can be viewed as a conservative response of the colonials to the British government's various schemes for dealing in a new and more rational way with the governance of its empire now that the French had been successfully ejected from North America. Anyone who runs through the colonial protests of those years cannot help being impressed by their underlying similarity. . . .

What analogy can there be between this history and that of the newly independent peoples? There was in America no long-drawn-out, underground independence movement as in India under Gandhi or in Ghana under Nkrumah. Independence became a goal for Americans only as a "dernier resort," [final choice] as Washington was fond of saying. The men who pushed the American Revolution were not nationalists compelled to spend years in the jails of the colonial power, but political leaders seeking only to continue their free governments as they knew them all their lives. Fully three-quarters of the men who signed the Declaration of Independence held office under the Crown before the Revolution and under state governments immediately after the Revolution. What other colonial country today can show a similar degree of continuity of leadership across the chasm of its revolution for independence?

How Do the Communists Explain the American Revolution?

Not all historians would agree with Carl Degler that the American Revolution exhibited conservative characteristics. For example, Russian historians provide their students with a radical interpretation. A section of the Russian encyclopedia gave a synopsis of this opposing view.[2]

The War for Independence was a bourgeois revolution. Popular masses won the victory over England, playing a decisive role in the revolutionary war against England. The Negroes took an active part in the struggle against the English. As a result of the War for Independence the American people freed themselves from the colonial oppression hampering the development of productive powers. Royal lands and a large part of the property belonging to the Loyalists were confiscated, slavery in the northern states was abolished, the Church was separated from the State, and suffrage was somewhat extended. Conditions for the rise in the northern USA of the capitalistic way of development in agriculture were created by the earlier elimination of the existing

[2]From *A Soviet View of the American Past,* edited by O. Lawrence Burnette, Jr., and William Converse Haygood. Copyright © 1960 by The State Historical Society of Wisconsin. Reprinted by permission of Scott, Foresman and Company.

elements of feudalism in land ownership and by the nationalization in 1787 of lands in the West. (footnote excluded) At the same time, under the influence of the industrial revolution in England and of the increasing demand for cotton by the English textile industry, in the South of the country a slave-holding economy was established. With the transition of the plantations to the growing of cotton, slavery—as K. Marx pointed out—changed into a commercial system of exploitation. The southern USA became the source of raw materials for the English textile industry.

K. Marx and F. Engels rated highly the historical significance of the Revolutionary War for Independence in North America and emphasized that it exerted a great influence on the development of the struggle against the feudal-absolutist order in Europe. V. I. Lenin considered the War for Independence one of the great, really liberating, really revolutionary wars.

What Was the Original Explanation of the Revolution?

The nature of the remarkable events of the American Revolutionary era and the need to explain them recently led some historians to study the Revolutionists' own interpretations of events. Gordon S. Wood defined what he called the "Whig" interpretation.[3]

It was the Revolutionaries themselves who first described the peculiar character of what they had been involved in. The revolution, as those who took stock at the end of three decades of revolutionary activity noted, was not "one of those events which strikes the public eye in the subversions of laws which have usually attended the revolutions of governments." Because it did not seem to have been a typical revolution, the sources of its force and its momentum appeared strangely unaccountable. "In other revolutions, the sword had been drawn by the arm of offended freedom, under an oppression that threatened the vital powers of society." But this seemed hardly true of the American Revolution. There was none of the legendary tyranny that had so often driven desperate peoples into revolution. The Americans were not an oppressed people; they had no crushing imperial shackles to throw off. In fact, the Americans knew they were probably freer and less burdened with cumbersome feudal and monarchical restraints than any part of mankind in the eighteenth century. To its victims, the Tories, the Revolution was truly incomprehensible. Never in history, said Daniel Leonard, had there been so much

[3]Gordon S. Wood, "Rhetoric and Reality in the American Revolution," *William and Mary Quarterly,* Third series (1966), pp. 4-7.

rebellion with so "little real cause." It was, wrote Peter Oliver, "the most wanton and unnatural rebellion that ever existed." The Americans' response was out of all proportion to the stimuli. The objective social reality scarcely seemed capable of explaining a revolution.

Yet no American doubted there had been a revolution. How then was it to be justified and explained? If the American Revolution, lacking "those mad, tumultuous actions which disgraced many of the great revolutions of antiquity," was not a typical revolution, what kind of revolution was it? . . .

The Americans, "born the heirs of freedom," revolted not to create but to maintain their freedom. American society had developed differently from that of the Old World. From the time of the first settlements in the seventeenth century, wrote Samuel Williams in 1794, "every thing tended to produce, and to establish the spirit of freedom." While the speculative philosophers of Europe were laboriously searching their mind in an effort to decide the first principles of liberty, the Americans had come to experience vividly that liberty in their everyday lives. The American Revolution, said Williams, joined together these enlightened ideas with America's experience. The Revolution was thus essentially intellectual and declaratory: it "explained the business to the world, and served to confirm what nature and society had before produced." . . .

The same logic that drove the participants to view the Revolution as peculiarly intellectual also compelled Moses Coit Tyler, writing at the end of the nineteenth century, to describe the American Revolution as "preeminently a revolution caused by ideas, and pivoted on ideas." That ideas played a part in all revolutions Tyler readily admitted. But in most revolutions, like that of the French, ideas had been perceived and acted upon only when the social reality had caught up with them, only when the ideas had been given meaning and force by long-experienced "real evils." The American Revolution, said Tyler, had been different: it was directed "not against tyranny inflicted, but only against tyranny anticipated." The Americans revolted not out of actual suffering but out of reasoned principle. "Hence, more than with most other epochs of revolutionary strife, our epoch of revolutionary strife was a strife of ideas: a long warfare of political logic; a succession of annual campaigns in which the marshalling of arguments not only preceded the marshalling of armies, but often exceeded them in impression upon the final result."

What Shortcoming Does This Patriotic Interpretation Exhibit?

This original interpretation of the Whigs justified the Revolution. However, it leaves unresolved questions which the opposition Royalists raised.

Gordon Wood also explained their interpretation, known as the Tory thesis.[4]

. . . [T]he recent publication of Peter Oliver's "Origin and Progress of the American Rebellion" is of major significance, for it offers us—"by attacking the hallowed traditions of the revolution, challenging the motive of the founding fathers, and depicting revolution as passion, plotting, and violence"—an explanation of what happened quite different from what we have been recently accustomed to. Oliver's vivid portrait of the Revolutionaries with his accent on their vicious emotions and interests seriously disturbs the present Whiggish interpretation of the Revolution. It is not that Oliver's description of, say, John Adams as madly ambitious and consumingly resentful is any more correct than Adams's own description of himself as a virtuous and patriotic defender of liberty against tyranny. Both interpretations of Adams are in a sense right, but neither can comprehend the other because each is preoccupied with seemingly contradictory sets of motives. Indeed, it is really these two interpretations that have divided historians of the Revolution ever since.

Any intellectually satisfying explanation of the Revolution must encompass the Tory perspective as well as the Whig, for if we are compelled to take sides and choose between opposing motives—unconscious or avowed, passion or principle, greed or liberty—we will be endlessly caught up in the polemics of the participants themselves. We must, in other words, eventually dissolve the distinction between conscious and unconscious motives, between the Revolutionaries' stated intentions and their supposedly hidden needs and desires, a dissolution that involves somehow relating beliefs and ideas to the social world in which they operate. If we are to understand the causes of the Revolution we must therefore ultimately transcend this problem of motivation. But this we can never do as long as we attempt to explain the Revolution mainly in terms of the intentions of the participants. It is not that men's motives are unimportant; they indeed make events, including revolutions. But the purposes of men, especially in a revolution, are so numerous, so varied, and so contradictory that their complex interaction produces results that no one intended or could even foresee. It is this interaction and these results that recent historians are referring to when they speak so disparagingly of those "underlying determinants" and "impersonal and inexorable forces" bringing on the Revolution. Historical explanation which does not account for these "forces," which, in other words, relies simply on understanding the conscious intentions of the actors, will thus be limited. . . . (footnotes excluded)

---

[4]*Ibid,* pp. 15-16.

WHAT WERE THE RESULTS OF THE REVOLUTION?

The results of the American Revolution have been as debatable as the causes. Did the Revolution really change life in America, or, was it merely a conserving effort of the patriots? Twentieth century historians have argued over this question for decades.

Generally speaking, these historical interpretations fall into two groups. Pre-World War II historians, the first group, stressed the genuinely revolutionary aspects of events in the age. To them, the Revolution destroyed the old society of pre-1776 and created a new one. Since the rebellion was a class revolution, the new society emerged as democratic. The common man had gained political power. Unfortunately for America, however, the old aristocrats regained control in the 1780's. With a few concessions to the radicals, the aristocrats wrote a federal Constitution which curbed many democratic gains won earlier.

The second group, post-World War II historians, have challenged this earlier interpretation. George Athan Billias synthesized this interpretation.[5]

Since World War II, a new group of scholars—the conservative historians—has emerged to challenge the interpretations set forth by the socio-economic historians. To these scholars the Revolution was a conservative movement. On the local level, the purpose of the Revolution was to perpetuate the existing democratic social order in the colonies. On the imperial level, its aim was to protect American rights and liberties against British encroachments.

The conservative scholars view American society as having been essentially democratic in the colonial era. Property-holding was widespread, they say, and most colonists qualified as members of the middle class. Political democracy flourished because small farmers owning their own land possessed the necessary qualifications for voting. Colonial society was already largely an open society; the common man, satisfied with his social status, felt no urge to precipitate a class conflict to achieve a greater degree of democracy.

If the colonists were content on the local level, why was there a Revolution? The answer given by some conservative historians is that British imperialism endangered this democratic way of life. Robert E. Brown asserts . . . that

---

[5]George Athan Billias, ed., *The American Revolution: How Revolutionary Was It?* American Problem Studies, pp. 6-7. Copyright © 1965 by Holt, Rinehart and Winston, Inc. Reprinted by permission of Holt, Rinehart and Winston, Inc.

imperial policies after 1763 threatened the middle-class democratic society in Massachusetts and the people rose in rebellion to defend the existing social order. Thus, for Brown the Revolution was *not* revolutionary; its purpose, indeed, was to preserve the *status quo.*

Conservative historians likewise emphasize the nonrevolutionary nature of the Revolution on the imperial level. Prior to the Revolution, they point out, the colonists enjoyed many traditional rights and liberties under the British constitution. When Parliament introduced changes in governing the empire after the French and Indian War, Americans resisted these innovations on the grounds that they were contrary to the constitution. After pleading with Parliament in vain to stop exercising powers unwarranted by constitutional precedents, the colonists rebelled. But American patriots proved to be "reluctant rebels," according to conservative scholars, because they remained loyal to British institutions and practices even while fighting the mother country. As . . . Daniel J. Boorstin shows, once Americans gained their independence they carried over into the new nation those traditional rights of Englishmen that they prized so highly–trial by jury, the concept of no taxation without representation, and the rights of free speech, free petition, and free assembly. Boorstin, like Brown, concludes that the Revolution was not revolutionary, but for different reasons. Americans were fighting to maintain old freedoms, not to achieve new rights.

What role, if any, did European ideas play in the American Revolution? Boorstin holds that the radical ideas of Enlightenment thinkers had little influence on the course of the Revolution; the American people showed their political "genius" by resisting the rash desire to remake all of society in accordance with the theories of European philosophers. Bernard Bailyn . . . takes issue with Boorstin. America had already achieved the social and political reforms advocated by European philosophers, Bailyn maintains. But America's patriot leaders employed Enlightenment ideas to justify these reforms that had taken place, and, by doing so, gave added impetus and thrust to changes still under way. Thus, in the history of ideas as in other areas there is sharp disagreement as to the revolutionary nature of the Revolution.

The controversy between the conservative and socio-economic historians raises as many questions as it answers. What impact did ideas, both European and American, have upon the Revolution? How was the historian to differentiate between reforms that represented accelerated evolution and those that constituted radical revolution? To what degree did the Revolution advance democracy? And finally, was the Revolution the cause of class conflicts, or did it exacerbate [make more severe] social cleavages that already existed?

This brief survey of conflicting interpretations shows that our view of the Revolution has been a constantly changing one. Each age seems to have rewritten the history of the Revolution to suit its needs. . . .

Historians will continue to study the Revolution because of its significance in giving birth to our nation. If in the child may be seen the emerging adult, then much that is unique in America's subsequent development can be traced back to its beginnings. Locked within the answer to the question, "How revolutionary was the Revolution?" lies the meaning of what America was, and is.

Summary

Revolutions for independence are not uncommon in the present. The first of these was the American Revolution. Historical interpretations of it have varied, for people have differed over its causes. Even contemporaries of the time produced conflicting conclusions over what initiated the struggle. Whatever the causes, modern historians generally agree that the revolution does not appear to have changed American life markedly.

Selected References:

George Athan Billias, *The American Revolution: How Revolutionary Was It?*, American Problem Series (New York: Holt, Rinehart and Winston, 1965).*
A synopsis of selected readings covering many aspects of the Revolution.

Edmund S. Morgan, ed., *The American Revolution: Two Centuries of Interpretation* (Englewood Cliffs, New Jersey: Prentice-Hall, 1965).*
Contains lengthy excerpts by noted historians who differ in their explanations.

______, *The Birth of the Republic, 1763-89* (Chicago: University of Chicago Press, 1956).*
A narrative and interpretive work which introduces the reader to major issues.

Clinton L. Rossiter, *Seedtime of the Republic* (New York: Harcourt, Brace and Co., 1953).
Discusses the influence of colonial ideas and institutions on causing the Revolution.

TERM PROJECTS:

A. If you were an English Tory, how would you have replied to the Declaration of Independence.

B. Explain the relationships of France, Holland and Spain with England during the Revolution.

CHECKUP FOR STUDY

Name: ____________________

1. Briefly stated, how revolutionary was the American Revolution?

2. How did Karl Marx view the American Revolution?

3. What does Gordon S. Wood mean by the word "Whig"?

4. Briefly explain the Tory arguments against the revolution.

To remove this page: Open the book as wide as possible several times to loosen this page from the binding. Lay the book flat on your desk and gently but firmly pull this page *straight up* and away from the binding from top to bottom.

5. How could a revolution be caused by ideas?

6. What are "underlying determinants"?

7. How did earlier historians interpret revolutionary actions?

8. Why did the colonists not participate in class warfare?

9.

10.

"Wake up! You're supposed to march in the Whisky Rebellion today."

Burr Shafer, *Through History with J. Wesley Smith,* New York: The Vanguard Press, 1950

5 An Unexpected Happening

POLITICAL PARTY: An organized body which promotes candidates for public office in order to win elections and gain control of government by constitutional means.

REFERENCE DATES:

1787-1788	*The Federalist* essays were published in support of the new Constitution
1790-1792	Differences of constitutional interpretation emerged between Hamilton and Jefferson
1796	First presidential election which involved political parties

1799-1800	Rift between Hamilton and Adams split Federalists
1800	So-called "Revolution of 1800" provided victory to Jefferson and his Democratic-Republican Party
1816	Last presidential election between Federalists and Jeffersonian Republicans

What is the Difference between Republicans and Democrats?

As elections in the recent past have shown, there appear to be few major differences between established Democratic and Republican Party philosophies. To assist us in identifying party allegiance, Will Stanton provided amusing insights.[1]

It takes no more than a glance for a Republican to spot a Democrat and vice versa, although to the outsider they may appear to be almost indistinguishable. It is true that their platforms and points of view do overlap—to about the extent that a dime covers a penny. However, there does remain this narrow border of difference, and this is the area I should like to explore.

The Democrats tend to think of themselves as the more open-handed party. Surprisingly, the Republicans agree. You have to have an open hand, they say, in order to reach into somebody else's pockets. They, in turn, think of themselves as more tightfisted. Again there is agreement. They already have theirs, the Democrats point out, and they're not going to let anyone take it away.

. . . .

In general, Democrats are people trying to get someplace—Republicans are people trying to stay where they are. Both feel the government should help them do it. . . .

Critical observers are fond of referring to the Democrats as the War Party and to the Republicans as the Depression Party. No one has ever explained who started all the wars and depressions before there were Republicans and Democrats. . . .

---

[1]Will Stanton, "The View From the Fence, or How to Tell a Democrat From a Republican." Reprinted by special permission of *Ladies Home Journal,* © November, 1962, p. 58. Downe Publishing, Inc.

Stanton also listed over two dozen humorous "hints which should result in positive identification" of Democrats and Republicans. Several examples of these follow.[2]

Democrats buy most of the books that have been banned somewhere. Republicans form censorship committees and read them as a group.

Republicans study the financial pages of the newspaper. Democrats put them in the bottom of the bird cage.

Republicans raise dahlias, Dalmatians and eyebrows. Democrats raise Airedales, kids and taxes.

Democrats make up plans and then do something else. Republicans follow the plans their grandfathers made.

Republicans sleep in twin beds—some even in separate rooms. That is why there are more Democrats.

WHY DID THE FOUNDING FATHERS OBJECT TO THE RISE OF POLITICAL PARTIES?

When George Washington became President in 1789, there were no political parties in the nation. What is more, the Founding Fathers desired none. They wanted a national government based upon the new Constitution which would be powerful enough to rule over local interest groups. Nationalists such as George Washington, James Madison, Alexander Hamilton and John Jay considered these local political interests as selfish "factions" which disregarded the common good of the nation. Noble E. Cunningham, Jr., emphasized this point.[3]

. . . The most striking attitude that permeated whatever was said or done in relation to early party formation was the idea that parties were evils to be avoided or, failing in that, devices whose dangerous tendencies were to be checked. Most of the thought given to the subject of parties reflected this negative approach. The framers of the Constitution clearly did not anticipate the party system, and even those who participated in the formation of parties rarely attempted to justify their actions in terms of a party system. Many contemporaries saw the early party struggle through which they lived in the

---

[2]*Ibid,* p. 59.

[3]Noble E. Cunningham, Jr., ed., *The Making of the American Party System, 1789 to 1809* (Englewood Cliffs, New Jersey: Prentice-Hall, 1965), p. 5.

simple terms with which so sophisticated a theorist as Thomas Jefferson once equated it: "the parties of Honest men, and Rogues, into which every country is divided." Although Jefferson wrote that "in every free and deliberating society there must, from the nature of men, be opposite parties" and suggested that "perhaps this party division is necessary," it is clear from Jefferson's action that he did not think in terms of a permanent party system. He himself never admitted the validity of the Federalist party, and he began his presidency following the party victory of 1800 with serious, though unsuccessful, efforts to reconcile parties and unite the electorate. Jefferson's affirmation in his inaugural address that "we are all republicans–we are all federalists" was no idle gesture.

Lacking a theoretical basis, American parties evolved from pragmatic experience. . . .

What Did Federalist Ten Argue?

It was with these sentiments in mind that James Madison wrote in November, 1787, what is commonly called *The Federalist,* No. 10, one of eighty-five essays in which he, along with Hamilton and Jay, argued for the ratification of the new Constitution by New York. In the tenth *Federalist* Madison amazed sophisticated politicians of the time, most of whom accepted the wisdom of the French philosopher, Montesquieu (1689-1755). Montesquieu had argued that a republican form of government was impossible in a large country. Diverse interest groups would tear it apart, he asserted. Madison predicted exactly the opposite. The size of the United States and its diversity of interests would guarantee stability and justice. Permanent parties would not arise to destroy it, asserted Madison.[4]

The other point of difference is, the greater number of citizens and extent of territory which may be brought within the compass of republican than of democratic government; and it is this circumstance principally which renders factious combinations less to be dreaded in the former than in the latter. The smaller the society, the fewer probably will be the distinct parties and interests composing it; the fewer the distinct parties and interests, the more frequently will a majority be found of the same party; and the smaller the number of individuals composing a majority, and the smaller the com-

[4]James Madison, Alexander Hamilton, and John Jay, *The Federalist*. This set of articles exists in numerous editions.

pass within which they are placed, the more easily will they concert and execute their plans of oppression. Extend the sphere, and you take in a greater variety of parties and interests; you make it less probable that a majority of the whole will have a common motive to invade the rights of other citizens; or if such a common motive exists, it will be more difficult for all who feel it to discover their own strength, and to act in unison with each other. Besides other impediments, it may be remarked that where there is a consciousness of unjust or dishonorable purposes, communication is always checked by distrust in proportion to the number whose concurrence is necessary.

Hence it clearly appears that the same advantage which a republic had over a democracy, in controlling the effects of faction, is enjoyed by a large over a small republic–is enjoyed by the Union over the States comprising it. . . .

The influence of factious leaders may kindle a flame within their particular States, but will be unable to spread a general conflagration through the other States. A religious sect may degenerate into a political faction in a part of a confederacy; but the variety of sects dispersed over the entire face of it must secure the national councils against any danger from that source. A rage for paper money, for an abolition of debts, for an equal division of property, or for any other improper or wicked project will be less apt to pervade the whole body of the Union than a particular member of it; in the same proportion as such a malady is more likely to taint a particular county or district, than an entire State.

How Did the Government Function Without Parties?

With the initiation of the Washington Administration, men in government tried to answer such questions as, What must we accomplish? and How shall we solve old problems–domestic and foreign debts, revenue shortages, treaties and alliances, territorial protection, and the rights of states, to mention a few? Problems such as these had led to the demise of the Confederation by 1789. Moreover, the new federal Constitution outlined only the functions of government, not its administrative policies. If the new nation was to survive, it would have to solve these problems. Lawrence S. Kaplan described how politicians attempted to fill this void in national policy.[5]

[5]Lawrence S. Kaplan, "The Decline and Fall of Federalism: Historic Necessity?" in Howard H. Quint, *et al.*, eds. *Main Problems in American History* (Homewood, Illinois, The Dorsey Press, 1964, I), pp. 107-108. Reprinted with permission.

The result was that in the first years of the federal republic, Federalism was a movement rather than a faction shared in one way or another by the entire country. Just as Washington could be elected and re-elected without opposition, so a Jefferson and a Hamilton could sit together in his Cabinet. In the Congress Madison of Virginia might be joined by Rufus King of New York on more issues than might separate them; if they disagreed, the differences initially were not particularly ideological or partisan. Frontier farmers west of the Appalachians could look upon the federal government with favor as a source of protection from Indian attack and British or Spanish intimidation. It is unlikely that their expectations were any less selfish or less sanguine than were those of eastern speculators awaiting the government's assumption of hitherto valueless securities. For a group which has been identified with pessimism and reaction, the buoyant optimism present in much of Washington's first administration was remarkably American, if un-Federalist.

What Initiated Party Development?

Political disagreement became evident by the end of Washington's first term. With deepening emotional commitments, men debated over what the national policy was to be. Common interest groups formed at the national level. By the mid-1790's, democratic societies, or political interest groups, emerged on the local scene. Informal factions which had sprung up to debate Hamilton's economic policy began to polarize over his foreign policy, either for or against his recommendations.

During the 1790's, these factions appeared more provincial than national, often developing over a specific issue. Few offered an all-encompassing program. Furthermore, loose organization resulted in frequent group dismemberment and reorganization, particularly after an election. Nevertheless, by the election of 1796, in contradiction to Madison's forceful argument, these factions had jelled into two distinct parties. Politicians eventually labeled the two parties Federalists (Washington, Hamilton and Adams being the leaders) and Democratic-Republicans (Jefferson and Madison leading this group).

When Did the Parties Begin?

Historians differ and are often ambiguous when referring to the creation of political parties during the 1790's. For about the first half of the twentieth century, the historian Charles Beard offered the most accepted explanation of how and when political parties began. His interpretation stressed a class conflict between capitalists, merchants, manufacturers and large property owners on the one hand and small farmers and poor workers on the other. Beard believed that two specific parties developed during the Constitutional Convention. One party, the wealthy class, began as convention "federalists," before emerging in the 1790's as Federalists. The opposing party, first called "anti-federalists," later became Democratic-Republicans. In 1800, Beard asserted, the latter crushed the former, thus ending a decade of capitalist rule and initiating agrarian democracy under Thomas Jefferson.

Recent historians have challenged Beard's interpretation. A leading modern critic, William N. Chambers, contended that "parties" in the 1790's originated not out of class conflict but from conditions aiding the building of the world's first republican government.[6]

> Thus the Federalist formation began as a capital faction, extended its lines into the states and communities, evolved a structure that proved durable, took on essential political functions, united a significant combination of interests, and developed an ideology and *élan*. We may speak of a Federalist party proper by the late months of 1793 and the early months of 1794–the period marked by Washington's adherence to Federalist advisers and attitudes, the ideological clash over foreign policy after the neutrality proclamation of April 1793, the final departure of Jefferson from the Cabinet, and a substantial consolidation of the Federalist voting alignment in Congress.
>
> . . . .
>
> . . . In America's great decade of political genesis, opposition to imperious Hamilton and his Federalist phalanx was forthcoming.
>
> Signs of antipathy appeared with Hamilton's fiscal and bank proposals. As early as February 1791, Jefferson noted regretfully the existence of a strong "sect," oriented toward "monarchy." The answer, "the only corrective of what is corrupt in our present (trend) of government," was "the augmentation of the numbers of the lower house, so as to get a more agricultural representation, which may put that interest above that of the stock-jobbers." Sixteen months later, in June 1792, Jefferson complained again that the "sect" espoused the Constitution, "not as a good and sufficient thing in itself, but only as a step to an English constitution, the only thing good and sufficient in itself, in their eye." The answer once again was an enlargement, in the

---

[6]William N. Chambers, *Political Parties in a New Nation: The American Experience, 1776-1809* (New York: Oxford University Press, 1963), pp. 49-52. Copyright © 1963 by Oxford University Press, Inc. Reprinted by permission.

elections of 1792, of the national "representation" to counter-balance the capital "stock-jobbers and king-jobbers."

Such comments signalized an emerging resistance, a resistance led at first by other men who were far more vigorous in opposition than Jefferson himself was yet inclined to be.

Why Were the Original Parties So Short-lived?

Less debatable than party origins, perhaps, are the reasons for Federalist Party decay after 1800. Lawrence Kaplan provided an interesting explanation for the decline.[7]

Did the election results signify a national rejection of the incumbent party? Federalism's narrow defeat suggests nothing of the sort. True, the country was stirred to a degree by the passions of the Kentucky resolutions. Undeniably, the Federalist war taxes were unpopular. On the other hand, Adams was shown to be more popular than he had been in 1796. And deservedly so. His action had spared the country war and released it from the entangling alliances with France. But the split within the Federalist ranks blurred the image of a party that offered everything the country would support in 1800—or in 1804—peace with Europe, stable government, and commercial expansion.

Hamilton's romantic ambitions, however, stripped the veil from the mortal failing of the Federalists: their propensity for self-destruction. It was hardly their rejection of democracy that defeated them; many Republicans shared this attitude. Their demise stemmed from a refusal to accept the responsibilities of politics in America, the ability to concede some objectives to win others. Had they not grown so ideologically rigid by 1800, they might have returned to power in 1804 or in 1808. Any party proclaiming Federalist principles that could win three successive presidential elections should certainly hope to win another in the immediate future. Their apocalyptic vision of America in 1800 and afterward doomed them more than the personality conflicts within the party itself. They could not or would not even recognize that Jefferson's administration was little more than a refinement of the government they had created. Had Republicanism genuinely defeated Federalism, Federalists today might have enjoyed the favor Americans often give to battlers for lost causes. By turning their backs on their country and their swords on themselves, they merit the special reputation Americans give to suicides.

---

[7]Kaplan, *op cit,* pp. 115-116.

What is Significant About these Early Parties?

William N. Chambers asserted that early American political parties were a landmark in world history.[8]

In 1790 Alexander Hamilton, as Secretary of the Treasury in the new government of the United States, proposed to Congress the first in a long series of measures aimed at the economic development of the new nation. Before he was finished he had brought into being a powerful political engine to advance his program, to support his determined effort to shape the destiny of the infant republic. In effect, he had founded the Federalist party. He began this task fourteen years after the declaration of American independence, seven years after the treaty of peace which followed the Revolutionary War.

In 1797 Thomas Jefferson boarded a coach at Monticello, the gracious home he had built on a Virginia hilltop. After three years of retirement devoted mainly to agricultural experiments and to country life, he was on his way to the nation's capital to assume fresh duties as Vice-President. Yet the trip of a week or so was more than a return to the chores of office. It was a crucial stage in a political odyssey which was to bring him at last to full acceptance of active leadership in the opposition Republican party, a political force which was unique for its time.

The two events symbolize the genesis and ultimate establishment of national political parties on the American scene. These political engines were not only the first parties to adventure on the precarious ground of politics in an emerging nation but also the first true parties of modern times, appearing well before such formations developed in England or other European countries. They were shaped slowly and painstakingly, as part of a general progress in which the American states moved from colonial dependence and revolutionary uncertainties to become a stable, democratic, modern republic. Like the nation itself, parties were the work not only of Hamilton and Jefferson, and of other great leaders like George Washington, the industrious James Madison, and the conscientious John Adams, but of nameless lesser workers as well. The final result was not only parties but a system of competing parties in interaction. Yet no man could have said in advance just what the outcome would be.

Summary

Modern political parties have their roots in the foundations of the American system of federal government. During the Washington Administra-

[8]Chambers, *op cit,* pp. 1-2.

tion national leaders frowned upon the creation of political parties in America and tried to deter their development. However, disagreements over the direction of federal policy led common interest groups to join together and ultimately form two political parties, one of which was short-lived.

SELECTED REFERENCES:

Joseph Charles, *The Origins of the American Party System; Three essays by Joseph Charles* (New York: Harper and Brothers, 1965).*
Several essays analyzing the subject. Dates for the rise of Jeffersonian Republicans can be challenged.

Paul Goodman, *The Federalists Vs. the Jeffersonian Republicans,* American Problem Studies (New York: Holt, Rinehart and Winston, 1967).*
A collection of excerpts from works by prominent historians who differ over the origins, development and decline of early political parties.

John C. Miller, *The Federalist Era: 1789-1801* (New York: Harper and Row, 1960).*
A comprehensive, yet compact, study of the period with recent interpretations.

Leonard D. White, *The Federalists, a Study in Administrative History* (New York: Macmillan & Co., 1956).
A study in administration with insights into the most minute decisions Washington had to make.

TERM PROJECTS:

A. Describe the political contributions of any one person during the Federalist Era, excluding presidents and cabinet members.

B. Analyze in detail any one major issue you listed in your answer to question 2 on the "Checkup For Study" for this Theme.

CHECKUP FOR STUDY

Name: ______________________________

1. Explain the relationship of the cartoon to this Theme topic.

2. What do you believe to be the difference between Democrats and Republicans today?

3. From your textbooks and library references, list all points of issue between Federalists and Democratic-Republicans before 1801.

4. What is the meaning of Jefferson's statement: "We are all republicans–we are all federalists"?

To remove this page: Open the book as wide as possible several times to loosen this page from the binding. Lay the book flat on your desk and gently but firmly pull this page *straight up* and away from the binding from top to bottom.

5. What were *The Federalist* essays?

6. Define a “faction.”

7. Explain in a few words why Federalism died out.

8. How have American parties been unique in comparison to those in other countries?

9.

10.

"Oh, Jefferson is a good man—but I'm not sure I like the idea of a[nother] civilian being President."

Burr Shafer, *Through More History with J. Wesley Smith,* New York: The Vanguard Press, 1953

6 The Modern Example

PUBLIC EDUCATION: A system of tax-supported schools which qualified officials administer according to law.

REFERENCE DATES:

1801-1809 Thomas Jefferson, third President

1819 Jefferson founded the University of Virginia at Charlottesville

c. 1825 A national movement to establish public education began

1852-1853	Massachusetts followed by New York initiated the first compulsory education acts
1902	First public junior college established at Joliet, Illinois

What Future Do Junior Colleges Hold in American Education?

One of the most startling aspects of modern education is the rapid development of the junior college. Until the recent generation, many high school graduates never went to college. Today the trend is toward post-high school education, and for many that experience will be in a public supported community or junior college. Recently, Edmund J. Gleazer described the trend in a junior college education.[1]

> This fall [1968] some 60 new two-year colleges opened, bringing the total to about 960. [This figure includes private as well as public institutions.] Expansion has been occurring at the rate of almost one a week for the past eight years, and it is likely to continue until most of the states have, like Florida and California, put community colleges within commuting range of nearly all their populations. Every state now has at least one junior college, and most urban areas have one or more.

More startling than this present expansion is Sidney G. Tickton's prediction for the future.[2]

> A hard look at the possibilities for the future leads me to believe that—
>
> 1. By 1985 there are likely to be no fewer than 1,000 public junior colleges, and they are likely to enroll between 4 and 5 million students.
>
> 2. On the average, public junior colleges are likely to be much larger than they are now—with the largest institutions enrolling up to 50,000 students, possibly in a network of branch locations.
>
> 3. Extensive systems of public junior colleges, such as those now found in California, are likely to be established in many states.

When Did Public Education Begin?

While the growth of the junior college is one of the most dynamic developments in recent public education, the idea of public education

---

[1]Edmund J. Gleazer, "The Junior College Explosion," *American Education,* Vol. V (1969), p. 12.

[2]Sidney G. Tickton, "What's Ahead for Public Junior Colleges?" *Junior College Journal,* Vol. XXXIV (1963), p. 9.

itself dates back to mid-seventeenth century New England. Massachusetts Bay and other colonies passed acts requiring towns to provide a school or a teacher for the education of the young. Nevertheless, public education was not commonplace before the nineteenth century. Robert Middlekauff noted the educational situation in the colonies.[3]

When an American colonist discussed a "public school," he was not talking about the institution familiar to us since the nineteenth century; usually he simply meant a school open to anyone who wished to attend. The chances were that the school was privately owned and financed. The designation "public" was given to distinguish it from a school catering exclusively to a special group —usually a religious sect.

. . . The state sometimes participated in organizing and financing schools, but its role (outside of New England) was small. Instead, several other agencies assumed the burdens of education; chief among them were the family, apprenticeship, and private schools of various sorts.

Of these institutions early in the colonial period, the family carried the greatest burden. In the primitive conditions of settlement, other agencies did not exist. Parents had to give their children education—if any was to be given. Frequently, of course, children went untutored or picked up rudimentary vocational training while they were working.

The family continued to be an important center of training even after colonial society developed. For colonial parents, like their English forefathers, frequently placed their children with other families for rearing and training. They had good reasons for doing so: some did not trust themselves to discipline their own children vigorously enough; others, wishing to see their children acquire certain skills, apprenticed them to masters capable of providing the appropriate knowledge.

What Caused Educational Deterioration After the Revolution?

The winning of freedom from England had a negative effect on American education. William G. Carleton asserted that for about half a century after Independence, American education in general deteriorated.[4]

---

[3]Robert Middlekauff, "Education in Colonial America," *Current History,* Vol. XLI (1961), pp. 5-6.

[4]William G. Carleton, "American Education After the Revolution," *Current History,* XLI (1961), pp. 9-10.

Provisions for formal education in America in the period following the American Revolution were miscellaneous and inadequate. . . . Students, mostly from the upper classes, were prepared . . . by private tutors or in Latin grammar schools, which in New England still had some town support but elsewhere were privately conducted.

Those above the pauper classes, but not being prepared for college, got the rudiments of reading, writing, spelling and arithmetic, as well as religious and moral training, in their homes, in church schools and in private schools. . . .

. . . .

What of the children of the masses, the children of the illiterate and the poor? Their parents could not teach them and could pay no church tithes or rate-bills. Neither could they afford the few pennies a week for the dame school. Consequently, most public attention was concentrated on pauper education, for it was felt that the children of the poor should be rescued from "corruption, lewdness, and blasphemy."

. . . .

In general, the educational practices . . . represented some deterioration in the conditions which had prevailed prior to the Revolution. Indeed, in a number of ways education in all parts of the United States, including New England, worsened in the decades following the Revolution. The endowments and charities maintained by the Crown and by wealthy individual American Tories had been cut off by the Revolution. The benevolences and schools of the Anglican Church declined. . . .

Why were Americans of the late eighteenth century and the early decades of the nineteenth century so little interested in maintaining formal educational institutions for their children? It must be remembered that as late as 1820 there were only 13 cities of 8,000 inhabitants or over in the whole country and that these "city" dwellers comprised only about five per cent of the country's population. The overwhelming majority of Americans lived on scattered farms and in isolated villages. Young people learned farming, livestock tending, meat-curing, food-preserving, sewing, rude carpentry, tool mending, hunting, trapping, and fishing from the older members of their family. In the towns and cities, one learned a craft or trade by being apprenticed at an early age to a master. Economic conditions, then did not bring any widespread popular demands for education. . . .

Why is Jefferson Respected by Educators?

In the midst of this educational deterioration, Thomas Jefferson formulated the rationale for our modern attitude toward public education. While he did not originate the idea itself, he has come to be identified with the philosophy that everyone should be educated to his capacity. For example, in a letter to George Washington in 1787, Jefferson asserted: "It is an axiom in my mind that our liberty can never be safe but in the hands of the people themselves, and that too of the people with a certain degree of instruction. This is the business of the state to effect, and on a general plan."[5]

These words were not idle thoughts. They were part of an imaginative philosophy of government which Carl Becker claimed to be the basis of American democracy.[6]

> Jefferson, like Franklin, attained an international as well as a national eminence. Like Franklin, he was familiar with all of the ideas of his time, contributed something to its accumulated knowledge, and was identified with its most notable activities and events. There was indeed scarcely anything of human interest that was alien to his curious and far-ranging intelligence. Nevertheless, his name is for us inevitably associated with a certain general idea, a certain way of regarding man and the life of man, a certain political philosophy. The word that best denotes that philosophy is democracy. More than any other man we think of Jefferson as having formulated the fundamental principles of American democracy, of what we now like to call the American way of life.

If Americans were to live in a successful democracy, they would have to be wise enough to make proper decisions. The welfare of the nation depended upon the education of youth, therefore, and a low family income should not be an obstacle to that education. James B. Conant summarized Jefferson's plan of education.[7]

> . . . The author of the Declaration of Independence put the highest value on education, but the total record shows that it was education as a whole that he constantly had in mind. He was concerned throughout his life, as in the first years of the Revolution, with education for everyone irrespective of family wealth or status, and his educational plan was part and parcel of his

---

[5]Thomas Jefferson, *Papers of Thomas Jefferson,* Vol. IX, ed. Julian P. Boyd *et al.* (Princeton: Princeton University Press, 1954), p. 151.

[6]Carl Becker, "What Is Still Living in the Political Philosophy of Thomas Jefferson," *American Historical Review,* Vol. XLVIII (1943), pp. 691-692.

[7]James B. Conant, *Thomas Jefferson and the Development of Public Education* (Berkeley: University of California Press, 1962), p. 3. Reprinted by permission of the Regents of the University of California.

revolutionary political thinking. He envisaged the commonwealth of Virginia as a model republic, socially and politically different from any society in the past. To that end he envisaged a new educational pattern composed of several parts. (footnote excluded)

First of all, free elementary schools were to be provided for all future citizens. Second, free education of a more advanced nature was to be provided for a selected group of poor boys through a series of residential grammar schools which were also to serve the well-to-do on a tuition basis. The selective process was to proceed in stages over a period of years. Third, a university education was to be provided at public expense for a selected few who would benefit from this education and who would, by virtue of this education, be ready to serve the state. Fourth, a true university was to be established in the state to accommodate this last group of students and others who were adequately prepared and could afford to pay. Such, in brief, are the four objectives of Jefferson's original plan for free schools in Virginia—his four proposals.

Did Jefferson Foresee Our Modern Educational System?

Jefferson and his philosophy should not be removed from the context of his period. Jesse P. Bogue warned us not to misread Jefferson's contribution.[8]

> We may see, then . . . a democratic society demands well-educated, intelligent people. The overwhelming majority of the citizens of this country believe this and are determined to have it so. To write this belief into public policy has been one of the longest and hardest fought battles for social welfare. It is almost common knowledge that Thomas Jefferson was one of the first American leaders who clearly and strongly advocated free public education. It was necessary for prosperity; without it democracy was unthinkable.
>
> Jefferson, although prophetic, worked under some of the limitations of his own time. He was unable, perhaps for practical reasons, to advocate free public education of more than three years for all children. His plan for basic education was devised primarily for the common welfare. He nevertheless thought of the program as a method for the discovery of talented youth who by further education would become leaders in society.

---

[8]Jesse P. Bogue, *The Community College* (New York: McGraw-Hill Book Company, 1950), pp. 4-5. Copyright © 1950. Used with permission of McGraw-Hill Book Company.

What Stimulated the Growth of Public Education?

Other than the rudimentary system of public education found in New England, tax-supported education did not exist in the United States until well into the nineteenth century. It was then that many and complex changes in society stimulated the growth of public education. One such change was economic–a transition was under way from the traditional agrarian way of life to an industrial society. Skilled and educated people came into demand, and manufacturing increased local taxable wealth, providing funds for public education. Another change was political–democracy and universal white male suffrage transformed the American political structure. If the masses were to govern, the masses must be educated. A third change was social–the population grew and became more diversified. The enormous influx of immigrants, possessing a variety of foreign values, led Americans to believe that public schools could help assimilate the newcomers and unify the nation. And finally, there was an immediate change which required mass education–the steam printing press provided the first modern cheap newspapers. To enlarge their sales, newspapers waged a campaign to teach reading.

William G. Carleton discussed this educational movement.[9]

> Beginning about 1825, a great educational awakening began in America, and during the following decades, particularly in the 1830's and the 1840's, decisive educational battles were fought which laid the firm foundations of America's system of free, tax-supported, democratic and non-sectarian schools.
>
> . . . .
>
> However, it must not be supposed that the proponents of free schools had an easy time of it. Opponents vigorously fought them every step of the way. The forces ranged against free schools were led by the aristocratic classes, the conservatives, the heavy taxpayers, and those who supported or had vested interest in the church and the private schools. Inertia, too, was on the side of the opposition.

How Developed Was Public Education by 1900?

Once initiated the public system of education expanded and grew to its present stature. Between the Civil War and the early twentieth century,

---

[9]Carleton, *op cit.*, pp. 10-11.

American education adjusted to the industrial and scientific revolutions and their impact on society. Ann M. Keppel described this change.[10]

> . . . This was a period of extended public support and, consequently, of remarkable growth in numbers of institutions and students. More important, schools and colleges assumed a multiplicity of tasks not previously considered within their domain. Paradoxically, although American public education surpassed that of any other nation in the world in scope and imagination, it was attacked as too narrow, too traditional, and inappropriate to the times.
>
> In response to the varied demands of a complex, heterogeneous society, the schools and colleges hesitantly but certainly reflected the fundamental changes in the economic, social, and intellectual life of the nation. America refashioned its education and, in the process, produced schools and colleges vastly different from their pre-Civil War predecessors.

Among the new educational developments during the second half of the late nineteenth century were the high school and state university. State legislatures and local communities worked together to provide more high schools, and the federal government helped the states develop public-supported universities.

The character of higher education changed too. Traditional courses in ethics, religion and the classics gave way to emphasis on liberal arts and science. Professional schools of law, medicine and dentistry opened, and leaders in these and other new fields became university presidents and deans. And, the enrollment of women increased dramatically to force coeducational programs to develop.

Twentieth century developments have included increased federal participation, enlarged enrollments and new courses and teaching methods. Whether the present structure needs changing is debatable. Some modern day protests against this system represent a questioning of the structure's applicability to the problems of today and the future.

Where Does the Junior College Fit In?

Although conceived in the late nineteenth century, the public junior college was more an experiment than a popular reality before the mid-

---

[10]Ann M. Keppel, "Educational Patterns in the United States," *Current History,* Vol. XLI (1961), p. 15.

twentieth century. Jesse P. Bogue placed junior college development in its historical perspective.[11]

The great impetus for the two-year colleges began in the early 20th century in conjunction with the growing interest in all education. That was the time high school enrollments started to increase in a spectacular manner; colleges and universities were attracting constantly greater numbers of students. The two-year college movement is, in many respects, all of a piece with the general upsurge of public interest for more and for different kinds of education.

Expansions in the number of colleges and in enrollments have been the result of the increasing public awareness of their unique functions. Originally, these institutions were regarded as means to provide two years of education in liberal arts and sciences. As times went on it became clear that there were many community needs that could be met by the organization of curricula designed for requirements in business, industry, agriculture, education, health and other types of services. . . . Moreover, adult education became a growing function in these colleges about the mid-1930's. Since that time, enrollments of special, part-time students in the adult age brackets have been very great.

Do Junior Colleges Reflect Jefferson's Philosophy?

While Jefferson never envisioned a junior college, the institution certainly reflects the imprint of his thinking, as Claude B. Boren suggested.[12]

There is widespread acceptance of the influence of the democratic tradition toward furthering the junior college movement. . . .

. . . The public junior college represents a natural extension of the public school system, and a partial realization of the democratic ideal that secondary school and college education should be available to everyone, rich and poor alike.

An additional part of the democratic tradition has to do with stress upon the value of the individual, and the belief that each individual should be allowed, even encouraged, to develop himself to the fullest extent of his abilities. . . . The guidance function of junior colleges represents an attempt to fulfill this aim.

---

[11]Jesse P. Bogue, *The Development of Community Colleges* (Washington, D.C.: American Association of Junior Colleges, 1957), pp. 2-3.

[12]Claude B. Boren, "Why a Junior College Movement?" *Junior College Journal,* Vol. XXIV (1954), pp. 348-349.

Summary

Educating all the people at public expense dates back to colonial America. Then it was more an ideal than a reality. Not until the nineteenth century did public education become commonplace. The public did not attend school en masse until after Thomas Jefferson had formulated the rationale for mass education and changes in society had required its acceptance. The junior college is a twentieth century example of the remarkable growth in public education.

Selected References:

James B. Conant, *Thomas Jefferson and the Development of Public Education* (Berkeley: University of California Press, 1962).
Three essays which trace Jefferson's educational ideals.

Current History, Vol. 41 (July, 1961).*
A series of articles which discuss the history of education and the role of government.

Gordon C. Lee, ed., *Crusade Against Ignorance: Thomas Jefferson on Education,* Classics in Education, No. 6 (New York: Bureau of Publications, Teacher's College, Columbia University, 1961).
A compilation of Jefferson's letters on education.

Merrill D. Peterson, *The Jeffersonian Image in the American Mind* (New York: Oxford University Press, 1960).*
The meaning of "Jefferson" to different generations.

Term Projects:

A. Compare and contrast the educational attitudes of Horace Mann with those of Thomas Jefferson.

B. Discuss the pros and cons of charging tuition at community colleges.

CHECKUP FOR STUDY

Name: ______________________________

1. What does this Theme title mean?

2. Compare the role of a colonial family in a child's education with that of your own family in your education.

3. Why did people lack interest in education in Washington's day?

4. In a few words, what was Jefferson's philosophy of education?

To remove this page: Open the book as wide as possible several times to loosen this page from the binding. Lay the book flat on your desk and gently but firmly pull this page *straight up* and away from the binding from top to bottom.

5. List those major points creating public interest in education.

6. When did public education grow dramatically?

7. Who opposed public education before the Civil War?

8. What is the relationship between Jefferson and junior colleges?

9.

10.

"Writing another one of your little protest songs, Mr. Key?"
The Saturday Evening Post, February 24, 1968, p. 62

7 Sitting On The Fence

NEUTRALITY: A national policy of not choosing sides during a war between other nations. The peaceful nation demands respect of its rights which it frequently gains through treaty.

REFERENCE DATES:

1807	H.M.S. *Leopard* attacked the U.S.S. *Chesapeake;* Embargo Act invoked until 1809
1811	"War Hawks" controlled Congress; Battle of Tippecanoe fought
1812	(June 18) Congress declared war on England; U.S. initiated a conquest of Canada

1814-1815	Hartford Convention discredited Federalist disunion plans
1814	British burned Washington D.C. and attacked Fort McHenry; Peace of Ghent ended war on Christmas Eve
1815	Battle of New Orleans won by Andrew Jackson

What Role Does Neutralism Play in the World Today?

Neutralism plays an important role in present world affairs. As a policy, neutralism is the basis for nonalignment in the Cold War. The nonaligned neutral countries, numbering over one-third of all nations, exert a strong influence on international events. Khalid I. Babaa defined the significance of neutralism.[1]

> The "Third Force," in the United States and outside it, is not a bloc in the literary sense of the word, but rather a "group" or "caucus" which convenes when the occasion arises to co-operate in settling international disputes that relate to the Cold War—and thus contributes to world peace and tranquility. From a neutralist or nonaligned point of view, international affairs after the Second World War developed in stages: the first, the immediate postwar stage, the second climaxed by the Suez invasion, and the third climaxed by the Cuban crisis. At the United Nations, the "Third Force" exercises influence in international affairs far greater than the economic or military strength of its adherents warrant. The Soviet Union identified itself with the aspirations of the nonaligned and neutralist states rather than the other way around. Neutralist countries share in common the endeavor to work for lessening international tension, to support the right of dependent peoples for self-determination, to oppose colonialism in all of its manifestations, and to struggle for disarmament and the prevention of atomic weapons for the sake of humanity at large. The neutralist states influence the decisions and tendencies of the United Nations, and the latter, in turn, influence the destinies of those states which find in the world organization not only protection from the dangers of global war, or local and limited ones, but also a confidence and dignity unequaled in modern history.

---

[1]Khalid I. Babaa, "The 'Third Force' and the United Nations," *Annals of The American Academy of Political and Social Scientists,* Vol. 362 (1965), p. 81.

WHY DID THE UNITED STATES BECOME NEUTRALIST?

The United States, too, once used neutralism as a guiding principle in foreign affairs. As a young nation, it sponsored the rights of neutrals, a policy which persisted well into the twentieth century. Richard W. Leopold detailed these origins.[2]

. . . Less than eleven weeks after declaring independence, the Continental Congress drafted a model plan for securing neutral rights through treaties. Reflecting both the nation's lack of sea power and its abundance of exportable grain, the plan set forth three objectives. The first was that neutral ships could carry without fear of capture all goods other than contraband, no matter who held the title. This theory that the neutral flag of the vessel protected its cargo was known as "free ships make free goods." The second goal was to give a narrow definition to contraband of war. Specifically, the United States wished to confine those articles that could be confiscated to arms and munitions and to exempt foodstuffs and naval stores. A final aim was to establish the right of neutrals to transport goods other than contraband from one unblockaded port to another, even to those which under normal conditions were closed to foreign nations.

This plan of September 17, 1776, did not correspond to eighteenth-century maritime practices. It was objectionable to England, Spain, and other countries who in time of peace monopolized the trade of their empires and who in time of war counted on their fleets to deprive the enemy of all seaborne commerce. The doctrine that free ships make free goods was not widely accepted, and a British Rule of 1756 forbade neutrals to enter during war those harbors from which they were barred in peace. The big-navy powers tended to expand, not contract, the contraband list and to declare a coast under blockade even when it was insufficiently patrolled. In the face of such opposition, the Plan of 1776 remained largely an ideal. Agreements incorporating its provisions were signed with France on February 6, 1778, with Holland on October 8, 1782, and with Sweden on April 3, 1783. No agreements could be obtained from England, Spain, or Russia. These omissions left American shipping unprotected during any war involving the Mistress of the Seas. Yet on May 7, 1784, Congress adopted a second and more ambitious plan. It proposed to abolish contraband entirely and to define blockades precisely. Only one treaty, that with Prussia on September 10, 1785, was concluded under the Plan of 1784.

---

[2]Richard W. Leopold, *The Growth of American Foreign Policy, A History* (New York: Alfred A. Knopf, 1962), pp. 30-32. © Copyright 1962 by Richard W. Leopold. Reprinted by permission of Alfred A. Knopf, Inc.

Undoubtedly the founding fathers expected the young republic to reap, not relinquish, the benefits of neutral rights in a global conflict. On July 11, 1787, Madison insisted that wartime trade was a source of wealth the United States ought not to deny its citizens. Jefferson expressed the hope on July 4, 1790, that "the new world will fatten on the follies of the old." After hostilities had commenced, President Washington urged Congress on December 7, 1796, to create a navy so as to prevent those violations of rights which might leave the neutral no option but to declare war. On May 16, 1797, President John Adams argued that it was imperative to consult other neutrals to safeguard those rights and that such consultation would not violate the policy of isolationism. In short, there was little disposition to withdraw into a continental economy whenever the world was at war. On the other hand, these early statesmen were neither foolhardy nor doctrinaire. Although not prepared to abandon neutral rights at the first sign of danger, they were unwilling to insist upon them at the cost of war. Between 1794 and 1812 they made many concessions to escape involvement in the European struggle, but they did not lose sight of their long-range goal, and they renewed their attempts after 1815 to vindicate those rights.

What Was the First Argument Madison Gave for the War of 1812?

When the United States felt that it was losing more by neutrality than it could gain by war, it fought. Historians frequently refer to this event, the War of 1812, as "the second war for independence." George Dangerfield evaluated President Madison's first argument in his request that Congress replace neutrality with a policy of war against England.[3]

The so-called War Message, when at length it was sent to Congress on June 1, 1812, may not rank high in polemical literature, but it was, as to four-fifths of its contents, a dignified and forcible presentation of the American case against Great Britain. It did not go back beyond the year 1803. It omitted "unrepaired wrongs of inferior magnitude," though these might have thronged its pages. It was content to offer, under five heads, a series of major British acts hostile to the United States as an independent and neutral nation.

" 'British cruisers,' the President began, 'have been in the continued practice of violating the American flag on the great highway of nations, and of carrying off persons sailing under it, not in the exercise of a belligerent right

[3]George Dangerfield, *The Era of Good Feelings* (New York: Harcourt, Brace & World, Inc., 1952), pp. 21, 22. Copyright, 1952, by Harcourt, Brace and reprinted with their permission.

founded on the law of nations against an enemy, but of a municipal prerogative over British subjects. British jurisdiction is thus extended to neutral vessels in a situation where no laws can operate but the law of nations and the law of the country to which the vessels belong. . . . The practice, hence, is so far from affecting British subjects alone that, under the pretext of searching for those, thousands of American citizens, under the safeguard of public law and of their national flag, have been torn from their country and from everything dear to them; have been dragged on board ships of war of a foreign nation and exposed, under the severity of their discipline, to be exiled to the most distant and deadly climes, to risk their lives in the battles of their oppressors, and to be the melancholy instruments of taking away those of their own brethren.' "

It may well be argued that, in continuing with the practice of impressing American seamen after the battle of Trafalgar had made her mistress of the seas, Great Britain had committed not only a crime, which was bad, but an error, which was worse. It is surely impolitic to goad with insults a country with whom it is increasingly to one's interest to stay at peace. It is sufficient to say that had Madison been able to allude, not to "thousands" of impressed Americans, but only to one, he would have had, then and there, his *casus belli* [cause for war]. Great Britain, however, had received no warning that America intended to make war on such a ground; and . . . impressment, though bitterly resented, had up to this point been officially considered as irrelevant to the main issues. It would not have been casuistical in the British had they maintained that, in putting impressment in its rightful place at the head of his list of grievances, Madison had not strengthened his argument but weakened it.

What Were the Second, Third and Fourth Arguments for War?

George Dangerfield analyzed three more points in Madison's war message.[4]

His second complaint was open to the same objection. He went on to say that British cruisers, not content with enforcing their country's municipal law upon an international highway, had violated the rights and peace of the coasts of America. "They hover over and harass our entering and departing commerce. To the most insulting pretensions they have added the most lawless proceedings in our very harbors, and have wantonly spilt American blood within the sanctuary of our territorial jurisdiction." This was irresistibly true: but this, too, strange as it may seem, had never before been advanced as a ground for war.

[4]*Ibid*, pp. 22-23.

The President then presented a third grievance which, upon any consideration, was unexceptionable. "Under pretended blockades, without the presence of an adequate force and sometimes without the practicability of applying one, our commerce has been plundered in every sea, the great staples of our country have been cut off from their legitimate interests." To make matters worse, the British had had the hypocrisy to declare "as the true definition of a legal blockade 'that particular ports must be actually invested and previous warning given to vessels bound to them not to enter.' "

Madison had now reached the heart of the matter. His fourth grievance referred to a gross extension of this system of pretended or "paper" blockades. "Not content with these occasional expedients for laying waste our neutral trade, the cabinets of Britain resorted at length to the sweeping system of blockades, under the name of orders in council, which has been molded and managed as might best suit its political views, its commercial jealousies, or the avidity of British cruisers." It was against the unflattering pretensions of these Orders-in-Council, which interdicted the coasts of Europe to American commerce and enforced the interdiction outside the harbor of New York, that Jefferson and Madison had aimed their policy of peaceful coercion. The President now permitted himself a display of bad temper not inappropriate to the complex system of robbery, whose ramifications he proceeded to summarize:

"It has become, indeed, sufficiently certain that the commerce of the United States is to be sacrificed, not as interfering with the belligerent rights of Great Britain; not as supplying the wants of her enemies, which she herself supplies; but as interfering with the monopoly which she covets for her own commerce and navigation. She carries on a war against the lawful commerce of a friend that she may the better carry on a commerce with an enemy—a commerce polluted by the forgeries and perjuries which are for the most part the only passports by which it can succeed."

Had the message ended at this point, it would have represented the legitimate complaint of a pacific, unmilitary nation which was being forced into war against its own will because of a gross violation of its neutral rights. . . .

Did the Maritime Issue Cause War?

Some historians, led by A. L. Burt, have accepted these four reasons—the maritime issue—as the primary cause of the War of 1812. Bradford Perkins summarized their viewpoint.[5]

[5]Bradford Perkins, ed., *The Causes of the War of 1812: National Honor or National Interest,* American Problem Studies (New York: Holt, Rinehart, and Winston, 1962), pp. 2-3.

The maritime interpretation stresses the impressment of American seamen, the orders in council interrupting American trade on the high seas, and the unprecedentedly broad blockade of enemy ports carried out by the Royal Navy. Impressment deprived the American marine of much needed seamen and undermined the honor of the young nation by showing that its flag could not protect those who served under it. Almost from the beginning of independence, at least since 1790, American statesmen protested against impressment. . . .

Ships and cargoes, as well as seamen, fell prey to the British. The dispute concerning these seizures was almost as old, as a matter of fact, as the controversy over impressment, for it went back to the early days of the Franco-British war begun in 1793. For more than a decade British policy fluctuated, and America chose to tolerate seizures that were not numerous enough to prevent a great commercial boom. Then, in 1805, Britain stepped up the pressure. . . . Despite several modifications, notably in the order in council of April 1809, British policy remained essentially unchanged until the war came. American protests were ignored or rejected until the final revocation of the orders in June, 1812. The anger engendered by interruption of American trade was increased by the fact that, through special licenses and other devices, Great Britain permitted her own subjects to carry on trade with Europe prohibited to the Americans. She was, in short, attempting to force her own goods onto the Continent as well as to prevent any of her commercial rivals from trading with her military enemy.

What Was Madison's Final Argument for War?

The maritime issue was not the only cause for entering the War of 1812. Madison had a fifth and final argument which George Dangerfield quoted and then commented upon.[6]

"In reviewing the conduct of Great Britain towards the United States *our attention is necessarily drawn to the warfare just renewed by the savages on one of our extensive frontiers*—a warfare which is known to spare neither age nor sex and to be distinguished by features particularly shocking to humanity. It is difficult to account for the activity and combinations which have for some time been developing themselves among tribes in constant intercourse with British traders and garrisons without connecting their hostility with that influence and with recollecting the authenticated examples of such interpositions heretofore furnished by the officers and agents of that government."

In these words, Mr. Madison connected the British with that singular chain

[6]Dangerfield, *op. cit.*, pp. 23-24.

of events which led to the battle of Tippecanoe. The diffidence of his language suggests the posturing of a man who is about to take a dive into very dangerous waters; and, indeed, the addition of the fifth grievance was not very wise or very helpful. For though the British record in their dealings with the Indians was an unsavory one–though there was nothing fanciful in the Western belief that they would not hesitate to loose upon the frontier all the horrors and miseries of an Indian war; though their innocence of people who were not yet ready to be guilty–it is only just to admit that, if they had had their way, there would have been no battle of Tippecanoe at all.

Did Madison Succumb to Frontier Pressure for War?

Expanding upon Madison's fifth argument for war, Julius Pratt dwelled upon the American frontier as the main cause for war against England.[7]

I. The belief that the United States would one day annex Canada had a continuous existence from the early days of the War of Independence to the War of 1812. From 1783 to about 1810 such annexation was thought of only as a matter for an indefinite future, the nation during those years having neither the strength, nor any sufficient motive, for taking Canada by force. The rise of Tecumseh, backed, as was universally believed, by the British, produced an urgent demand in the Northwest that the British be expelled from Canada. This demand was a factor of primary importance in bringing on the war.

II. The South was almost unanimous in its demand for the Floridas, for agrarian, commercial, and strategic reasons, and in the spring of 1812 appeared to be in a fair way to accomplish its purpose. In the Southwest, at the same time, there was a lively interest in Mexico and widely prevalent opinion that it was ready to fall into American hands.

III. Even within the Republican party, there was already a distinct sectional rift between North and South, and neither section was anxious to see the other increase its territory and population. But if both could gain at the same time, and in something like equal proportion, such objections would be obviated on both sides. There is good evidence that, before the declaration of war, northern and southern Republicans came to a definite understanding that the acquisition of Canada on the north was to be balanced by the annexation of the Floridas on the south. Thus the war began with a double-barrelled scheme of territorial aggrandizement.

---

[7]Julius Pratt, *Expansionists of 1812* (New York: The Macmillan Company, 1953 ed.), pp. 12-14.

IV. Both Madison and Monroe, especially the latter as Secretary of State, were wholly in sympathy with the proposal for annexing Florida. The invasion of East Florida by General Mathews in March and April, 1812, was effected with the full knowledge of the administration. Special circumstances forced the government to repudiate Mathews, but the territory he had taken from the Spanish was held for over a year, until Congress had twice refused to sanction the occupation. At the same time, Monroe's official correspondence shows that he never really desired or expected the annexation of Canada.

V. It appears that in the all round failure of the expansionist plans, sectional feeling played a larger part than is commonly supposed. The sectional bargain with which the war had begun broke down. Opposition from northern Republicans combined with Federalists forced the abandonment of East Florida. On the other hand, it is evident that in the utter failure of the efforts to take Canada, not only want of skill and preparation, but also a lack of enthusiasm on the part of the administration and of certain southern men in Congress played a part.

VI. Finally, in the expansionist program with which the war opened, we have the first general appearance of the idea which later received the name of "Manifest Destiny." Although enthusiasts like Jefferson had dreamed years before of a nation destined to embrace the continent, the date usually given for the dawn of "Manifest Destiny" is about 1830. Yet both in the Congressional debates of 1812 and in the contemporary press, particularly that of the Southwest, we find the idea repeatedly expressed. "Where is it written in the book of fate," asked the editor of the Nashville *Clarion* (April 28, 1812), "that the American republic shall not stretch her limits from the Capes of the Chesapeake to Nootka sound, from the isthmus of Panama to Hudson bay?"

Summary

As some modern nations have today, America once incorporated the principle of neutrality in its foreign policy. In 1812, however, the United States temporarily abandoned its neutralist policy. President Madison and a majority in Congress felt that the nation was losing more by neutrality than it would lose by war. Thus the United States declared war on England. Among the principal motives for war were British disrespect for American neutral rights at sea and a fear of British-instigated attacks by Indians on the frontier. After the War of 1812, the United States returned to its policy of neutrality.

Selected References:

A. L. Burt, *The United States, Great Britain, and British North America from the Revolution to the Peace after the War of 1812* (New Haven: Yale University Press, 1940).

The maritime argument–impressment and ship-seizure caused the war.

Reginald Horsman, *The Causes of the War of 1812* (Philadelphia: University of Pennsylvania Press, 1962).*

An attempt to synthesize various causes into a clear explanation.

Bradford Perkins, ed., *The Causes of the War of 1812: National Honor or National Interest?* American Problem Studies (New York: Holt, Rinehart and Winston, 1962).*

A composite of brief essays and abstracts from larger works on the subject.

Julius W. Pratt, *Expansionists of 1812* (New York: The Macmillan Company, 1953 ed.).

The Western argument–land hunger, Indian defense and potential profit caused the war.

Term Projects:

A. Compare the arguments for neutralism which newly emerging African nations espouse to those which the United States defended in the early nineteenth century.

B. Write a lengthy answer to the following question: If you were President Madison, what would you have done to avoid war?

CHECKUP FOR STUDY

Name: ______________________________

1. How does this Theme title relate to the cartoon?

2. Define "third force."

3. Briefly stated, why did the United States become a neutralist?

4. What were the maritime issues?

To remove this page: Open the book as wide as possible several times to loosen this page from the binding. Lay the book flat on your desk and gently but firmly pull this page *straight up* and away from the binding from top to bottom.

5. What did England have to do with the frontier?

6. Did America ever invade Canada before 1812? If so, when?

7. Why was Florida so attractive to Americans?

8. List and define all new words you learned in this Theme.

9.

10.

"Fellow citizens! Are you tired of having to pay five cents for meat? Ten cents for butter? Twelve cents a dozen for eggs? Then vote for . . ."

Burr Shafer, *The Wonderful World of J. Wesley Smith,*
New York: The Vanguard Press, 1960

8 Doing Our Thing

SUFFRAGE: The right or privilege to vote; the franchise.

REFERENCE DATES:

1824	Andrew Jackson won the popular vote but lost the election (1825) in the House
1829-1837	Andrew Jackson elected seventh President
1830	Webster-Hayne debate; Maysville Veto; Indian Removal Act

1831	Anti-Masonic Party introduced the political convention and party platform; Jackson re-elected
1832	South Carolina Ordinance of Nullification; Bank of U.S. recharter vetoed
1836	Vice President Martin Van Buren elected eighth President

SHOULD 18-YEAR-OLDS VOTE?

One of the most important political questions of our age is the issue of establishing a national voting age at 18 years. President Richard Nixon supports such a change, as did his predecessor, Lyndon Johnson. Both desire a constitutional amendment to lower the minimum voting age to 18. Yet the issue still remains in debate.

Their requests are not novel, for the idea goes back over a quarter century. Senator Arthur Vandenburg of Michigan proposed the change in 1942 and former President Dwight Eisenhower repeated that demand in 1954. On the other hand, another former President, Harry Truman, once urged a 24-year age limit.

The following excerpts summarize arguments for and against the issue.[1]

FOR THE VOTE

1. *The Draft:* For years men between the ages of 18 and 21 have been summoned to defend the U.S. in time of war. . . .

To deny such men the right to vote is far worse than "taxation without representation." It is, in the words of General Eisenhower, "sacrifice without representation."

2. *Involvement*: "These young people today," says Senator Birch Bayh (D-Ind.), "are vastly more literate and socially conscious than their counterparts of a few generations ago. They don't get their kicks swallowing goldfish or sitting on flagpoles or crowding into telephone booths. Instead, they work actively for both political parties, they work for civil rights and equal oppor-

---

[1]"Vote at 18: Overdue or Premature?" *Senior Scholastic* XCIII (September 27, 1968), pp. 20-21.

tunity for all, they are in the Peace Corps, the Teacher Corps, VISTA, and a host of other constructive and meaningful causes that have added a new strength of purpose to our nation. . . .

3. *Obligations*: Young people today are allowed, and in many cases required, to assume many obligations of citizenship. They may work—and pay taxes on their income. . . .

. . . Many become parents before they are 21. Shouldn't these young parents have a voice in local and national issues that concern the welfare of their family?

Against the Vote

1. *Immaturity:* Says Congressman Emanuel Celler (D-N.Y.): "When we consider how easily the adolescent is inflamed, how passionately he attaches himself to 'causes,' how imperative it is for him at that age to see in patterns of black and white without shadings lest he falter in his commitments, we can readily understand why the demagogue, and the dictator, and the hypnotic orator have been able, historically, to capture the youth of the land."

2. *States' Rights:* Senator Richard B. Russell (D-Ga.) . . . points out, the U.S. Constitution gives the states, not the federal government, the power to set up voting qualifications.

3. *The Draft*: If we follow the "fight and vote" argument to its logical conclusion, we arrive at the ridiculous proposition that "if you're too old to fight, you're too old to vote."

When and Where Did Democracy Originate?

For generations, social scientists have studied the nature of American politics. Generally they disagree over when and where American democracy (government by the people) originated, how it developed, and what impact, if any, Andrew Jackson had on the subject.

Theories on the origins of American democracy have gone through three phases. Initially, nineteenth century historians wrote in terms of the "Teutonic Germ" theory. In brief, this hypothesis asserted that the origins of American institutions date back to the primitive customs of Teutonic tribes in early Germany. The Anglo-Saxons transferred these customs to England and, upon another transfer, from England to the New World, the "germs" of democracy matured and emerged triumphant in America.

At the end of the nineteenth century, Frederick Jackson Turner[2] challenged the germ theory. He argued that democracy "came out of the American forest, and it gained a new strength each time it touched a new frontier." Turner added, "the history of our institutions, our democracy, is not a history of imitation, or simple borrowing; it is the history of the evolution and adaptation of organs in response to changed environment, a history of the origin of new political species."

Since the turn of the twentieth century, Turner's thesis has been the focal point of an intense debate among historians. Generally, the consensus among modern historians tends to deny the validity of Turner's interpretation. Ray Allen Billington outlined these two viewpoints.[3]

1. *The Attack:* . . . Western man, they stated, was well along the road toward perfecting a workable democratic theory before he was influenced by the forests of America. The rise of the English middle class to economic power, the Protestant Reformation, and the gradual spread of fee simple land ownership to replace serfdom were all landmarks in this progression. Hence democracy *was* carried to the New World on the *Sarah Constant* and the *Mayflower*. Had it originated in the American forest it would have developed in New France and New Spain as it did in the English colonies. Secondly, critics of Turner have argued that such democratic practices as manhood suffrage, equitable legislative representation, and concentration of power in the legislature rather than the executive have been eastern in origin and have been imitated in western constitutions.

2. *The Defense:* . . . Scholars point out that the frontier provided an ideal breeding ground for the growth of democratic governments. This was the case for two reasons. On the one hand, the low man-land ratio allowed a wider distribution of property rights than in older communities, with a corresponding insistence on political participation natural among those with a stake in society. On the other hand, the relatively common level of economic and social status stimulated belief in egalitarianism, just at a time when lack of national or external controls made self-rule a "brutal necessity." In this situation governmental structures had to be created, and with no prior leadership structure existing, every man had an opportunity to win office if his abilities warranted such an award.

---

[2]Turner, *The Frontier in American History*. See Theme One for a brief discussion of Turner's significance in the development of American historical thought.

[3]Ray Allen Billington, *The American Frontier*. Publication Number 8 (Washington, D.C.: Service Center for Teachers of History, 1965), pp. 15-16. Reprinted by permission of the Service Center for Teachers of History of The American Historical Association.

When Did Mass Suffrage Democracy Emerge in America?

Historians have debated, too, the question of whether mass suffrage democracy existed in America before the Revolution. Arguments over this issue have raged for a century. Originally historians asserted that it did; then some said it did not; and today, historians appear badly divided over the question. Whatever the answer, modern democracy, which includes mass suffrage, did not prevail until after the War of 1812, as Richard D. Heffner explained.[4]

Ever since the emergence of Jacksonian Democracy in the 1820's and 1830's, the most pervasive myth to dominate American political thinking has been our rather naive–and mistaken–equation of equality with freedom, of democracy (or majority rule) with liberty. Long before the age of Jackson, of course, Thomas Jefferson had set forth the proposition that "all men are created equal" as the philosophical basis of the Declaration of Independence. And as far back as the so-called "Revolution of 1800," majority rule had triumphed in America when the Federalist party–a minority party of "the rich and the well-born"–was permanently driven from national office by the numerically superior Jeffersonian Democrats. Yet our early leaders, even the Jeffersonians, were themselves essentially far from equalitarian in outlook. They believed in government *of* and *for* the people, but not *by* the people. And, more important, they were much too dedicated to the principles of individual liberty and freedom ever to equate them necessarily and irrevocably with equality and democracy.

Thus it was not until Jackson's time that equalitarianism became the overriding theme of American life, with majority rule its most convenient rule of thumb. . . .

Why Did Jefferson Fail to Gain Such Popular Support?

Expanding upon the relationship of Jefferson and Jackson to democracy, Charles M. Wiltse explained why Jefferson failed to gain the popular support which Jackson enjoyed.[5]

---

[4]Richard D. Heffner, ed., Introduction to *Democracy in America,* by Alexis de Tocqueville (New York: The New American Library, 1956), pp. 9-10. © by Richard D. Heffner. Reprinted by arrangement with The New American Library, Inc.

[5]Charles M. Wiltse, *The New Nation: 1800–1845* (New York: Hill and Wang, 1961), p. 100.

Jackson's appeal to the common people was sounder than Jefferson's had been, if only because there were now more of them qualified to vote and because they came closer to a common level; but the democracy of 1828 was a "popular" party in only a limited sense. It was the same combination of interests that had elected Jefferson in 1800—a coalition, in Van Buren's phrase, of "the planters of the South and the plain Republicans of the North"; but the plain Republicans tended to be the hand workers, the artisans, and the tradespeople of the cities, with a sprinkling of northern farmers and a leaven in every section of the rising middle class. More broadly still, the democracy of Jackson's day was very like the combination of northern and western liberals, southern conservatives, and big-city bosses that elected Wilson, Roosevelt and Truman. The real issues were often masked, and did not emerge until later, because these various elements wanted different and sometimes irreconcilable things.

. . . The well-oiled Crawford machine became, with the blessing of Crawford himself, the Jackson machine, powerful enough to win all but two national elections between 1828 and 1860. That the machine had remained in working order to compass his own defeat was largely Adams' fault, for he, like Monroe, had so little appreciated the role of the President as party leader that he had not only refused to remove political opponents from office, he had even reappointed most of those who served fixed terms. Yet these office-holders, most important of whom were the collectors of customs, were Crawford partisans who were key figures in state political organizations. Their services to the Jackson cause were to prove invaluable.

How Did Jackson Affect American Democracy?

The lifting of suffrage restrictions and the increased exercise by the people of their voting right introduced what some historians have termed "Jacksonian Democracy." For over a century, historians have differed over the definition of this ambiguous term, for it raises an important question: Did Andrew Jackson introduce democracy? Or, to put it another way, did the forces of democracy make Jackson President?

The fact that there are several interpretations of "Jacksonian Democracy" and that each interpretation is, to some extent, valid, illustrates how difficult it is to make firm conclusions in matters of historical interpretation. Charles G. Sellers, Jr., warned students of the problem of trying to find a "right" answer.[6]

---

[6]Charles G. Sellers, *Jacksonian Democracy*. Publication Number 9 (Washington, D.C.: Service Center for Teachers of History, 1958), p. 12. Reprinted by permission of the Service Center for Teachers of History of the American Historical Association.

. . . It may be well to remind ourselves that an interpretation is not necessarily wrong merely because a writer seems to have been impelled toward that interpretation by a particular frame of reference. The conclusions of honest men, working within limits set by an abundance of reliable and relatively unmalleable evidence, must have some basis in the reality of the past they seek to interpret. This may suggest that each school of Jacksonian historiography has been correct up to a point, and that the real problem of interpreting Jacksonian Democracy is to define the proper relationship among the various elements emphasized by the different schools.

Will historians ever be able to resolve the relationship of Jackson and the development of American democracy? Alfred A. Cave expressed his opinion that historians never will.[7]

. . . The Jacksonian movement may have been so highly pluralistic as to render impossible its definition within the framework of any single concept. In their way, the frontier democracy, urban labor, and entrepreneurial theses may all be quite valid. The question may in the future resolve itself into the problem of tracing the relationships between the often conflicting, frequently contradictory elements which composed the party of Andrew Jackson. . . .

One thing is probable: the spirit of detachment, of analysis, will not in the near future lead to a complete and total objectivity in dealing with the turbulent Age of Jackson. As long as the relationship of the business community to government, of government to the citizen, and of the states to the national government remains controversial, the Jacksonian movement will be an object of controversy. The passage of time has dulled the partisan conflict of Whig versus Jacksonian; it has not totally effaced that conflict. By careful effort, the historian may minimize the distortions of the past produced by his own partisanship and by the frame of reference of the present; as a competent scholar he should struggle to do so. It is doubtful, however, that he will completely succeed.

When and How Did Mass Suffrage Expansion Occur?

It is important to consider several other points on the expansion of mass suffrage.

Voter Participation: Richard P. McCormick asserted that voter participation was not great before 1840.[8]

---

[7]Alfred A. Cave, *Jacksonian Democracy and the Historians* (University of Florida Monographs, No. 22, Gainesville), pp. 85-86.

[8]Richard P. McCormick, "New Perspectives on Jacksonian Politics," *American Historical Review,* Vol. XLV (1960), p. 301.

. . . None of the Jackson elections involved a "mighty democratic uprising" in the sense that voters were drawn to the polls in unprecedented proportions. When compared with the peak participation recorded for each state before 1824, or with the contemporaneous gubernatorial elections, or most particularly with the vast outpouring of the electorate in 1840, voter participation in the Jackson elections was unimpressive. The key to the relatively low presidential vote would seem to be the extreme political imbalance that existed in most states as between the Jacksonians and their opponents. Associated with this imbalance was the immature development of national political parties. Indeed, it can be highly misleading to think in terms of national parties in connection with the Jackson elections. As balanced, organized parties subsequently made their appearance from state to state, and voters were stimulated by the prospect of a genuine contest, a marked rise in voter participation occurred. Such conditions did not prevail generally across the nation until 1840, and then at last the "mighty democratic uprising" took place.

Non-Western Contribution: Chilton Williamson suggested that suffrage expansion originated in the East.[9]

In view of the extent to which western suffrage history was a recapitulation of the suffrage history of the eastern seaboard, it is difficult to believe that the New West was unique or that it made any new contribution to the growth of suffrage democracy.

Democratic Party: While leading Democrats such as Andrew Jackson, Martin Van Buren and Thomas Hart Benton made anti-manhood suffrage statements before 1828, the Democratic Party under their leadership did provide the initiative for suffrage reform. They vigorously attacked property tests and taxpaying qualifications. However, Chilton Williamson cautioned historians on the reason for such action.[10]

. . . The manner of voting involved the question of whether voting should be easy or difficult and this, in turn, involved matters of democratic philosophy and of party advantage and expediency as well. When the leaders of either major party thought they would benefit from removing obstacles to voting, they made every effort to do so.

---

[9]Chilton Williamson, *American Suffrage from Property to Democracy, 1760-1860* (Princeton: Princeton University Press, 1960), pp. 221-222.

[10]*Ibid*, p. 272.

World Importance: Chilton Williamson noted the uniqueness of American democracy in the world.[11]

The almost total elimination of property as a qualification for voting and the adoption of democratic techniques to encourage the voter to exercise his privileges proved how successful had been the suffrage reform movement by the time of the Civil War. Although the future proved that much had to be accomplished by later generations, it was an impressive fact, of world significance, that the movement to eliminate property as a test for voting had achieved so great a degree of success by 1860. Manhood suffrage without democracy, as conceived at that time, existed in the France of Napoleon III and the German Empire of Bismarck, but not in the America of 1860.

Have Suffrage Rights Changed Since the Mid-Nineteenth Century?

Many modifications in suffrage laws have occurred since the Civil War. Three Amendments to the Constitution illustrate this change.

Article XV Negro Suffrage: The right of citizens of the United States to vote shall not be denied or abridged by the United States or any State on account of race, color, or previous condition of servitude. (adopted in 1870)

Article XIX Woman Suffrage: The right of citizens of the United States to vote shall not be denied or abridged by the United States or by any State on account of sex. (adopted in 1920)

Article XXIV Anti-Poll Tax: The right of citizens of the United States to vote in any primary or other election for President or Vice President, for electors for President or Vice President, or for Senator or Representative in Congress, shall not be denied or abridged by the United States or any State by reason of failure to pay any poll tax or other tax. (adopted in 1964)

Summary

The present question of voting age minimum relates much to the historical development of expanded suffrage in the United States. Aspects of

---

[11] *Ibid,* p. 280.

that development include such controversial issues as the origins of democracy in America, when the majority of men gained the right to vote, what impact their vote had on American politics and whether Andrew Jackson was responsible for mass suffrage. Whatever the case, by the mid-nineteenth century the importance of mass suffrage in America lay in its uniqueness in the world.

Selected References:

James L. Bugg, *Jacksonian Democracy: Myth or Reality?* American Problem Studies (New York: Holt, Rinehart and Winston, 1962).*
Excerpts from noted historical works on Jackson categorized into schools of interpretation.

Marcus Cunliffe, *The Nation Takes Shape: 1789-1837* (Chicago: University of Chicago Press, 1959).*
Though not solely on the Jackson era, the theme provides both a valuable background and an explanation of the age.

Edward Pessen, *Jacksonian America: Society, Personality, and Politics* (Homewood, Illinois: The Dorsey Press, 1969).*
A synthesis of early and modern scholarship describing the age. Also included is a comprehensive bibliography.

Glyndon G. Van Deusen, *The Jacksonian Era: 1828-1848* (New York: Harper & Row, 1959).*
An attempt to synthesize historians' debates over issues of the era.

Term Projects:

A. Compare Jacksonian Democrats to Whigs of the age with reference to party principles and voter strength.

B. In an essay describe how manhood suffrage has helped and obstructed honest government.

CHECKUP FOR STUDY

Name: ______________________________

1. Should Congress give the eighteen-year-old the right to vote? Why?

2. Explain the following: "Turner's forests were germ free and pure."

3. Comment on the following: "Jefferson believed in government by the people."

4. Why is "Jacksonian Democracy" so difficult to define?

To remove this page: Open the book as wide as possible several times to loosen this page from the binding. Lay the book flat on your desk and gently but firmly pull this page *straight up* and away from the binding from top to bottom.

5. Where did American democracy emerge first?

6. What motivated the expansion of mass suffrage?

7. How did the extent of American suffrage compare to that of European suffrage by 1860?

8. In what ways has suffrage expanded since the Civil War?

9.

10.

"No building permit, Mr. Thoreau! What do you mean, you 'burned it in protest'?"

James F. Wickens

9 Flowers Before The Children

REFORM: The correction of an abuse or error by amendment, improvement or removal. To change a condition.

REFERENCE DATES:

1824	Charles G. Finney began his revivalist career in upper state New York
1828	American Peace Society founded in New York City
1836-1850	Ralph Waldo Emerson led the Transcendentalist revolt against Unitarianism
1841-1860	Brook Farm (Mass.), the most notable reform community, existed

1845-47	Henry Thoreau lived in isolation at Walden Pond (Mass.)
1848	Seneca Falls (N.Y.) Convention demanded equal rights for women

What Has Been the Social Impact of Youthful Non-Conformists?

Generally evident on many college campuses and in many cities today are non-conforming young people, commonly called "hippies." On campuses, they have done much to change both the external appearance and the internal workings of the colleges. Where once crew-cuts and white buck shoes prevailed, hippies have appeared attired in long hair, beards, flowing robes, beads and bare feet. In the society as a whole, not only have they changed fashions, these young people have also contributed new meanings to old words, challenged moral codes and narcotics laws, and attempted to reevaluate the purpose of life itself. Upon investigating San Francisco's Haight-Ashbury district, John R. Howard categorized and described variations in hippie conformity and non-conformity.[1]

. . . Four hippie types [emerge] . . . : the visionaries, the freaks and heads, the midnight hippies, and the plastic hippies. The visionaries are utopians who pose an alternative to existing society. They repudiate conventional values on the grounds that they induce status anxiety and a fetish for material acquisition. The community that they developed in Haight-Ashbury can be viewed as a kind of experiment in social organization. Freaks and heads are the more drug-oriented hippies. They surround the use of drugs with an elaborate mythology suggesting a variety of benefits to be derived from "going out of one's mind." Midnight hippies are older people, mostly in their thirties, who, having become integrated into straight society, cannot adopt the hippie style of life, but, who are, nevertheless, sympathetic to it. They articulate and rationalize the hippie perspective to the straight world. Plastic hippies are young people who wear the paraphernalia of hippies (baubles, bangles, and beads) as a kind of costume. They have entered into it as a fad, and have only the most superficial understanding of the ideology. The visionaries sought over a two-year period in Haight-Ashbury to implement their view of the good society. External pressure and certain internal contradictions in their social system led to a breakdown of the experiment. By the summer of 1968,

---

[1]John R. Howard, "The Flowering of the Hippie Movement," *Annals of the Academy of Political and Social Science,* 382 (1969), p. 43.

many had left the city to set up rural communes, with the hope of being able to survive in a less hostile environment. . . .

Why Is Modern Non-Conformist Behavior Not Original?

Much of what passes for modern non-conformist behavior, such as that just described, is not original. Many of the eccentric ways have roots in or similarities to non-conforming groups in another era, antebellum (*ante:* before; *bellum:* war, or Civil War) America.

Common to both antebellum avant-gardists and modern non-conformists, the search for an abstract meaning of life provides one area for comparison. Today people claim to seek this meaning through meditation. They practice Zen Buddhism, Hindu philosophy, yin-and-yang cosmology and Yoga. Many use hallucinatory drugs for "trips."

Antebellum reformers took "trips," too. The age was fraught with religious, mystical and "scientific" investigations and conclusions. Spiritualists heard rappings and received messages from departed souls in the spirit world. "Scientists" mesmerized sick patients to health. Shakers released repressed emotions and measured spiritual energy in a special dance. Evangelists drove camp-meeting converts into repentant expressions of animal noises and lament. Perfectionists attempted to rid society of sin through acts of free love. And, transcendentalists (those who believed in a philosophy that stressed a spiritual or abstract experience over one which was rational or tangible; thus, those for whom truth transcended reason) studied and even meditated over the Hindu holy book, *Bhagavad-Gita.*

Then there is the matter of dress. Imaginative to some observers and ridiculous to others, modern unconventional dress habits have led to controversy. Before the Civil War, feminist (one who demanded equal rights for women) Amelia Bloomer caused quite a stir with her fashions, too. She designed knee-covering dresses with pantelettes underneath. Many conventional Americans chided such garb as ludicrous, fit only for women of ill repute. Nevertheless, this wardrobe was functional. It improved women's mobility in the early industrial age.

Beyond such superficial parallels, however, the student of history should be wary of comparing non-conformist groups in the two ages. For example, hippies are generally negativists. They relieve their frustrations with American society by "tuning-in" and "dropping-out." Thus, they have not sought to produce positive solutions to modern problems.

In contrast, the non-conformists of the antebellum era participated actively in attempts to change society. C.S. Griffin described these antebellum efforts.[2]

. . . During the years from 1830 to 1860 a host of reformers in a variety of reform movements together examined and attacked every American institution, every idea, every conceivable sin, evil, or burden of suffering. Against slavery stood thousands of abolitionists; against the horrors of war stood a small army of pacifists; against liquor drinking, drunkenness, and the neighborhood saloon stood cadres of prohibitionists striving to make cold water the national beverage. While some reformers worked to wipe out prostitution, saving the whores from sin and shame and their clients from temptation, other reformers—good Protestants, they—labored in various ways to destroy Roman Catholicism. Still other reformers tried to redeem criminals by changing the prison environment, to help the mentally incompetent and the physically disabled toward happier lives, to provide public schools and colleges to educate the nation's children and lyceums to inform adults. Although most Americans continued to believe that traditional political and economic institutions best promoted the general welfare, many of their fellow citizens argued that communitarian or socialistic societies promised more, and a few men claimed that all coercive institutions were evil. Most Americans continued to accept one or another of the orthodox Protestant creeds, and there were numberless reformers seeking to bring the entire nation to Christ. But hard beside them other religious zealots created new cults and sects to offer men better ways toward a proper relation with that Spirit, or those spirits, which lay beyond space and time. The yeasty ferment of reform buoyed up Americans who would make women the political and social equals of men—hell had no fury like a women's-righter scorned; who would drastically change the people's dietary habits and modes of dress; who hewed away at the ancient institution of monogamy, letting lovers fall where they might.

What Initiated Reform Movements?

By the 1830's, moral self-righteousness and conservatism combined to bring forth antebellum reform. Of this moral impulse, John L. Thomas traced reform origins and their political implications.[3]

---

[2]C. S. Griffin, *The Ferment of Reform, 1830-1860* (New York: Thomas Y. Crowell, 1967), pp. 2-3.

[3]John L. Thomas, "Romantic Reform in America, 1815-1865," *American Quarterly*, Vol. XVII:4 (1965), pp. 656-657.

Out of a seemingly conservative religious revival there flowed a spate of perfectionist ideas for the improvement and rearrangement of American society. Rising rapidly in the years after 1830, the flood of social reform reached its crest at mid-century. . . .

Romantic reform in America traced its origins to a religious impulse which was both politically and socially conservative. With the consolidation of independence and the arrival of democratic politics the new nineteenth-century generation of American churchmen faced a seeming crisis. Egalitarianism and rising demands for church disestablishment suddenly appeared to threaten an inherited Christian order and along with it the preferred status of the clergy. . . . Between 1815 and 1830 nearly a dozen moral reform societies were established to counter the threats to social equilibrium posed by irreligious democrats. . . .

How Did Antebellum Reformers Try to Change Society?

Reformers in Europe and America during the first half of the nineteenth century used four approaches to change their societies, according to Arthur Bestor, Jr.[4]

Individualism, now largely associated with conservative thinking, we can recognize as an authentic philosophy of reform in the hands of an Adam Smith or a Jefferson, and in the ringing words of Emerson's Phi Beta Kappa Address of 1837, "If the single man plant himself indomitably on his instincts, and there abide, the huge world will come round to him." *Revolution,* too, is a possible path to social change, as present to our experience as it was to the eighteenth or nineteenth century. In between we recognize, as a third alternative, the multitude of reform movements, best described as *gradualistic,* which employ collective action but aim at an amelioration of particular conditions, not a total reconstruction of society.

Communitarianism does not correspond exactly to any of these. It is collectivistic not individualistic, it is resolutely opposed to revolution, and it is impatient with gradualism. . . .

Two of these approaches to reform, revolution and gradualism, need not bother us. During this era, American reformers did not attempt to change life through revolution as did the Europeans. And few gradualistic reform movements made much significant headway other than the

---

[4]Arthur Bestor, Jr., *Backwoods Utopias* (Philadelphia: University of Pennsylvania Press, 1950), p. 4.

abolition of slavery. An examination of the other two methods, communitarianism and individualism, follows.

WHAT WAS COMMUNITARIANISM?

Some reformers decided to change society by example. They created small, voluntary, isolated communities which incorporated solutions to America's social ills. As Arthur Bestor, Jr., noted, "A microcosm of society . . . could undergo drastic change in complete harmony and order, and the great world outside could be relied on to imitate a successful experiment without coercion or conflict."[5]

Between 1825 and the Civil War (1861), nearly one hundred of these communities arose, and in most instances, disappeared. Different communities experimented with a wide variety of ideas, including vegetarianism, trade unionism and free love. Inhabitants of some communities owned property outright and those in others treated property as communal. Unknowingly, perhaps, each group of reformers was following the concept of the medieval monk, St. Benedict, who viewed the monastery as a little model State which by example could reform Christianity.

Arthur Bestor, Jr., noted the reasons for the popularity of antebellum communitarianism.[6]

> The communitarian idea was peculiarly attractive because alternative methods of social reform appeared to have reached a dead end during this particular period. Individualism seemed incapable of answering the nineteenth-century need for collective action. Revolution had revealed itself as a dangerous two-edged sword in the quarter-century of French and European history between 1789 and 1815. And the problems created by industrialization appeared to have so far outdistanced the ability of gradual methods to solve them that society itself was retrograding. Drastic reform was the demand, but drastic reform without revolution. Such a program the secular communitarians offered, and during the half-century following 1815 they were listened to with attention, only finally losing influence in the last third of the nineteenth century when gradual methods began at last to prove themselves effective.

---

[5]*Ibid*, p. 4.

[6]*Ibid.*, pp. 7-8.

What Was Individualism?

While some antebellum reformers used group action, a few others stressed individualism, or a doctrine which places the interests of the individual above those of the society. Notable for this type of thought was Henry David Thoreau, who lived for two years (1845-1847) in isolation on Ralph Waldo Emerson's property at Walden Pond. Out of this experience, Thoreau expressed his thoughts on individualism in a famous essay, "Civil Disobedience."[7]

> I heartily accept the motto,—"That government is the best which governs least"; and I should like to see it acted up to more rapidly and systematically. Carried out, it finally amounts to this, which also I believe,—"That government is best which governs not at all"; and when men are prepared for it, that will be the kind of government which they will have. Government is at best but an expedient; but most governments are usually, and all governments are sometimes, inexpedient. . . .
>
> . . . .
>
> The authority of government . . . is still an impure one; to be strictly just, it must have the sanction and consent of the governed. . . . The progress from an absolute to a limited monarchy, from a limited monarchy to a democracy, is a progress toward a true respect for the individual. . . . There will never be a really free and enlightened State, until the State comes to recognize the individual as a higher and independent power, from which all its own power and authority are derived, and treats him accordingly.

What Brought Antebellum Reform to an End?

By mid-century, of all the reforms initiated, only temperance (the abstinence from use of alcoholic beverages) and nativism (opposition to immigrants, particularly Roman Catholics) had gained popularity. Most other reforms had met temporary or permanent failure. C. S. Griffin explained why many reforms failed to take hold.[8]

---

[7]Henry David Thoreau, "Civil Disobedience," in *The Writings of Henry David Thoreau,* Vol. X (Boston: Houghton, Mifflin & Co., Riverside edition, 1893), pp. 131, 169.

[8]Griffin, *op. cit.,* pp. 68-69.

> Yet the very diversity of American life and American reform movements prevented any one reform from capturing overwhelming public support. Like the American economy, antebellum reform worked on the free enterprise system. . . .
>
> Whatever progress the reformers made, then, depended on what the people generally would accept. Relative successes and failures bore no relation whatever to the intrinsic worth of any reform, or to a reformer's sincerity and earnestness of purpose. . . .

Thus reformers faltered in their objective to change society quickly. Most old social values remained intact.

HOW DID THE CIVIL WAR AFFECT THE REFORM MOVEMENT?

As it turned out, by the time of the Civil War, the most important reform of all, the abolition of slavery, had thrust forward to command more and more attention. John L. Thomas described the impact of abolitionism and war on the reform spirit.[9]

> The collapse of the communitarian movement in the 1850s left a vacuum in social reform which was filled by the slavery crisis. At first their failure to consolidate alternative social and educational institutions threw the reformers back on their old perfectionist individualism for support. It was hardly fortuitous that Garrison, Mann, Thoreau, Howe, Parker, Channing, Ripley and Emerson himself responded to John Brown's raid with a defense of the liberated conscience. But slavery, as a denial of freedom and individual responsibility, had to be destroyed by institutional forces which could be made to sustain these values. The anti-slavery cause during the secession crisis and throughout the Civil War offered reformers an escape from alienation by providing a new identity with the very political institutions which they had so vigorously assailed.
>
> The effects of the Civil War as an intellectual counter-revolution were felt both in a revival of institutions and a renewal of an organic theory of society. The war brought with it a widespread reaction against the seeming sentimentality and illusions of perfectionism. It saw the establishment of new organizations like the Sanitary and the Christian Commissions run on principles of efficiency and professionalism totally alien to perfectionist methods. Accompanying the wartime revival of institutions was a theological reorientation directed by Horace Bushnell and other conservative churchmen whose long-standing opposition to perfectionism seemed justified by the war. The extreme

---

[9]Thomas, *op. cit.*, pp. 679-680.

individualism of the ante-bellum reformers was swallowed up in a Northern war effort that made private conscience less important than saving the Union. Some of the abolitionists actually substituted national unity for freedom for the slave as the primary war aim. Those reformers who contributed to the war effort through the Sanitary Commission or the Christian Commission found a new sense of order and efficiency indispensable. Older perfectionists, like Dorothea Dix, unable to adjust to new demands, found their usefulness drastically confined. Young Emersonians returned from combat convinced that professionalism, discipline and subordination, dubious virtues by perfectionist standards, were essential in a healthy society. A new emphasis on leadership and performance was replacing the benevolent amateurism of the perfectionists.

Is Antebellum Reform Relevant to the Present?

To a degree, the heritage of the antebellum reformers has been persistent. David Brion Davis pointed out this relationship.[10]

The main issues raised by the reformers are still very much alive. We have by no means solved the problems of racial and sexual discrimination. We still dream of extending the intimate love of the private family to a wider circle of social relationships, and yet debate, as did the ante-bellum reformers, the justifications for monogamous marriage, the proper role of woman, and the best methods of child-rearing. We are still perplexed by the discrepancy between our penal institutions and our ideal of reforming and rehabilitating criminals. We argue endlessly over the most effective methods for redeeming what Theodore Parker called "the dangerous classes of society" and what we now term "the culturally deprived." If we are usually more cynical than the ante-bellum reformers, we have not abandoned their dream of a world without war. Indeed, the radical protest movements of the 1960s have hauntingly echoed the ante-bellum ideal of nonresistance, the "come-outer" spirit of disengagement from a sinful society, and the reliance on individual conscience as opposed to all forms of corporate and bureaucratic power.

In short, we continue to believe that without social criticism a nation is doomed to complacency, stultification, and hardening injustice. We like to think that American history is something more than a record of diverse groups and interests struggling for power. And if we are to find in our heritage some trace of the unfolding of an ideal, some evidence, however imperfect, of a continuing tradition of discontent, of repudiating the status quo, of

[10]David Brion Davis, *Ante-Bellum Reform* (New York: Harper and Row, 1967), pp. 2-3.

insisting that things can and should be better, then we must see the antebellum reformers in part as they saw themselves: as the legitimate heirs of the American Revolution, as champions of the ideals of the Declaration of Independence.

Summary

Today's rebellion against social customs is not unique. Even hippie non-conformity is not startlingly novel. Non-conformity existed in antebellum America, unsuccessful and restricted as it may have been in its attempt to reform society. Communitarianism and individualism flourished briefly among a self-elected few, many of whom lived in New England. The main issues which reformers raised have relevance to present social problems.

Selected References:

E. Douglas Branch, *The Sentimental Years, 1836-1860* (New York: Hill and Wang, 1962 edition).*
A description of the culture of the age.

Whitney R. Cross, *The Burned-Over District, The Social and Intellectual History of Enthusiastic Religion in Western New York, 1800-1850* (Ithaca: Cornell University Press, 1950).*
The social significance of evangelicalism and its relationship to the origins of antebellum reform.

C. S. Griffin, *The Ferment of Reform, 1830-1860* (New York: Thomas Y. Crowell Co., 1967).*
A short but thought-provoking analysis which surveys recent scholarship on the theme.

Alice Felt Tyler, *Freedom's Ferment: Phases of American Social History to 1860* (Minneapolis: University of Minnesota Press, 1944).*
Though uncritical of the reformers, a simple but excellent synthesis of reform movements.

Term Projects:

A. Compare and contrast communitarianism with modern communism.

B. Describe why the South failed to participate in antebellum reform and literary developments.

CHECKUP FOR STUDY

Name: ______________________________

1. What does the Theme title mean?

2. Why would a hippie feel out of place among antebellum reformers?

3. What connection did Protestantism have with reform?

4. What insights into history does study of the reformers offer?

To remove this page: Open the book as wide as possible several times to loosen this page from the binding. Lay the book flat on your desk and gently but firmly pull this page *straight up* and away from the binding from top to bottom.

5. Why did many reformers fail by the 1850's?

6. Why did abolitionism eventually dominate the reform movement?

7. What antebellum issues are alive today?

8. List any fiction written in the reform era (1820-1860) which you have read.

9.

10.

"My brother has an idea that we should grow beards and manufacture cough drops."

Burr Shafer, *The Wonderful World of J. Wesley Smith,* New York: The Vanguard Press, 1960

10 On Your Mark; Get Set; Go!

INDUSTRIAL REVOLUTION: The replacement of hand tools by power-driven tools, accompanying the transfer of manufacturing from the home and/or shop to the factory. (The word "revolution" is misleading. Taken literally, it means a rapid and dynamic change which is rarely the case in industrialization.)

REFERENCE DATES:

1811 National Road begun; reached Vandalia, Ill. (1838)

1813	Textile manufacturing factory system started at Waltham, Massachusetts
1825	Erie Canal opened with enormous success
1830	Baltimore and Ohio Railroad began operations as first common carrier to handle freight in U.S.
1843-1860	Rostow's "take-off" of industrial growth in the United States
1860	U.S. ranked second in world value of manufacturers behind Great Britain

Can Underdeveloped Nations Imitate the American Industrial Experience?

Many newly emerging nations, underdeveloped and in need of assistance, desire immediate wealth and prestige through industrialization. These new nations reason that the industrial powers had used technology to dominate them as colonials. It is only reasonable, therefore, that many of these new nations upon independence see industrial technology as a solution to many of their economic problems. Moreover, they argue that the first colonial nation to win independence, the United States, was able to propel itself into world power and wealth by industrialism. If the Americans did it, cannot people in Africa or Asia do the same?

Perhaps, but there is danger in thinking that producers of primary products can become industrialized quickly, avoiding America's mistakes and capitalizing upon its successes. Carl Degler warned us of the pitfalls in such a comparison.[1]

Another analogy often made between the history of the United States and the newly emergent nations is that America began as an underdeveloped country, successfully making the transition to industrialization without government controls or interference with individual initiative. Therefore, it is argued, if Americans could do it in the past, then these new nations can today. Why, then, many Americans today ask in rising anger, do these nations

---

[1]Carl Degler, "The American Past, An Unsuspected Obstacle in Foreign Affairs." Reprinted from *The American Scholar,* Vol. XXII, Number 2 (Spring 1963), pp. 193-194. Copyright © 1963 by the United Chapters of Phi Beta Kappa. By permission of the publisher.

need foreign aid, why do they lean so sympathetically toward socialistic measures and state intervention in economic affairs?

Again the answer must be that the analogy is wrong. It is true that in the early years of the Republic the United States was largely agrarian in economy, deceptively similar in character to those traditional societies now emerging into statehood. But the United States was an agricultural society in which the ratio between man and land was low. . . .

Moreover, the American land was fresh, often rich and ready to yield ample crops. As a result, from the beginning of the nation food and raw materials for export were always abundant. Early in their careers on the land, men produced a surplus for sale to support a growing urban and, later, industrial population. What a contrast there is with the poor, worn-out soil of much of Africa south of the Sahara, where a surplus is difficult for the most vigorous farmer to come by. It is true that in many of the underdeveloped countries, like India or Indonesia, the yields *per acre* are far higher than Americans have ever achieved. But the yields *per man* are discouragingly low because the labor is unassisted by adequate tools, machines, good seeds or fertilizers —or even by healthy manpower. And it is yields per man that determine whether labor can be released from agriculture for other tasks.

An American in the early nineteenth century, as a result of his own hard labor, could accumulate a surplus, even buy more land (and, if he lived in the South, more slaves) and greatly improve his material position in his own lifetime. The thirty-eight million immigrants who entered the United States between 1820 and 1930 were living testimony to the belief in and the actuality of the opportunity. . . .

. . . As agricultural productivity rose, more men could be spared from farming to serve in the industrial labor force in the expanding cities. The very prosperity of the countryside meant that an internal market for manufacturers was already in being. Furthermore, the generally high wages in the cities—as compared with contemporary Europe, to say nothing of Asia, Africa and South America today—provided a still better and wider market for manufactures in the urban centers by the close of the century. . . .

DID AMERICAN INDEPENDENCE STIMULATE ECONOMIC GROWTH?

Political independence is no guarantee of economic progress. August C. Bolino suggested that at best the early American economy was stationary.[2]

---

[2]August C. Bolino, *The Development of the American Economy,* second edition (Columbus, Ohio: Charles E. Merrill Books, 1966), p. 61. Used by permission of Charles E. Merrill Publishing Co.

When the Revolution ended, America was a small, mainly agrarian country. The early years were difficult ones, since independence resulted in much physical destruction of productive facilities, and foreign trade was reduced. The war, which sprang partly from colonial resentment to British taxation, brought the very results that the new citizens had fought to prevent.

There is considerable controversy as to whether any economic growth occurred after the Revolution. There appeared to be little prospect for growth, and since population grew from 3.9 million to 5.3 million between 1790 and 1800, it is possible that real per capita income actually fell.

Gilbert C. Fite and Jim E. Reese described the continuation of the colonial-type economy after political independence.[3]

. . . Most industry was still in the handicraft stage, and a substantial part of the manufacturing was done in the home. Commercial manufacturing, with the exception of a few heavy industries, was carried on in small shops by skilled craftsmen. Almost every village had a sawmill and a flour mill. In addition to the mills, the larger towns usually had a number of small industries operated by tailors, shoe makers, jewelers, blacksmiths, and coopers. The large commercial industries, the iron works, flour mills, paper mills, potash plants, breweries, tanneries, brick yards, and fulling mills showed little change in the years immediately following the Revolution. Water power was almost the only source of energy, but, with the exception of the textile industry, its use was confined to the heavy work in flour mills, saw mills, and iron foundries. Mechanization was probably carried further in the flour mills than in any other industry, and the American mills were considered superior to their European counterparts.

What Was Life Like in the America of 1800?

In some ways, perhaps, the physical and economic conditions of the United States in 1800 resemble those of underdeveloped nations today. Henry Adams vividly portrayed those conditions in America.[4]

---

[3]Gilbert C. Fite and Jim E. Reese, *An Economic History of the United States,* second edition (Boston: Houghton, Mifflin & Co., 1965), p. 208.

[4]Henry Adams, *History of the United States of America During the First Administration of Thomas Jefferson,* Vol. I (New York: Charles Scribner's Sons, 1889), pp. 1-2, 16-18.

Even after two centuries of struggle the land was still untamed; forest covered every portion, except here and there a strip of cultivated soil; the minerals lay undisturbed in their rocky beds, and more than two-thirds of the people clung to the seaboard within fifty miles of tidewater, where alone the wants of civilized life could be supplied. The centre of population rested within eighteen miles of Baltimore, north and east of Washingon. Except in political arrangement, the interior was little more civilized than in 1750, and was not much easier to penetrate than when La Salle and Hennepin found their way to the Mississippi more than a century before.

A great exception broke this rule. Two wagon-roads crossed the Allegheny Mountains in Pennsylvania. . . .

. . . .

If the physical task which lay before the American people had advanced but a short way toward completion, little more change could be seen in the economical conditions of American life. . . . The Saxon farmer of the eighth century enjoyed most of the comforts known to Saxon farmers of the eighteenth. The eorls and ceorls of Offa and Ecgbert could not read or write, and did not receive a weekly newspaper with such information as newspapers in that age could supply; yet neither their houses, their clothing, their food and drink, their agricultural tools and methods, their stock, nor their habits were so greatly altered or improved by time that they would have found much difficulty in accommodating their lives to that of their descendants in the eighteenth century. In this respect America was backward. Fifty or a hundred miles inland more than half the houses were log-cabins, which might or might not enjoy the luxury of a glass window. Throughout the South and West houses showed little attempt at luxury; but even in New England the ordinary farmhouse was hardly so well built, so spacious, or so warm as that of a well-to-do contemporary of Charlemagne. . . . The ordinary cultivator planted his corn as his father had planted it, sowing as much rye to the acre, using the same number of oxen to plough, and getting in his crops on the same day. He was even known to remove his barn on account of the manure accumulated round it, although the New England soil was never so rich as to warrant neglect to enrich it. The money for which he sold his wheat and chickens was of the Old World; he reckoned in shillings or pistareens, and rarely handled an American coin more valuable than a large copper cent.

How Had Life Changed by the Civil War Era?

The American economy of 1800 was but a memory by the eve of the Civil War. The industrial revolution had changed the United States visibly. George Rogers Taylor characterized the national economy in 1860.[5]

> By 1860 the colonial orientation of the American economy . . . had disappeared, and a national economy had taken its place. No longer were more than nine-tenths of American agriculture and industry concentrated within a narrow strip extending no farther inland than a hundred miles from the Atlantic coast, nor was dependence upon foreign trade and European markets the most universal characteristic of the economy. . . . Changes . . . especially those of the transportation revolution, had resulted in the creation of a new and really national economic orientation.
>
> . . . American importers and exporters were beginning to compete on more nearly equal terms with British merchants.
>
> . . . The extreme dependence on foreign markets for disposing of American wheat and tobacco had been greatly reduced. This followed not only from the increasing diversification of American agriculture and industry but also from the tremendously expanded home market for domestic products.
>
> . . . .
>
> . . . Banking and finance had become a separate calling which was further differentiated with the rise of commercial banks, savings banks, insurance companies, note brokers, clearinghouses, and stock exchanges. With the rise of factories, manufacturing had become separated from marketing, and with the transportation revolution the actual moving of goods in foreign and domestic trade had become largely the responsibility of common carriers. . . .
>
> New York had firmly established itself as the great distributing center of the nation for both domestic and foreign goods. Here, centered in Pearl Street, were the jobbers and wholesalers to whose establishments came by coastwise vessel and railroad train country retailers from the South and West. . . .
>
> This emerging national economy of 1860 had a new orientation. The great cities of the East no longer faced the sea and gave their chief attention to shipping and foreign trade. Their commerce centered increasingly now at the railroad stations rather than at the docks, and the commercial news from Mobile, Memphis, Louisville, Cleveland, and Chicago was awaited with greater interest than that from Liverpool, Marseilles, or Antwerp. But though the American economy now faced the rapidly developing West, the leadership and the organizing genius remained concentrated in the great eastern cities. There, on Wall Street, State Street, and Broad Street, the leaders of the emerging era of finance capitalism were beginning to appear. By means

---

[5]George Rogers Taylor, *The Transportation Revolution, 1815-1860* (New York: Rinehart & Co., 1951), pp. 396-398.

of well-placed investments, by speculation and manipulation on the stock and produce exchanges, and by membership on the boards of directors of banks, insurance companies, cotton mills, and railroads, these rising entrepreneurs, the successors of the older sedentary merchants, were soon to play the directing role in the emerging national economy of stocks and bonds and debentures.

How Do Economists Explain This Dramatic Change Between 1800 and 1860?

The startling difference between life in 1800 and that in 1860 came as a result of industrialization. Economists generally agree that it was the Napoleonic Wars which stimulated American economic growth. Technological developments and periods of prosperity aided economic expansion, so that by about 1840 conditions were ripe for industrial expansion at an accelerated rate. August C. Bolino depicted this transitional period.[6]

> Although the United States was plagued with all the problems of any underdeveloped country, including shortage of capital, absence of adequate technology, and insufficient supply and demand for its products, soon there were signs that growth would occur. There were ample natural resources, the political climate was favorable for growth, and the prospects of increasing foreign demand for our goods could not have appeared more promising, since the war between France and Great Britain created markets from both sources.

Fite and Reese added other reasons for the rapid transition of America's prepared economy into industrial capitalism.[7]

> . . . Factors involved in the quickening economic pace following the 1830's included larger industrial establishments based on a growing market, improved economic organization involving greater specialization and division of labor, imports of large quantities of foreign capital to be invested first in canals and later in railroads, and a remarkable westward expansion which not only increased the supply of staple crops for export but acquired gold in California.

---

[6]Bolino, *op. cit.*, p. 62.

[7]Fite and Reese, *op. cit.*, p. 132.

What Caused the Dramatic Industrial Growth After About 1840?

Exactly what happened to cause a rapid industrial growth in the generation preceding the Civil War is hotly debated by economic historians. Economists of today generally gravitate to one of two basic theories to explain the development. One fact is sure, however. Both sides agree that the critical period of industrialization occurred before the Civil War, not during and/or after that great event, as historians had believed for many years.

What Is "Take-off?"

One of the first economists to theorize that the industrial boom occurred before the Civil War was Walter W. Rostow.[8] According to his theory, when the economy satisfied the preconditions for industrial growth, the traditional agrarian economy succumbed to sustained economic development which he calls "take-off." These preconditions included the following: the spreading of ideas that economic progress is a necessary good for the nation and/or the individual; expanded education; leadership from new enterprising men willing to invest and take a risk; increased investments in "transport, communications, and in raw materials in which other nations may have an economic interest." As agriculture improved and technology developed, manufacturing appeared. The nation was ready for "take-off." Rostow dates this event in America as 1843 to 1860.

August C. Bolino presented one of the clearest explanations of Rostow's thesis.[9]

> Rostow believes that the working capital for industrialization must come from rapid increases in output in agriculture and mining. Agriculture plays a special role: it supplies more food to meet the food problem and to help pay for foreign exchange for capital development; it stimulates capital development in farm machinery, fertilizer, and seeds; and it provides a rising real income for taxation. This tax money can be used to pay for social over-

---

[8]Walter W. Rostow, *The Stages of Economic Growth: A Non-Communist Manifesto* (Cambridge: University Press, 1960).

[9]Bolino, *op. cit.*, pp. 63-64.

head costs—those investments in schools, roads, and other social needs that are a necessary concomitant of growth.

The takeoff is just a new way of looking at some old-fashioned concepts of economic development. We can define it as an industrial revolution that depends on the plowing back of profits in certain key industries. Rostow dates the American takeoff from 1843 to 1860 and states that it was postponed by the high welfare gains that were possible by exploiting land and natural resources. He lists three requirements for takeoff: (1) the rate of investment must exceed 10 per cent, (2) one or more manufacturing sectors must develop with high growth rates, and (3) there must emerge a political, social, and institutional framework that exploits these impulses to expansion.

Requirement number two states that general economic growth is thus dependent on the growth of leading sectors, a development that is related to a diffusion of new cost-reducing processes and innovations that bring about advances in other sectors that are supplemental to the leading ones. According to Rostow, the introduction of the railroad has been the most powerful single initiator of takeoffs in the western world, because the growth of railroads resulted in an increase in the demand for coal, iron, shovels and other capital goods.

What Other Interpretation Is There?

In opposition to the Rostow theory, Douglass C. North offered an alternative explanation of the acceleration in industrial development.[10] North emphasized the importance of international trade. August Bolino explained North's thesis.[11]

> . . . The gist of his argument is that the growth of an economy depends on the success of the export sector, the characteristics of exports, and the way the income is spent. North stresses the initiating role of a successful export sector. Up to that time, the domestic market is small and very scattered, specialization is limited by the size of the market, hence self-sufficiency persists.
>
> When a significant export market develops, the domestic market increases also, money income rises, and division of labor results. This sets in motion a series of occurrences that lead to sustained economic growth. Credits earned from exports help to finance essential imports, especially capital goods.

---

[10] Douglass C. North, *The Economic Growth of the United States, 1790-1860* (Englewood Cliffs, New Jersey: Prentice-Hall, Inc., 1961).

[11] Bolino, *op. cit.*, p. 64.

The rate of growth of any region is thus seen to depend on its natural endowments, transport costs, and any technological changes that affect the terms of trade. These developments are accompanied by an increase in productive capacity, a growth of population, an increase in entrepreneurial talents, and a rising productivity. North emphasizes that this productivity stems from technological advances that are a fairly automatic response to the growth of industries under this competitive market structure.

Summary

Noting the example of the United States, newly independent and underdeveloped nations believe that rapid industrialization will bring them the material prosperity which Americans enjoy. The United States gained virtually no economic independence and relatively little prosperity by separating from England. Not until American industrialization occurred, the time and cause of which are still under debate, was the United States able to generate the enormous wealth it possesses in the twentieth century.

Selected References:

Henry Adams, *The United States in 1800* (Ithaca, N.Y.: Cornell University Press, 1955).*
A vivid portrayal of American life at this time.

Douglass C. North, *Growth and Welfare in the American Past: A New Economic History* (Englewood Cliffs, New Jersey: Prentice-Hall, Inc., 1966).
A non-technical appraisal of American economic history.

Walter W. Rostow, *The Stages of Economic Growth: A Non-Communist Manifesto* (Cambridge: University Press, 1960).
A technical description of the development of manufacturing.

George Rogers Taylor, *The Transportation Revolution, 1815-1860,* vol. IV, The Economic History of the United States (New York: Rinehart & Co., 1951).
The significance of transportation in economic developments of the period.

TERM PROJECTS:

A. Either analyze the growth or evaluate the importance of one improvement in transportation during the first half of the nineteenth century.

B. How did technology change American life between 1815 and 1860?

CHECKUP FOR STUDY

Name: ______________________________

1. Why do underdeveloped countries desire foreign aid?

2. What do Saxons have to do with Jeffersonian America?

3. Comment: "They don't build houses like they used to in the time of Washington and Jefferson. Those were the good old days."

4. List some of the major economic changes which occurred between 1800 and 1860.

To remove this page: Open the book as wide as possible several times to loosen this page from the binding. Lay the book flat on your desk and gently but firmly pull this page *straight up* and away from the binding from top to bottom.

5. Comment: "By signing this Declaration of Independence," boasted a delegate in 1776, "we are improving the well-being of every American."

6. Comment: "The United States won total independence–in every facet of life–with the Treaty of Paris in 1783."

7. What is the meaning of "take-off" as used in this Theme?

8. Describe briefly the major arguments that North used against Rostow.

9.

10.

"Don't worry, amigo. Let the Gringos capture our beloved Mexico City. After they drink the water, the city will be ours again."

James F. Wickens

11 God, Gringos and Guns

MANIFEST DESTINY: A mid-nineteenth century term denoting the conviction of United States citizens that God had destined them to rule all of North America. Supposedly, though not necessarily in fact, all conquered non-citizens were to enjoy the benefits of American democracy and rights.

REFERENCE DATES:

1836 Texas won independence and became a republic

1845	U.S.-Mexican border dispute erupted; Slidell mission failed; Texas admitted as the 28th state
1846	Congress declared war on Mexico; California declared its independence; Oregon Treaty ratified
1847	Americans captured Mexico City
1848	Treaty of Guadalupe-Hildalgo ratified

What Is the Chicano Movement?

Now evident in California and the American Southwest, is the Chicano Movement. A slang derivative of "Mexicano," "Chicano" generally applies to those persons of Mexican descent born in the United States. Older generations used the terms "Mexican-American" and "Spanish-speaking American." The younger generation prefers "Chicano," for it also symbolizes a different kind of person, one involved in a mass movement demanding equal rights and justice. The roots of this movement are in the distant past. Independent expressions of resistance and frustration with Anglo-Saxon America date back to the War with Mexico. Recent manifestations of discontent include the "Huelga" (farm workers' strike in California) and the Los Angeles school boycott of 1967. Wanted are educational improvements and ethnic studies programs, for people of Mexican descent have the lowest educational attainment and income levels in the American Southwest, according to a UCLA Mexican-American Study Project in 1967.

Chicanos have applied history in their argument for equality. In the following excerpt from a leaflet passed out among students in southern Alameda County, California, the Chicanos expressed their controversial viewpoint.[1]

After America illegally usurped one-half of Mexico, after America cleared its conscience through the euphemism "Manifest Destiny" and a token payment [of] $15 million, the brutal process of destroying Mexican people's self-

[1]"Chicanos on the Move," mimeographed leaflet (Hayward, California: Mexican-American Student Committee, February, 1969).

concept, culture, and dignity began. The educational system has followed suit in the exploitative mechanism of imperalism.

. . . .

The educational system hides its own inadequacies for teaching Spanish-speaking people by inventing the myth of the language barrier of our children. With our original tongue severed, we rejected the forced attempts to shove the alien "English" language down our throats. . . .

. . . The Guadalupe-Hidalgo Treaty (Mexican-American War, 1848) essentially guaranteed the honoring of land grants and cultural autonomy for the Mexican people. Because of the blatant violation of this treaty by the United States, we are forced to make these minimal reasonable demands. They represent our reassertion of our own unique soul and cultural heritage.

How Have Mexicans Viewed the War?

Some people south of the border would undoubtedly sympathize with the Chicano viewpoint, for bitterness over the war still persists. J. Patrick McHenry described this attitude.[2]

There is not a Mexican today who does not feel somewhat bitter about the war of 1847.

It is said that the word "gringo" came out of this war. American troops while marching along often broke out with a lusty rendition of the ancient ballad "Green Grow the Rushes, Oh!" and the Mexicans, mispronouncing and misinterpreting the words, shortened it to "Grin Go," which thereafter became a name for Americans or American-looking English-speaking people living in Mexico.

By the end of July the last regiment of American marines had been evacuated from Mexico. The Mexican people were depressed and disillusioned. Their mines and farms had been neglected for so long that commerce had practically come to a standstill, and their roads were overrun by gangs of armed bandits whose brutal crimes were going unpunished. . . .

In support of these comments, Ramón Eduardo Ruiz pointed out that Mexican scholars engaged in historical fantasy.[3]

---

[2]J. Patrick McHenry, *A Short History of Mexico* (Garden City, New York: Doubleday & Co., 1962), pp. 114-115.

[3]Ramón Eduardo Ruiz, *The Mexican War: Was It Manifest Destiny?* American Problem Studies (New York: Holt, Rinehart and Winston, 1963), p. 1.

For historians and laymen alike of that country, the war is one of the tragedies of history. Unlike the Americans who have relegated the conflict to the past, Mexicans have not forgotten. Mexico emerged from the war bereft of half of its territory, a beaten, discouraged, and divided people. Dreams of international prominence had vanished forever. The treaty of Guadalupe Hidalgo outlined clearly the scope of their disaster. Mexican scholars are still engrossed with "what might have been" if General Antonio López de Santa Anna had vanquished the invaders from the north.

As tragic as this war may have been, not all Mexicans agreed with the convictions shared by those noted above. Hubert Herring described the opposing viewpoint.[4]

. . . In the judgment of Lesley Simpson, Mexico had been "defeated in advance by hatreds, jealousies, poverty, despair, indifference and apathy," an opinion shared by many Mexicans. The disastrous defeat worked a great upheaval in Mexico. It brought about not only economic chaos, with the loss of credit and man power, but also a shattering sense of moral defeat. Now the people knew how weak, how corrupt, how inexpert their leaders were; they knew how far they must travel to gain unity and strength. In 1850 an American traveler described the country: "Impoverished, haughty, uneducated, defiant, bigoted, disputatious, without financial credit, beaten in arms, far behind the age of mechanical progress or social civilization, Mexico presents a spectacle in the 19th Century . . . that moves reflective men to compassion." Thoughtful Mexicans, in honest self-criticism, considered "the disgraces of the war and the scandal of civil discord," and some at least hoped "that the hard lesson that we received will serve us to reform our conduct, obliging us to take the necessary precautions to avoid repetition of those disgraceful events; . . . we must prepare ourselves to stop in time the blows with which ambition and perfidy threaten us." There were, however, many Mexicans who wished that the United States had carried its conquest further in order to assure tranquillity to their troubled country.

How Have Americans Viewed the War?

The war with Mexico was, for many Americans, part of the American success story, as Ramón Eduardo Ruiz suggested.[5]

---

[4]Hubert Herring, from *A History of Latin America* (New York: Alfred A. Knopf, 1964), pp. 323-324. © Copyright 1955, 1961 by Hubert Herring, 1968 by Helen Baldwin Herring. Reprinted by permission of Alfred A. Knopf, Inc.

[5]Ruiz, *op. cit.*, p. 1.

No war waged by the United States has won more striking victories than the Mexican War 1846-1848. After an unbroken string of military triumphs from Buena Vista to Chapultepec and the occupation of their first foreign capital, Americans added the sprawling territories of New Mexico and California to their domain. The United States had also fulfilled its Manifest Destiny, that belief of American expansionists that Providence had willed them a moral mission to occupy all adjacent lands. No American can deny that war had proved profitable.

Accepting the American victory as fact, Samuel Flagg Bemis denied that winning the war was profitable.[6]

. . . James K. Polk allowed Mexico to begin the war, and this, too, without any dishonorable action on his part to precipitate it. The war added a vast domain to the United States, at a total cost of $118,250,000–in addition to the several thousands of lives on both sides–fifteen millions for the "purchased" territory, $3,250,000 for the released claims, and $100,000,000 for the military cost of the war. The acquisition of the new regions brought to a head the bitter and long dormant controversy over the status of slavery in the territories of the United States, which was eased temporarily by the Compromise of 1850, only soon to be upset–following the election of President Franklin Pierce in the Democratic triumph of 1852–by the Kansas-Nebraska Act and the tragic train of events which led directly to the secession of the southern states and the Civil War. That war cost the United States over a half million men, untold human suffering, and, if we add the cost of interest on debt and pensions up to the present time, an amount of money equal to the total wealth of the country, North and South, at the beginning of the war in 1861. Notwithstanding all this it would be well-nigh impossible today to find a citizen of the United States who would desire to undo Polk's war, and the treaty of Guadalupe Hidalgo. . . .

Regardless of the fact that the war was a success, profitable or not, prominent Americans of the era criticized the nation's action against Mexico. Hubert Herring recorded this dissent.[7]

In the United States, despite the general popularity of the war, there was an unhappy sense of poor sportsmanship that grew with the years. Abraham Lincoln, a congressman when the war began, challenged the administration by asking whether the first American blood had not indeed been shed on

[6]Samuel Flagg Bemis, *A Diplomatic History of the United States* (New York: Holt, Rinehart and Winston, 1955 ed.), p. 244.

[7]Herring, *op. cit.*, p. 324.

Mexican soil. Ulysses S. Grant, in his last years, described the war as "the most unjust ever waged by a stronger against a weaker nation." Robert E. Lee expressed himself in similar fashion. American historians generally regard it as one of the less glorious episodes in the history of the United States, although they accept it as a step in the inevitable American expansion to the Pacific.

What Role Did Manifest Destiny Play in Causing the War?

Manifest Destiny played an important role in causing the war. Whether it was the primary cause is still a much debated issue among historians. Coined in late 1845 by John L. O'Sullivan, editor of the *New York Morning News,* "Manifest Destiny" expressed the rationale for the American existence. Extending the American way of life was the holy mission God had vested in His chosen people, the Americans. Typical of northern Democratic newspapers, the *New York Sun* propounded this attitude.[8]

> The [Mexican] race is perfectly accustomed to being conquered, and the only new lesson we shall teach is that our victories will give liberty, safety, and prosperity to the vanquished, if they know enough to profit by the appearance of our stars. To *liberate* and *ennoble*–not to *enslave* and *debase*–is our mission. Well may the Mexican nation, whose great masses have never yet tasted liberty, prattle over their lost phantom of nationality. . . . If they have not–in the profound darkness of their vassal existence–the intelligence and manhood to accept the ranks and rights of freeman at our hands, we must bear with their ignorance. But there is no excuse for the man educated under our institutions, who talks of our "wronging the Mexicans" when we offer them a position infinitely above any they have occupied, since their history began, and in which, for the first time, they may aim at the greatness and dignity of a truly republican and self-governing people.

This conviction of American superiority had deep roots in the past. According to Ramón Eduardo Ruiz, the belief dated back to Jamestown.[9]

---

[8]*New York Sun* editorial (October 22, 1847), as quoted in *The War with Mexico: Why Did It Happen?* ed. Armin Rappaport (Chicago: Rand McNally, 1964), p. 45.

[9]Ramón Eduardo Ruiz, reprinted from Quint, et al., *Main Problems in American History,* Vol. I (Homewood, Illinois: The Dorsey Press, 1964 ed.), pp. 251-252.

Manifest Destiny voiced the expansionist sentiment that had gripped Americans almost from the day their forefathers had landed on the shores of the New World in the seventeenth century. Englishmen and their American offspring had looked westward since Jamestown and Plymouth, confident that time and fate would open to them the vast West that stretched out before them. Manifest Destiny, then, was first territorial expansion–American pretensions to lands held by Spain, France, and later Mexico; some even spoke of a United States with boundaries from pole to pole. But Manifest Destiny was greater than mere land hunger; much more was involved. Pervasive was a spirit of nationalism, the belief that what Americans upheld was right and good, that Providence had designated them the chosen people. In a political framework, Manifest Destiny stood for democracy as Americans conceived it; to spread democracy and freedom was the goal. Included also were ideals of regeneration, the conquest of virgin lands for the sake of their development, and concepts of Anglo-Saxon superiority. All of these slogans and beliefs played a role in the Mexican question that culminated in hostilities in 1846.

Of course, not all Americans saw expansionism as the American mission. Eighty-five year old former Secretary of Treasury (1801-1814) Albert Gallatin vigorously opposed the war. He defined the role of America differently.[10]

> Your mission was, to be a model for all other governments and for all other less favored nations, to adhere to the most elevated principles of political morality, to apply all your faculties to the gradual improvement of your own institutions and social state, and, by your example, to exert a moral influence most beneficial to mankind at large. Instead of this, an appeal has been made to your worst passions; to cupidity, to the thirst of unjust aggrandizement by brutal force; to the love of military fame and of false glory; and it has even been tried to pervert the noblest feelings of your nature. The attempt is made to make you abandon the lofty position which your fathers occupied, to substitute for it the political morality and heathen patriotism of the heroes and statesmen of antiquity. . . .

Did Sectional Interests Cause the Mexican War?

Not all historians agree that Manifest Destiny caused war in 1846. Some have contended that sectional interests were responsible. In the cen-

[10]Albert Gallatin, *Peace with Mexico* (New York: E. O. Jenkins, 1847), p. 13.

tury since the conquest of Mexico, American historians have implicated different sections of the nation.

Initially, the South bore the brunt of the blame. Contemporaries of the time such as Abraham Lincoln, Daniel Webster and Henry Thoreau denounced southern slave owners for conspiring to cause the war. They charged that slave owners desired to expand the South so that they could fill up Mexican lands with slaves. Southern "slave power" threatened to expand at northern expense. A half century later northern historians still expressed such sentiments.

The next section cited for causing the war was the West. Land hungry and eager to expand, the West sent more than half of the 69,540 volunteers to fight Mexico despite its sparse population at this time. The well populated northern states could only muster about one out of ten volunteers. "It was not merely the question of Texas that set all these [western] troops in motion," asserted William E. Dodds in 1912. "The West wanted most or all of Mexico. . . ."

More recently, Norman A. Graebner challenged these interpretations. He maintained that commercial interests centered in the East were primarily responsible for war.[11]

> Polk alone could fulfill the expansionist goals of the forties. Although he was an advocate of agrarian democracy, his expansionist outlook as President was as narrowly mercantile as that of Webster or Winthrop. He accepted the wisdom of compromise in Oregon for the precise reasons that the Whigs and the metropolitan press called for a settlement along the forty-ninth parallel. His war-time expansionist policy was aimed primarily at San Francisco and San Diego, and as the war neared completion Polk acknowledged no other objectives to Congress. . . .

Did Polk Cause the Mexican War?

Sectional feelings were present during John Tyler's presidency, but no war resulted. Yet Tyler's successor, James K. Polk went to war with Mexico. During his administration and in the century and one-quarter since, some contemporaries of the time and historians have pointed their finger at President Polk himself. His reputation as an expansionist pre-

[11]Norman A. Graebner, *Empire on the Pacific: A Study in American Continental* Expansion (New York: The Ronald Press, copyright 1955), p. 224.

ceded him to the presidency in 1845. Moreover, once there, in a famous cabinet session on May 9, 1846, Polk asserted his right to commence war without a Mexican attack.[12]

> The Cabinet held a regular meeting to-day; all the members present. I brought up the Mexican question, and the question of what was the duty of the administration in the present state of our relations with that country. The subject was very fully discussed. All agreed that if the Mexican forces at Matamoras committed any act of hostility on Gen'l Taylor's forces I should immediately send a message to Congress recommending an immediate declaration of War. I stated to the Cabinet that up to this time, as they knew, we had heard of no open act of aggression by the Mexican army, but that the danger was imminent that such acts would be committed. I said that in my opinion we had ample cause of war, and that it was impossible that we could stand in *status quo,* or that I could remain silent much longer; that I thought it was my duty to send a message to Congress very soon and recommend definitive measures. I told them that I thought I ought to make such a message by tuesday next, that the country was excited and impatient on the subject, and if I failed to do so I would not be doing my duty. I then propounded the distinct question to the Cabinet and took their opinions individually, whether I should make a message to Congress on tuesday, and whether in that message I should recommend a declaration of War against Mexico. . . .

Some historians have asserted that President Polk was hell-bent to fight Mexico. His *Diary* indicated a determination to obtain New Mexico and California by any means. Other historians have exonerated the President, asserting that, despite Mexico's diplomatic rebuffs, Polk persisted in patient negotiation of issues relating to Texas. A historical judgment of this question requires further study of these points of view.

Summary

The present-day Chicano Movement to some degree expresses the Mexican bitterness resulting from the Mexican-American War of 1846-1848. Historians still debate why the United States went to war. Some argue for the profit motive. Others see Manifest Destiny as the primary reason

---

[12]Milo M. Quaife, ed., *The Diary of James Knox Polk,* Vol. I, (Chicago: A. C. McClurg, 1910), p. 384.

for fighting. Still others contend that sectional interests caused the embroilment or charge President Polk with personal responsibility for not preventing war.

Selected References:

José F. Ramírez, *Mexico during the War with the United States,* trans. Walter V. Scholes (Columbia, Missouri: University of Missouri Press, 1950).
Life, events and viewpoints from the Mexican side of the war.

Ramón Eduardo Ruiz, ed., *The Mexican War, Was It Manifest Destiny?* (New York: Holt, Rinehart and Winston, 1963). An analysis and collection of excerpts on the issue.

Otis A. Singletary, *The Mexican War* (Chicago: University of Chicago Press, 1960).
A synopsis of the military aspects of the war.

Albert K. Weinberg, *Manifest Destiny: A Study of National Expansion in American History* (Baltimore: Johns Hopkins Press, 1935). An extensive investigation of American thought on expansion.

Term Projects:

A. Evaluate Polk's contributions to the causes of the Mexican War.

B. From a Mexican viewpoint, describe the causes and results of the war with the United States.

CHECKUP FOR STUDY

Name: ______________________

1. Define "Manifest Destiny" in your own words.

2. How would Mexican historical fantasy treat the California gold rush?

3. Why was Mexico so easy to defeat?

4. Do you consider the Mexican War profitable for the U.S.? Why?

To remove this page: Open the book as wide as possible several times to loosen this page from the binding. Lay the book flat on your desk and gently but firmly pull this page *straight up* and away from the binding from top to bottom.

5. Why did many prominent Americans criticize the war?

6. Briefly describe the meaning of the American "mission"?

7. Why did northern historians blame the South for the Mexican War?

8. What specifically did mercantile interests want?

9.

10.

"Another thing we don't like about it, Mrs. Stowe,
it wouldn't sell in the South."

Burr Shafer, *The Wonderful World of J. Wesley Smith*,
New York: The Vanguard Press, 1960

12 Losing Our Cool

SECESSION: The formal withdrawal from an organization, as the withdrawal of one section of a nation from the nation as a whole.

REFERENCE DATES:

1854 Kansas-Nebraska Act; organization of the Republican Party

1860 Abraham Lincoln elected sixteenth President; South Carolina seceded

1861	Confederate States of America formed; Fort Sumter fired upon; the Civil War began
1862	Battle of Antietam, high point of Confederacy; Preliminary Emancipation Proclamation issued (effective January 1, 1863)
1864	Sherman marched to the sea; the Milligan Case; Lincoln reelected
1865	The Appomattox surrender; Lincoln assassinated; Thirteenth Amendment ratified

What Causes Secession in Africa?

Secession and civil war are not uncommon in our modern world. Africa, in particular, has had several bitter cases during the past decade where warfare resulted from political separatist movements. The most devastating, perhaps, has been in Nigeria. Lloyd Garrison visited the scene and wrote of this event.[1]

> Also at stake was an old principle with an intriguing new meaning—self-determination. Africa had won its first round for self-determination in gaining independence from colonialism. Now it was facing a second: the demand of Africa's many ethnic groups to shape their own destinies without being bound to the colonial-imposed concept of "territorial integrity."
>
> . . . .
>
> The war's causes were built into the fabric of Nigeria, a nation born an accident of colonial history—and, in reality, several nations within a nation. Even before the current crisis, each of Nigeria's three major peoples had felt itself so endangered by the others that it had threatened to secede. In fact, only a last-minute compromise prevented the Northern Region from withdrawing before independence in 1960, so fearful were its Moslem rulers of being submerged by the less numerous but better educated Yoruba and Ibo Christians to the south.

What Caused Secession in America?

Whether the foregoing explanation of civil war in Africa will remain unchanged in history books, only time will tell. Time heals all wounds, some

[1]Lloyd Garrison, "Biafra vs. Nigeria: The Other Dirty Little War," *New York Times Magazine,* 31 March 1968, p. 37.

say, and in the writing of history, time aids in removing contemporary bias and emotion from the written page.

In the case of the American Civil War (1861-1865), time appears to have provided little assistance to the historian. For over a century writers have flooded the historical marketplace with explanations of the causes of the war. In practically each case, a multitude of rebuttals have followed. It may be that students will never be able to find a simple answer to the question: What caused the Civil War? Any attempt to do so now requires a pair of intellectual hip boots to wade through the flood of printed answers.

On the surface, the reason for so many conflicting interpretations appears simple. In a war which pitted brother against brother, one need only determine which brother was fighting for the just cause. The intellectual complexities of the problem prove far more vexing, however, as Thomas N. Bonner plainly revealed.[2]

> Historians in general . . . continue to use the term "cause" as if it had definite and precise meaning. Does causation mean to them only regularity of sequence? Or does it imply the predictability of events? Does it mean that like causes have like effects? What does it mean when one speaks of the causes of the Civil War? . . .
>
> Most writers on the Civil War, however, have not troubled to define terms in describing the background and causes of that struggle. This has been true even of the recent revisionists, who have dramatically echoed the denial of the Peace Democrats that slavery was a morally irrepressible force in causing war. No critical attention has been given even to such key concepts as causation and inevitability. . . .

In the remainder of this Theme we will examine the causes of war as cited by the two belligerent presidents, Jefferson Davis and Abraham Lincoln. The issues which these two men presented provide arguments representative of those which historians have developed during the past century.

Did a Conspiracy Cause War?

Before, during and after the American Civil War, politicians and writers in each section had suggested that the other was conspiring to convert

---

[2]Thomas N. Bonner, "Civil War Historians and the 'Needless War' Doctrine," *The Journal of the History of Ideas,* Vol. XVII (1956), pp. 193-194.

the entire nation to its own way of life. Southern Democrats feared the Republicans, referring to them as "Black Republicans," for they threatened the southern way of life. Jefferson Davis reflected this fear.[3]

As soon, however, as the Northern States, that prohibited African slavery within their limits, had reached a number sufficient to give their representation a controlling vote in Congress, a persistent and organized system of hostile measures against the rights of the owners of slaves in the Southern States was inaugurated and gradually extended. A series of measures was devised and prosecuted for the purpose of rendering insecure the tenure of property in slaves.

Fanatical organizations, supplied with money by voluntary subscriptions, were assiduously engaged in exciting amongst the slaves a spirit of discontent and revolt. Means were furnished for their escape from their owners, and agents secretly employed to entice them to abscond.

On the other hand, northerners, particularly abolitionists, spoke of "Slave Power," the ruthless and secret attempt to transform all of America into a den of slavery. Although not an abolitionist before the war, and never particularly rabid, Lincoln nonetheless became an abolitionist as the war progressed. By the end of the hostilities, Lincoln too could see a Slave Power threat to the Union, as he stated.[4]

One-eighth of the whole population were colored slaves, not distributed generally over the Union, but localized in the Southern part of it. These slaves constituted a peculiar and powerful interest. All knew that this interest was, somehow, the cause of the war. To strengthen, perpetuate, and extend this interest was the object for which the insurgents would rend the Union, even by war; while the government claimed no right to do more than to restrict the territorial enlargement of it.

Was the Cause Constitutional?

The Constitution of 1787 was vague and ineffective in answering many questions over the division of powers. Was the Union sovereign over

---

[3]Jefferson Davis, address to Confederate Congress, April 29, 1861. All quotes from Davis are from this address, which can be found in *The Rebellion Record,* Vol. I, ed. Frank Moore (New York: G. P. Putnam, 1864), pp. 166-175.

[4]Abraham Lincoln, Second Inaugural Address, March 4, 1865. All quotes from Lincoln's addresses can be found in *Abraham Lincoln: Complete Works,* Vol. II, eds. John G. Nicolay and John Hay (New York: The Century Company, 1915), pp. 1-7, 55-66, 656-657.

the states, or were the states sovereign over the Union? Did the constitutional Fathers mean "the united states," or did they mean "the states united," as John C. Calhoun had claimed. Both sections argued the point for decades, and both shifted their positions when necessary. On the question of secession, however, there was no compromise of issues. Jefferson Davis argued the secessionist view.

Here it may be proper to observe that, from a period as early as 1798, there had existed in all of the States of the Union a party almost uninterruptedly in the majority, based upon the creed that each State was, in the last resort, the sole judge as well of its wrongs as of the mode and measures of redress. Indeed, it is obvious that under the law of nations this principle is an axiom as applied to the relations of independent sovereign States, such as those which had united themselves under the constitutional compact.

In reply, Lincoln voiced opposing convictions.[5]

The States have their status in the Union, and they have no other legal status. If they break from this, they can only do so against law and by revolution. The Union, and not themselves separately, procured their independence and their liberty. By conquest or purchase the Union gave each of them whatever of independence or liberty it has. The Union is older than any of States, and, in fact, it created them as States. Originally some dependent colonies made the Union, and, in turn, the Union threw off their old dependence for them, and made them States, such as they are. Not one of them ever had a State constitution independent of the Union. Of course, it is not forgotten that all the new States framed their constitutions before they entered the Union—nevertheless, dependent upon and preparatory to coming into the Union.

Did Slavery Cause the War?

Fundamental to both the conspiracy thesis and the constitutional debate was the question of slavery. Was slavery morally right or morally wrong? No other issue before the war caused more heated public debate. Both sides appealed to the Bible, history and law to support their claim of moral correctness. Jefferson Davis cited the southern defense of slavery.

---

[5]Lincoln, address to United States Congress, July 4, 1861.

In the meantime, under the mild and genial climate of the Southern States, and the increasing care for the well-being and comfort of the laboring classes, dictated alike by interest and humanity, the African slaves had augmented in number from about six hundred thousand, at the date of the adoption of the constitutional compact, to upwards of four millions.

In a moral and social condition they had been elevated from brutal savages into docile, intelligent, and civilized agricultural laborers, and supplied not only with bodily comforts, but with careful religious instruction, under the supervision of a superior race. . . .

Early in his presidency, Abraham Lincoln did not attack slavery where established, but he did limit its expansion.[6]

Apprehension seems to exist among the people of the Southern States that by the accession of a Republican administration their property and their peace and personal security are to be endangered. There has never been any reasonable cause for such apprehension. Indeed, the most ample evidence to the contrary has all the while existed and been open to their inspection. It is found in nearly all the published speeches of him who now addresses you. I do but quote from one of those speeches when I declare that "I have no purpose, directly or indirectly, to interfere with the institution of slavery in the States where it exists. I believe I have no lawful right to do so, and I have no inclination to do so." Those who nominated and elected me did so with full knowledge that I had made this and many similar declarations, and never recanted them.

Later in his presidency, Lincoln condemned slavery as unjust before God.[7]

The Almighty has his own purposes. "Woe unto the world because of offenses! for it must needs be that offenses come; but woe to that man by whom the offense cometh." If we shall suppose that American slavery is one of those offenses which, in the providence of God, must needs come, but which, having continued through his appointed time, he now wills to remove, and that he gives to both North and South this terrible war, as the woe due to those by whom the offense came, shall we discern therein any departure from those divine attributes which the believers in a living God always ascribe to him? Fondly do we hope—fervently do we pray—that this mighty

---

[6]Lincoln, First Inaugural Address, March 4, 1861.

[7]Lincoln, Second Inaugural Address.

scourge of war may speedily pass away. Yet, if God wills that it continue until all the wealth piled by the bondman's two hundred and fifty years of unrequited toil shall be sunk, and until every drop of blood drawn with the lash shall be paid by another drawn with the sword, as was said three thousand years ago, so still it must be said, "The judgments of the Lord are true and righteous altogether."

Was the Cause Economic?

In the early twentieth century, after the impact of the industrial revolution was apparent, historians led by Charles A. Beard considered sectional economic differences at the root of the Civil War. Each section desired specific economic legislation to benefit itself. Another historian, Louis M. Hacker, once claimed: "Civil War was nothing less than a conflict between two different systems of economic production; and with the victory at the Presidential polls in 1860 of the higher order, the young industrial capitalism of the North and Middle West, a counter-revolutionary movement was launched by the defenders of the lower order, the slave lords of the South."

Jefferson Davis presented the southern economic viewpoint.

> The people of the Southern States, whose almost exclusive occupation was agriculture, early perceived a tendency in the Northern States to render a common government subservient to their own purposes by imposing burthens on commerce as protection to their manufacturing and shipping interests.
>
> Long and angry controversies grew out of these attempts, often successful, to benefit one section of the country at the expense of the other, and the danger of disruption arising from this cause was enhanced by the fact that the Northern population was increasing, by emigration and other causes, more than the population of the South.

Abraham Lincoln represented a party with northern and western economic interests. To understand his party's view, the student should examine five points in the 1860 Republican Platform. Where applicable, major laws enacted under Lincoln follow each point.[8]

---

[8]*Proceedings of the First Three Republican National Conventions o*ȷ *1856, 1860, and 1864* (Minneapolis: Charles W. Johnson, 1893), pp. 132-133. Italics have been added.

12. That, while providing revenue for the support of the general government by duties upon imports, sound policy requires such an *adjustment of* these *imposts* as to encourage the development of the industrial interests of the whole country; and we commend that *policy of national exchanges,* which secures to the working men liberal wages, to agriculture remunerating prices, to mechanics and manufacturers an adequate reward for their skill, labor, and enterprise, and to the nation commercial prosperity and independence. (Morrill Tariff, March 2, 1861; National Bank Act, February 25, 1863, and amended June 3, 1864.)

13. That we protest against any sale or alienation to others of the public lands held by actual settlers, and against any view of the free homestead policy which regards the settlers as paupers or suppliants for public bounty; and we demand the passage by Congress of the complete and satisfactory *homestead measure* which has already passed the House. (Homestead Act, May 20, 1862.)

14. That the Republican party is opposed to any change in our naturalization laws or any State legislation by which the rights of citizenship hitherto accorded to *immigrants* from foreign lands shall be abridged or impaired; and in favor of giving a full and efficient protection to the rights of all classes of citizens, whether native or naturalized, both at home and abroad. (Immigration Act, July 4, 1864.)

15. That appropriations by Congress for *river and harbor improvements* of a national character, required for the accommodation and security of an existing commerce, are authorized by the Constitution, and justified by the obligation of Government to protect the lives and property of its citizens.

16. That a *railroad to the Pacific Ocean* is imperatively demanded by the interests of the whole country; that the Federal Government ought to render immediate and efficient aid in its construction; and that, as preliminary thereto, a daily overland mail should be promptly established. (Pacific Railroad Act, July 1, 1862.)

Was the Civil War Inevitable?

Was the Civil War a costly step forward in American progress, or was it an avoidable mistake? Just before the United States entered World War II, a group of "revisionist" historical interpretations appeared. Influenced perhaps by their southern background, these historians condemned antebellum leaders for blundering the nation into war. By their stupid, irrational, exaggerated and uncompromising positions, the revisionists charged, antebellum agitators created a needless crisis and plunged the nation into civil war.

In the past generation the revisionist thesis has come under increasing criticism. In fact, a few of these historians appear to have reevaluated their interpretations. Avery O. Craven, for example, modified his position to raise the important question of inherent weakness within the democratic structure of government. Can a democracy resolve major domestic issues to satisfy the needs of most all those affected? Interestingly enough, President Lincoln pondered this same question a century earlier, after the attack on Fort Sumter.[9]

> . . . In this act, discarding all else, they have forced upon the country the distinct issue, "immediate dissolution or blood."
>
> And this issue embraces more than the fate of these United States. It presents to the whole family of man the question whether a constitutional republic or democracy—a government of the people by the same people—can or cannot maintain its territorial integrity against its own domestic foes. It presents the question whether discontented individuals, too few in numbers to control administration according to organic law in any case, can always, upon the pretenses made in this case, or on any other pretense, break up their government, and thus practically put an end to free government upon the earth. It forces us to ask: "Is there, in all republics, this inherent and fatal weakness?" "Must a government, of necessity, be too strong for the liberties of its own people, or too weak to maintain its own existence?"

Summary

Sectional withdrawals within nations in modern times are reminiscent of the American experience one century ago. At that time, after the South seceded from the Union, contemporaries then and historians since have argued over the most controversial aspect of the war which followed: Why did secession occur? Primary causes under debate include a conspiracy, constitutional failure, the immorality of slavery, economic competition between sections, and the inevitability of war.

Selected References:

David Donald, ed., *Why the North Won the War* (Baton Rouge: Louisiana State University Press, 1960).*
A variety of answers to the question.

[9]Lincoln, Address of July 4, 1861.

Thomas J. Pressly, *Americans Interpret Their Civil War* (Princeton: Princeton University Press, 1954).
An extensive introduction to many historical writings on the subject.

Edwin C. Rozwenc, *The Causes of the Civil War,* Problems in American Civilization (Boston: D. C. Heath & Co., 1961).*
Excerpts from leading schools of interpretation.

Kenneth M. Stampp, *The Peculiar Institution* (New York: Alfred A. Knopf, 1956).*
Slavery in the antebellum South, objectively analyzed.

TERM PROJECTS:

A. Investigate the following question: why did the North win the War?

B. Why do historians frequently rank Lincoln as the nation's greatest President?

CHECKUP FOR STUDY

Name: ______________________________

1. Why is the term "cause" so difficult to define?

2. In the conspiracy argument, what did Davis mean by "fanatical organizations"?

3. Why was "Slave Power" a threat to the Union?

4. Which do you think had sovereignty over the other in 1860, the states or the union? Why?

To remove this page: Open the book as wide as possible several times to loosen this page from the binding. Lay the book flat on your desk and gently but firmly pull this page *straight up* and away from the binding from top to bottom.

5. What were Lincoln's policies with regard to slavery?

6. Why would Republican economic promises not have satisfied southerners?

7. What weakness in the democratic structure of government encourages secession?

8. What do you think caused the Civil War?

9.

10.

"Just what is it that you people want, anyway?"

Playboy, December 1968, Vol. 15

13 Unfinished Business

RECONSTRUCTION: The process of political reunion whereby seceded states rejoined the nation.

REFERENCE DATES:

1865	Slavery abolished (Amendment 13); Black Codes enacted
1866	Ku Klux Klan founded; Civil Rights Act passed over Presidential veto
1868	Unsuccessful attempt to impeach President Andrew Johnson; Fourteenth Amendment passed

1870	Fifteenth Amendment enacted; first Negroes entered Congress
1875	Another Civil Rights Act passed (invalidated, 1883)
1877	Wormley House bargain: Union troop withdrawal ended Reconstruction

How Have Americans Redefined Their Democracy?

Four years of bloody Civil War had apparently settled the question of secession and slavery in the United States. The nation would never tolerate either again. Unresolved by the struggle, however, was an acceptable definition of "rights"—both states' rights and civil rights.

In 1964, nearly a century later, the Supreme Court upheld a new definition of civil rights which guaranteed federal enforcement of laws for all citizens, regardless of race, with respect to life, liberty and property. In doing so, the Court enhanced the protection of the individual by reducing arbitrary state control, and thus permitted all persons equal opportunity to enjoy individual freedoms previously withheld from some minority groups. This Supreme Court decision upheld a law which President Lyndon Johnson approved over the faltering opposition of southern Democrats and conservative Republicans, led by Senator Barry Goldwater. Briefly stated, the Civil Rights Act of 1964 reduced the multitude of state restrictions which whites had placed on non-whites.[1]

The Civil Rights Act of 1964, signed into law by President Johnson July 2, contained new provisions to help guarantee Negroes the right to vote, guaranteed access to public accommodations such as hotels, motels, restaurants and places of amusement; authorized the Federal Government to sue to desegregate public facilities and schools; extended the life of the Civil Rights Commission for four years and gave it new powers; provided that federal funds could be cut off where programs were administered discriminatorily; required most companies and labor unions to grant equal employment opportunity; established a new Community Relations Service to help work out civil rights problems; required the Census Bureau to gather voting statistics by race; and authorized the Justice Department to enter into any pending civil rights case.

---

[1]*Congressional Quarterly, Almanac, 88th Congress, 2nd Session,* 1964, Vol. XX (Washington, D.C.: 1964), p. 338.

When challenged, the public accommodations section of the act won Supreme Court approval (*Heart of Atlanta Motel* v. *United States,* 1964). Similarly, the following year, the Supreme Court upheld the Voting Rights Act, or Civil Rights Act of 1965 to end literacy tests and enforce laws against poll taxes (*South Carolina* v. *Katzenbach*).

What Was "Radical" Reconstruction?

The great amount of civil rights legislation during the mid-1960's, which incorporated previous civil rights laws, had led a few historians to refer to this period as the "Second Reconstruction" era. Actually, this term refers back to civil rights legislation passed during the "first" Reconstruction (1865-1877) era. The Supreme Court invalidated these early attempts soon afterward.

Reconstruction history is controversial and demands much study of the various issues which arose after the Civil War. Central to many disputes is a definition of federalism itself. Which body, the executive or legislative, should have power over the readmission into the Union of the defeated secessionist states? What were the legitimate areas of federal and state authority? President Lincoln, as President Andrew Johnson after him, asserted that he personally was the ultimate determiner of reunion. Both requested a quick and lenient readmission of the rebel states. Opposed to this plan was a group called "radical" Republicans, led by Senator Charles Sumner and Representative Thaddeus Stevens. Before 1867, as a minority group with an appeal to the majority of Congressmen, the radicals dominated the Reconstruction process. For several years thereafter, they continued to control Congress. Historians call their legislative actions "Radical Reconstruction."

For three-quarters of a century after Reconstruction, writers interpreted the radicals' policies as vindictive attempts by northerners to punish the South for its secession. During the past generation, however, many historians have viewed radical Reconstruction as a sincere attempt to provide freedmen (freed slaves) with the same rights that whites enjoyed. (For serious qualifications of this interpretation, see Theme 23.) LaWanda and John H. Cox rendered some insights into this changing interpretation.[2]

---

[2]LaWanda and John H. Cox, *Politics, Principle, and Prejudice, 1865-1866: Dilemma of Reconstruction America* (New York: The Free Press of Glencoe, 1963), p. 208.

Thus what had once been an advanced, or "Radical," position within Republican ranks, by 1866 had become accepted and moderate. To most opponents of equal civil status, however, the principle still appeared "Radical." Herein lies one clue to the confusion in the use of the term "Radical" which plagues any serious student of the period. The term is inescapable; yet a man labeled a "Radical" by one set of contemporaries or historians is often found designated a "moderate" by another group of contemporaries or historians. All would agree that Charles Sumner, Thaddeus Stevens, and Wendell Phillips, extreme men though not of one mind, were the prototypes of Radicalism. The term *radical,* however, has often been used to identify, and castigate, all Republican opponents of Andrew Johnson. Many of these men were almost as critical of Sumner, Stevens, and Phillips as were their Conservative adversaries. Few followed Stevens in his demand for confiscation; most were ready to abandon or drastically compromise Sumner's aim of Negro suffrage. Though they wished to proceed with caution, there was no strong desire among them for an indefinite postponement of restoration by reducing the South to the status of "territories" or "conquered provinces." In other words, many Radicals were moderate men. The Radical opponents of President Johnson were united in one demand–that of national protection for the freedmen. On other issues of Reconstruction they held widely divergent views.

Thus, while the radicals were able to unite to pass the Civil Rights Bill of 1866, the Freedmen's Bureau Bill and the Radical Reconstruction Bills, they lost by one vote in their attempt to impeach President Johnson.

How Did Expanded Civil Rights Reduce States Rights?

The freeing of slaves at the conclusion of the Civil War created fear among some southern whites that Negroes would become their social equals. To keep the freedmen in their place, many southern states passed "Black Codes." Most extreme in Mississippi and Louisiana, these state laws denied Negroes most basic rights and freedoms guaranteed Caucasians by the Constitution.

To combat these inequities, radical Republicans enacted the Civil Rights Act of 1866 over President Andrew Johnson's veto. This new civil rights law offered freedmen rights of citizenship equal to those of the white man. Also enacted over President Johnson's veto were several Reconstruction Acts in 1867-68 which, among other things, granted

Negro suffrage. By this time, too, northern and western states had provided enough votes to ratify the Fourteenth Amendment to the Constitution. Chase C. Mooney explained the need for this amendment.[3]

The power to create a citizen and to grant a citizen certain rights rested with the states before the adoption of the Constitution, and no one was considered eligible for national citizenship unless he was a citizen of a state. . . . One could be a citizen of a state without being a citizen of a nation–so Chief Justice Taney said in the Dred Scott case of 1857. . . .

. . . [Thus] the duality of the government, state and federal, led to a duality of privileges and immunities. Confusion as to who were citizens and who had the power to confer citizenship was removed by the adoption of the fourteenth amendment in 1868.

. . . .

The fourteenth amendment was considered necessary because many supporters of the Civil Rights Act of April 9, 1866 . . . doubted the constitutionality of that congressional legislation. Why? Because the granting of those rights and privileges was traditionally within the exclusive province of the state governments.

Radical Charles Sumner was not satisfied simply that the ex-slave had gained the right to vote. From his deathbed he provided the leadership for the passage of another Civil Rights Act in 1875 which gave them equal accommodations in public places.[4]

Be it enacted, That all persons within the jurisdiction of the United States shall be entitled to the full and equal enjoyment of the accommodations, advantages, facilities, and privileges of inns, public conveyances on land or water, theaters, and other places of public amusement; subject only to the conditions and limitations established by law, and applicable alike to citizens of every race and color, regardless of any previous condition of servitude.

. . . .

That no citizen possessing all other qualifications which are or may be prescribed by law shall be disqualified for service as grand or petit juror in any court of the United States, or of any State, on account of race, color, or

---

[3]Chase C. Mooney, *Civil Rights: Retrospect and Prospects,* Publication No. 37 (Washington, D.C.: Service Center for Teachers of History, 1961), pp. 3-4. Reprinted by permission of the Service Center for Teachers of History of the American Historical Association.

[4]*U.S. Statutes at Law,* XVIII, pp. 355 ff.

previous condition of servitude; and any officer or other person charged with any duty in the selection or summoning of jurors who shall exclude or fail to summon any citizen for the cause aforesaid shall, on conviction thereof, be deemed guilty of a misdemeanor. . . .

What Motivated Radicals to Act As They Did?

How sincere these radical Republican actions were is a matter of interpretation. Some historians have asserted that behind the radical effort to grant freedmen the suffrage was an attempt to seduce four million ex-slave votes for the Republican Party, thereby assuring its political power in the South. These historians refer to this power as "Black Republicanism," a term which incorrectly implied that ex-slaves ran and corrupted southern governments under Republican protection. By and large, Negroes together with radicals ran southern state governments honestly. Moreover, their control was brief, for in most instances white Democratic conservatives took over before the end of Reconstruction.

Recently, Kenneth M. Stampp challenged the older interpretation of Reconstruction which considered radical Republicans as devils and white southerners as redeeming saints. In Stampp's view, radical Republicans provided much of the mobility of the Civil War years, and most of the idealism of the Union cause. These high motives continued into the Reconstruction era.[5]

In the nineteenth century most white Americans, North and South, had reservations about the Negro's potentialities—doubted that he had the innate intellectual capacity and moral fiber of the white man and assumed that after emancipation he would be relegated to an inferior caste. But some of the radical Republicans refused to believe that the Negroes were innately inferior and hoped passionately that they would confound their critics. The radicals then had little empirical evidence and no scientific evidence to support their belief—nothing, in fact, but faith. Their faith was derived mostly from their religion: all men, they said, are the sons of Adam and equal in the sight of God. And if Negroes are equal to white men in the sight of God, it is morally wrong for white men to withhold from Negroes the liberties and rights that white men enjoy. Here, surely, was a projection into the reconstruction era of the idealism of the abolitionist crusade and of the Civil War.

---

[5]Kenneth M. Stampp, *The Era of Reconstruction, 1865-1877* (New York: Vintage Books, 1967), pp. 12-13. Copyright © 1965 by Kenneth M. Stampp. Reprinted by permission of Alfred A. Knopf, Inc.

Radical idealism was in part responsible for two of the most momentous enactments of the reconstruction years: the Fourteenth Amendment to the federal Constitution which gave Negroes citizenship and promised them equal protection of the laws, and the Fifteenth Amendment which gave them the right to vote. The fact that these amendments could not have been adopted under any other circumstances, or at any other time, before or since, may suggest the crucial importance of the reconstruction era in American history. Indeed, without radical reconstruction, it would be impossible to this day for the federal government to protect Negroes from legal and political discrimination.

Stampp concluded that Reconstruction was a finale to nineteenth century reform.[6] (For a discussion of the latter, see Theme 9.)

. . . The radicals of the reconstruction era were either the reformers of the prewar years or men who had been strongly influenced by their moral imperatives. In fact, radical reconstruction ought to be viewed in part as the last great crusade of the nineteenth-century romantic reformers. Since the radicals were in politics, we may assume that they had learned to accommodate themselves to some of the practical realities of public life and that their pristine innocence may have eroded in the passing years. Nevertheless, it is likely that the radicals were, if anything, somewhat *less* opportunistic in their purposes and a little *more* candid in their public utterances than the average American politician has been. Their pleas for justice for the Negro, their objection to the Johnson governments on the ground that the Black Codes were restoring a form of slavery, cannot be discounted as pure hypocrisy. To the practical motives that the radicals occasionally revealed must be added the moral idealism that they inherited from the abolitionists.

How Did the States Retain Their Suffrage Power?

Although the states ratified the Fifteenth Amendment to the Constitution in 1870, providing suffrage rights for black males, but not for Indians or for women of any race, the Supreme Court reduced the scope of the new amendment. Chase C. Mooney pointed out this reversal.[7]

The amendment conferred suffrage on no one; the right of suffrage was not considered one of the necessary attributes of national citizenship. . . .

[6] *Ibid*, pp. 101-102.

[7] Mooney, *op. cit.*, pp. 8-9.

The right to vote in the states came from the states. The right of protection from discriminatory prohibitions by the states came from the United States. . . . The states may determine the electorate, but the voters may exercise their right freely and without molestation in regard to national elections—a distinction between having the privilege and exercising the privilege!

The Court . . . had made national government responsible for life, liberty, property and equal protection against interference by the states, but it left to the states the power they had always had of protecting these rights from impairment by individuals.

What Happened to the Black's Civil Rights?

All of these efforts by radicals were of little avail. In the Civil Rights Cases of 1883, the Supreme Court invalidated civil rights laws which, the court argued, interfered with states' rights. The essence of the majority opinion follows.[8]

When a man has emerged from slavery, and by the aid of beneficent legislation has shaken off the inseparable concomitants of that state, there must be some stage in the progress of his elevation when he takes the rank of a mere citizen, and ceases to be the special favorite of the laws, and when his rights as a citizen, or a man, are to be protected in the ordinary modes by which other men's rights are protected. There were thousands of free colored people in this country before the abolition of slavery, enjoying all the essential rights of life, liberty and property the same as white citizens; yet no one, at that time, thought that it was any invasion of his personal status as a freeman because he was not admitted to all the privileges enjoyed by white citizens, or because he was subjected to discriminations in the enjoyment of accommodations in inns, public conveyances and places of amusement. Mere discriminations on account of race or color were not regarded as badges of slavery. . . .

Slightly over one decade later, in 1896, the Supreme Court killed any black person's hope for equality. In the famous decision, *Plessy* v. *Ferguson* the doctrine of "separate but equal" won legal sanction.[9]

We consider the underlying fallacy of the plaintiff's argument to consist in the assumption that the enforced separation of the two races stamps the

[8]*Civil Rights Cases,* 109 U.S. 3 (1883).

[9]*Plessy* v. *Ferguson,* 136 U.S. 537 (1896).

> colored race with a badge of inferiority. If this be so, it is not by reason of anything found in the act, but solely because the colored race chooses to put that construction upon it. The argument necessarily assumes that if, as has been more than once the case, and is not unlikely to be so again, the colored race should become the dominant power in the state legislature, and should enact a law in precisely similar terms, it would thereby relegate the white race to an inferior position. We imagine that the white race, at least, would not acquiesce in this assumption. The argument also assumes that social prejudices may be overcome by legislation, and that equal rights can not be secured to the negro except by an enforced commingling of the two races. We cannot accept this proposition. If the two races are to meet on terms of social equality, it must be the result of natural affinities, a mutual appreciation of each other's merits and a voluntary consent of individuals. . . .

This lawful segregation remained for over half a century. Not until 1954, when the Supreme Court, in *Brown* v. *Board of Education* required integration of public schools, did the individual rip away significant power from the states. A decade later the Civil Rights Acts of 1964 and 1965 legally crushed most other forms of segregation, although *de facto* (actual) school segregation continues as does housing segregation.

Why Did Blacks Fail to Gain Equality After Reconstruction?

Rather than rebelling over their inferior status, blacks for the most part submitted to their inequities. Thomas D. Clark and Albert D. Kirwan outlined the freedmen's reasons for doing so.[10]

> At the end of the Civil War and for many years thereafter the congenital inferiority of the Negro was all but universally agreed on, not only in the South but in the North and among the learned as well as the uneducated. . . .
>
> With the abandonment of the Negro by his northern protectors after 1877, he was again returned to the mercy of native whites. But there would be a difference now. Under slavery the vast majority of non-slaveowning whites had been largely isolated from the Negro, and there had been only a labor issue between the white man and his slave. Under the new order there would be created a race issue. In a sense and to a degree, all whites had been aristocrats under slavery because they were free. After redemption, white men who

[10]Thomas D. Clark and Albert D. Kirwan, *The South Since Appomattox: A Century of Regional Change* (New York: Oxford University Press, 1967), pp. 305-306.

had seen Negroes occupy superior positions to their own during radical reconstruction were resolved that it should not happen again. Accordingly, they set about creating a caste system based, not on law as was slavery, but on biological inferiority. In this new order the Negro would be the bottom layer, regardless of wealth or personal merit; even lower than he had been in slavery, for then he had looked down upon the poor white. And it became the principal aim of the new southern society to see that the Negro did not rise above this lowly position.

The tragedy of Reconstruction, that black people did not win lasting equality with whites, is the tragedy of American history. It remains an intense blight on our present era and a burden left to a future generation to resolve.

Summary

Civil rights legislation in the 1960's was not the first of its kind. The passage of laws to provide equality also occurred after the Civil War. Radical Republicans tried to protect the freedmen by reducing state power over their civil rights. However, these reformers failed in their attempt to change social conditions and bring about equality. The then-conservative Supreme Court reduced the potency of the new laws, thus legalizing segregation.

Selected References:

John Hope Franklin, *Reconstruction After The Civil War* (Chicago: University of Chicago Press, 1961).*
Revising earlier interpretations, this work examines the subtleties of the era.

Seth M. Scheiner, *Reconstruction: A Tragic Era?* American Problems Studies (New York: Holt, Rinehart and Winston, 1968).*
A compilation of excerpts from noted historical works on the subject.

Kenneth M. Stampp, *The Era of Reconstruction, 1865-1877* (New York: Alfred A. Knopf, 1965).*
A brief synthesis of myth-busting interpretations.

C. Vann Woodward, *The Strange Career of Jim Crow*, 2nd revised edition (New York: Oxford University Press, 1966).*
The most complete one-volume analysis of black segregation.

TERM PROJECTS:

A. Investigate the elections of 1868 and 1876. Then explain how the following would vote and why: northern Democrats; western farmers; southern whites; southern blacks; eastern industrialists.

B. Compare and contrast the position of blacks in the South at the conclusion of the Civil War in relation to that at the end of Reconstruction.

CHECKUP FOR STUDY

Name: ______________________________

1. Why do civil rights acts reduce states' rights?

2. Why was a definition of federalism controversial in reconstruction?

3. Why is "radical" a difficult term to define?

4. Why does expanded civil rights reduce states' rights?

To remove this page: Open the book as wide as possible several times to loosen this page from the binding. Lay the book flat on your desk and gently but firmly pull this page *straight up* and away from the binding from top to bottom.

5. Compare the Civil Rights Act of 1875 to that of 1964.

6. Why is "Black Republicanism" historically an inaccurate term?

7. Briefly state "radical" motives behind Reconstruction.

8. Why did the business of Reconstruction go unfinished?

9.

10.

"All right! Which one of you sidewinders let the air out of my tires?"

The New Yorker, June 17, 1961, p. 33

14 Cowboys and In'juns

MYTH: A traditional story of unknown authorship which has an alleged, but not necessarily true, historical basis.

REFERENCE DATES:

1861-1876	Most intense period of Indian warfare
1862	Homestead Act passed
1866	Long Drive initiated, moving cattle north from Texas
1875	Successful development of barbed wire fencing
1887	Dawes (Severalty) Act, a failing attempt to assimilate Indians; the end of the cattle boom

1890	U.S. Census revealed that a frontier line no longer existed; Ghost Dance War, the last major slaughter of the Indians

How Does the Cowboy Image Affect Your Life?

Out of the past and into the modern living room come the hoof beats of many a great horse opera, and with them the romantic myth of the cowboy. His image is ever-present, as David Brion Davis depicted.[1]

> Yet more than a half-century after the passing of the actual wild and woolly cowboy, we find a unique phenomenon in American mythology. Gaudy-covered Western or cowboy magazines decorate stands, windows, and shelves in "drug" stores, bookstores, grocery stores and supermarkets from Miami to Seattle. Hundreds of cowboy movies and television shows are watched and lived through by millions of Americans. Nearly every little boy demands a cowboy suit and a Western six-shooter cap pistol. Cowboys gaze out at you with steely eye and cocked revolver from cereal packages and television screens. Jukeboxes in Bennington, Vermont, as well as Globe, Arizona, moan and warble the latest cowboy songs. . . . Adolescents and even grown men in Maine and Florida can be seen affecting cowboy, or at least modified cowboy garb, while in the new airplane plants in Kansas, workers don their cowboy boots and wide-brimmed hats, go to work whistling a cowboy song, and are defiantly proud that they live in the land of lassos and sixguns.

When Was the Cowboy Prominent?

American cowboys originated in Texas soon after that province won its independence from Mexico in 1836. They adopted many of the talents which Mexican vaqueros had developed. Cowboys worked for a few businessmen who paid them \$25 to \$40 per month to round up wild cattle and drive them to distant markets in Cincinnati, Chicago, New Orleans and Los Angeles. This business remained piecemeal, based upon demand, until Civil War hostilities interrupted its operation. During

---

[1]David Brion Davis, "Ten-Gallon Hero," *American Quarterly,* Vol. VI:2 (1954), pp. 111-112. Copyright, 1954, Trustees of the University of Pennsylvania. Reprinted by permission.

that conflict, most of the cattle remained in Texas where they multiplied to probably five million.

After the war was over the demand for cattle was high enough to bring $40 per head. Thus the five million steers in Texas were worth roughly $200,000,000. Shrewd businessmen hired cowboys to round up the roaming longhorn and drive them (the "Long Drive") to railheads (cowtowns at the end of the railroad line being built westward). There, dealers shipped them to eastern markets.

During the 1870's, cattle ranching developed on the rich grasslands of the Great Plains where steers multiplied rapidly. Colorado, Wyoming, Montana and Dakota, for example, had virtually no cattle in 1860, the year Lincoln won the presidency. Yet, by 1870 these territories had over 176,000 steers. In the decade which followed, that number increased to more than two million. The day of the cowboy was at hand.

What Was Cowboy Life Like?

Cowboys of the nineteenth century had a hard life. Their main jobs were to "line-ride" and to "round-up." That is, they patrolled along unfenced open range boundaries to keep different ranchers' cattle separated, and they gathered up cattle twice a year to brand and to ship them to market. Frequently a cowboy worked up to twenty hours a day. John Baumann, a young English immigrant who resided in Texas, described the cowboy's life from firsthand experience.[2]

> . . . I have no hesitation in warning any restless, roving spirits who may be attracted by picturesque descriptions of a cowboy's life that, unless they are prepared to toil during the long summer months both by day and by night, for small pay and on scant fare, to be in the saddle from early dawn until sunset both Sundays and weekdays, to abstain from comfort and civilization for the greater part of every year, and so to wear themselves out with exposure and manifold fatigues as to be reckoned old and past their work while still young in years, they had better remain at home and leave cowboy life alone.

But what about the romantic cowboy life? Ray Allen Billington answered that question.[3]

---

[2]John Baumann, "On a Western Ranche," *The Fortnightly Review* 41 (1887), p. 516.

[3]Ray Allen Billington, *Westward Expansion: A History of the American Frontier*, third edition (New York: The Macmillan Co., 1967), p. 684.

Eastern imagination, in turn, has given the nation one of its most enduring legends: the myth of the glamorous cowboy. Actually the clean-cut heroes of Hollywood and the television screen bear little resemblance to the hard-working men who tended cattle in the heyday of the open range. Cowboys, as one of them put it, were simply hired hands on horseback, doomed to a life of dull routine as they "rode line" separating the unfenced ranches, doctored sick animals, or drifted herds from pasturage to pasturage. Little wonder that when they "hit town" on rare occasions they indulged in the riotous conduct that has come to typify them for cinema addicts the world over. There was little romance in their lonely lives; even the widely publicized "ten-gallon" hats, chaps, knotted handkerchiefs, and colorful shirts that they sometimes wore to charm strangers were often displaced by a working garb of overalls, a cast-off army overcoat that had seen service in the Civil War, and a derby hat. Even their individualism has been exaggerated; many joined a labor union, the Knights of Labor, and a group struck one ranch during the 1884 roundup. The true heroes of the Cattle Kingdom were not the cowboys, but the ranchers whose shrewd management allowed the conquest of a new frontier.

The day of the cowboy came rapidly to an end by 1890 after the rich profits from cattle ranching turned into shocking losses. Historians have offered many reasons for this painful finale to the boom, among them, overgrazing, harsh winter weather and competition for land from farmers and sheepherders. It seemed that the cowboy would become a forgotten figure of the past.

Why Has the Cowboy Become Mythical?

"In 1900," David Brion Davis noted, "it seemed that the significance of the cowboy era would decline along with other brief but romantic episodes in American history." Yet, while the cowboy era died, it did not fade away in the popular fancy. Davis suggested the reasons for the origin of this myth.[4]

The cowboy hero and his setting are a unique synthesis of two American traditions, and echoes of this past can be discerned in even the wildest of the modern horse operas. On the one hand, the line of descent is a direct evolution

---

[4]Davis, *op. cit.*, pp. 112-114.

from the Western scout of Cooper and the Dime Novel; on the other, there has been a recasting of the golden myth of the ante-bellum South. The two were fused sometimes in the 1880's. . . .

. . . .

. . . In our mythology, the cowboy era is timeless. . . . There is, it is true, a nostalgic sense that this is the last great drama, a sad knowledge that the cowboy is passing and that civilization is approaching. But it never comes. This strange, wistful sense of the coming end of an epoch is not something outside our experience. It is a faithful reflection of the sense of approaching adulthood. . . . We know that adulthood, civilization, is inevitable, but we are living toward the end of childhood, and at that point "childness" seems eternal; it is a whole lifetime. But suddenly we find it is not eternal, the forests disappear, the mountains are settled, and we have new responsibilities. When we shut our eyes and try to remember, the last image of a carefree life appears. For the nation, this last image is the cowboy.

What About Women and Fighting?

Two elements in many Westerns are women and fighting. The fact and fiction about women rarely coincide, according to Davis.[5]

. . . There were few women in the West in the Chisholm Trail days and those few in Dodge City, Abilene, and Wichita were of dubious morality. The cowboy's sex life was intermittent, to say the least. He had to carry his thirst long distances, like a camel, and in the oases the orgies were hardly on a spiritual plane.

. . . .

. . . A woman in the Western drama is somebody to rescue, somebody to protect. . . . This role would lose its value if the heroine surrendered herself to the cowboy immediately. So the more she struggles with herself, the more she conquers her Eastern reservations and surmounts difficulties before capitulating, the more it enhances the hero.

Fighting also plays an important role in the myth, as Davis wrote.[6]

Of course, most cowboy books and movies bristle with violence. Wild fist fights, brawls with chairs and bottles, gun play and mass battles with crashing

---

[5]*Ibid,* pp. 117-118.

[6]*Ibid,* p. 123.

windows, fires, and the final racing skirmish on horseback, are all as much a part of the cowboy drama as the boots and spurs. These bloody escapades are necessary and are simply explained. They provide the stage for the hero to show his heroism, and since the cowboy is the hero to the pre-adolescent, he must prove himself by their standards. Physical prowess is the most important thing for the ten- or twelve-year-old mind. They are constantly plagued by fear, doubt, and insecurity, in short by evil, and they lack the power to crush it. The cowboy provides the instruments for their aggressive impulses, while the villain symbolizes all evil. The ethics of the cowboy band are the ethics of the boy's gang, where each member has a rôle determined by his physical skills and his past performance. . . .

That such violence was a fact is hard to prove. *Time* reported the realities of fighting.[7]

. . . The reader is told that a cowboy seldom fought with a gun and never with his fists, but elected what the modern delinquent calls a shiv (knife); [and] that the most gunplay in Dodge City was caused by non-cowboys. . . .

What Aspect of Cowboy History Does Fiction Delete?

While novels, movies and television serials have added women and fighting to the cowboy scene, they have omitted the black man, who contributed a large part to western life. *Time* revealed the following facts about the West, stereotyped as lily-white.[8]

. . . Among the cowboys who rode the ranges from Texas to Montana, driving millions of cattle to market, were more than 5,000 Negroes. . . .

. . . Most came from Texas; all began their trade as slaves who were brought West when their masters moved to Texas and acquired cattle. They learned to ride, rope and brand cattle from their white owners, and from local Indians and Mexicans.

. . . "The demands of their job made the white cowboys transcend much of their prejudice. . . ." A typical trail crew of eight cowboys would include two or three Negroes.

---

[7]"Coruna Long, Ars Brevis," review of *The American Cowboy* by Joe B. Frantz and Julian Ernest Choate, Jr., *Time,* 14 November 1955, p. 136.

[8]"Shaded Heroes," review of *The Negro Cowboys* by Philip Durham and Everett L. Jones, *Time,* 26 February 1965, p. 103.

. . . Among [them] . . . was Nat Love, a rootin' tootin' former slave who wrote that his prowess with gun and lariat earned him the title of "Deadwood Dick," . . . the original inspiration for the fictional (and white) hero of 33 dime Westerns by Edward L. Wheeler.

Were Indians "Good Guys" or "Bad Guys"?

While writers of cowboy stories have omitted the Negro, they retained the Indian. No matter how many Indians the white man has killed in decades of written and acted stories, unending numbers have continued to pop up at just the right time to allow the hero to exterminate another "varmint" and win the West for the "good guys" of American mythology.

Indians were not always a blight to the white man either in reality or story telling. Many Americans can recall the tale of kind Indians who greeted the early English settlers, taught them how to grow corn and shared the mythical Thanksgiving dinner in peace. Few can explain, however, why the early Europeans regarded the Indian as a noble being. Oliver La Farge explained why colonial era Europeans saw the Indians in so favorable a light.[9]

. . . Ever since the white men first fell upon them, the Indians of what is now the United States have been hidden from white men's view by a number of conflicting myths. The oldest of these is the myth of the Noble Red Man or the Child of Nature. . . .

. . . .

It was in the earliest period of the Noble Red Man concept that the Indians probably exerted their most important influence upon Western civilization. . . . French and English of the early Seventeenth Century encountered, along the East Coast of North America from Virginia southward, fairly advanced tribes whose semi-hereditary rulers depended upon the acquiescence of their people for the continuance of their rule. The explorers and first settlers interpreted these rulers as kings, their people as subjects. They found that even the commonest subjects were endowed with many rights and freedoms, that the nobility was fluid, and that commoners existed in a state of remarkable equality.

---

[9]Oliver La Farge, "Myths That Hide the American Indian," *American Heritage* 7 (October, 1956), pp. 5-6. Copyright © 1956 by Oliver La Farge. Reprinted by permission of Consuelo La Farge.

Constitutional monarchy was coming into being in England, but the divine rights of kings remained firm doctrine. All European society was stratified in many classes. A somewhat romanticized observation of Indian society and government, coupled with the idea of the Child of Nature, led to the formulation, especially by French philosophers, of the theories of inherent rights of all men, and of the people as the source of the sovereign's authority. The latter was stated in the phrase, "consent of the governed." Both were carried over by Jefferson into our Declaration of Independence. . . .

How Did Indians Take on the Image of Savages?

Just as the image of the noble Indian served the needs of eighteenth century white men, so too did the image of the ruthless and faithless savage fill a need for nineteenth century Americans. The nation was on the move westward, and the Indians with their land stood in the way. They were a barrier to "progress." Exterminating them rid America of an obstacle in the path to greatness and wealth. Since cowboy stories depict this era, rather than an earlier one, authors of Westerns have generally portrayed Indians in unflattering terms. William T. Hagan described the realities of the removal of Indians.[10]

Following the War of 1812, the character of Indian-American relations changed. The Unted States felt less need to conciliate the Indian nations as the threat of British intervention failed. . . . The peremptory demands made on the Indians for more and more land reflected both the weakened positions of the tribes and the flood of settlers to the frontier. . . .

. . . .

The wave of wagon trains across the plains in the early 1840's turned into a flood in the 1850's. The Indians watched dismayed while the emigrants and their stock destroyed timber and pastures along the streams and frightened away the buffalo herds. Incidents multiplied as the tribesmen hung around the caravan routes, driving off stock at every chance and killing an occasional white who had ventured too far from his companions. The whites retaliated by indiscriminate killings inspired by revenge and sheer nervousness. The guilty whites and Indians seldom paid the price for their misdeeds; it was simpler to blame an entire people for the excesses of a few.

---

[10]William T. Hagan, *American Indians* (Chicago: University of Chicago Press, 1961), pp. 66, 92-93.

By the last half of the nineteenth century, the plight of the American Indian was pathetic. Not only had their population declined rapidly, from an estimated three-quarters of a million in 1600 to one-quarter of a million in 1880, but the living conditions on reservations for those who had survived were deplorable. Belatedly, reformers began to champion improvements in rights, respect and standard of living for the Indians. One of these reformers, Helen Hunt Jackson, a special government commissioner for Indian affairs, investigated Indian conditions and wrote about them. In one of her influential books, Mrs. Jackson condemned the "good guys" of western myth, the white men, and defended the "bad guys," the Indians.[11]

> It makes little difference, however, where one opens the record of the history of the Indians; every page and every year has its dark stain. The story of one tribe is the story of all, varied only by differences of time and place; but neither time nor place makes any difference in the main facts. . . .
>
> . . . The old tales of the frontier life, with its horrors of Indian warfare, have gradually, by two or three generations' telling, produced in the average mind something like an hereditary instinct of unquestioning and unreasoning aversion which it is almost impossible to dislodge or soften.
>
> There are hundreds of pages of unimpeachable testimony on the side of the Indian; but it goes for nothing, is set down as sentimentalism or partisanship, tossed aside and forgotten.

What Was the Result of Reform Efforts for Indians?

Although reformers aroused popular sentiment against Indian extermination, federal programs to improve their well-being proved ineffective and insufficient. The Indian standard of living remained pathetically low in the half century which followed Helen Hunt Jackson's disclosures because federal policies did not fit Indian needs, as William T. Hagan noted.[12]

> Most of them [policies] were old standbys—Christianize the aborigines, educate them, and introduce them to private property. The variable factor was the condition under which these policies would be applied.

[11]Helen Hunt Jackson, *A Century of Dishonor,* (Boston: Roberts Brothers, 1885), pp. 337-338.

[12]Hagan, *op. cit.*, p. 121.

The federal government abandoned this kind of Indian policy in 1934 for one designed to foster tribal culture and unity. Even so, although the average Indian's living standard improved over that of the pre-1934 era, his position in life was still low, even in comparison to that of other minorities. One shrewd observer of Indians commented. "It's not a matter of being Indian. It's a matter of being poor." William T. Hagan elaborated on the poverty of the Indian.[13]

> . . . Today the red men are one of the minorities in our population, perhaps on the average the most impoverished and poorest prepared of all our minority groups. Although hampered by race prejudice in some areas, in others the Indian classification is a defense against the discrimination their dark-skinned neighbors suffer.

Summary

The present images of the cowboy and the Indian do not match the realities of their pre-twentieth century existence. The cowboy's life was a difficult one. It lacked much of the romance Westerns ascribe to it, particularly with relation to working, fighting and loving. Absent from the myth entirely were the blacks. The Indian, on the other hand, started out in the American myth as a "good guy" Noble Red Man. Then in the nineteenth century he turned into a "bad guy" Red Savage. In fact, both representations are myths, useful to the whites, but meaningless—or worse —to the Indians.

Selected References:

William Brandon, ed., *The American Heritage Book of Indians* (New York: American Heritage Publishing Co., 1961).*
A survey of Indians in American history with illustrations.

Philip Durham and Everett L. Jones, *The Negro Cowboys* (New York: Dodd & Mead, 1965).
A revision of lily-white history which has deleted the contribution of the black man on a horse.

[13]*Ibid*, p. 168.

Henry Nash Smith, *Virgin Land: The American West as Symbol and Myth* (New York: Vintage Books, 1957).*
A study of how the nineteenth century West helped to shape the American society.

William T. Hagan, *American Indians* (Chicago: University of Chicago Press, 1961).*
A thorough analysis of the American Indian, past and present.

TERM PROJECTS:

A. Evaluate the circumstances which delayed settlement of the Great Plains.

B. Explain how federal Indian policies in the 19th century contributed to the inferior position of American Indians today.

CHECKUP FOR STUDY

Name: ______________________________

1. List several historical distortions you remember seeing in a Hollywood Western.

2. What were "line-riding" and "rounding-up"?

3. Describe a real cowboy's attire.

4. What are the origins of the cowboy myth?

To remove this page: Open the book as wide as possible several times to loosen this page from the binding. Lay the book flat on your desk and gently but firmly pull this page *straight up* and away from the binding from top to bottom.

5. Why does the cowboy image appeal to Americans?

6. Why do you suppose Western writers omitted blacks?

7. How could a Noble Red Man become a faithless savage?

8. If she were alive today, how would Helen Hunt Jackson evaluate the Indian's present position in American society?

9.

10.

"Another monstrosity."

Look, February 18, 1969, p. 42

15 Home Sweet Home

CITY: An inhabited place of 2,500 persons or more (in this theme). In the eighteenth century, the terms "town" and "city" were synonymous. Since that time, as opposed to the town, the city has come to imply larger concentrations of people, sometimes numbering in the millions.

REFERENCE DATES:

1776	Philadelphia was the largest U.S. city
1789	The new nation began with six urban centers
1840	New York became the largest city in the U.S.
1860-1910	The modern city emerged

1890-1910	Era of intensive political reform in urban centers
1920	U.S. Census reported 51.4 percent of the national population lived in cities

What Is Right and Wrong With City Life?

"Cities have always been the fireplaces of civilization," wrote Theodore Parker, transcendentalist author and underground railroad leader of the antebellum era. Today, according to a recent Census estimate, about seventy percent of Americans live in urban areas, and that percentage is increasing with each passing year. Like it or not, Americans have become urban creatures. Why do so many live in cities? The advantages are numerous, as *Senior Scholastic* outlined.[1]

> Cities are a place of opportunity for thousands of people with varying and specialized interests, skills, and ambitions. . . .
>
> Cities, too, are centers of learning and culture. . . . City people set the styles–in clothing, in hairdos, in the latest fads and slang.
>
> . . . Those who seek an escape from the "humdrum" life or restrictions of the small town or farm may find a new freedom. Those coming from foreign countries to settle most often find a "colony" of people who speak their language or serve their native food in local restaurants. This ethnic diversity adds to a city's excitement and interest. Chinatown and French restaurants, for instance, are attractions in New York and San Francisco. . . .

On the other hand, plenty appears wrong with city life. "Name a problem," noted *Senior Scholastic,* "almost any one–and chances are that some American city has it."[2] While the list of problems is almost endless, four major ills are worth noting.[3]

> [Decay:] . . . Slums remain a prominent feature of every single U.S. city. For the cities, slums are a double-edged problem. Because they harbor and foster more crime, more disease, more welfare clients, more unemployment, more drug addiction, they require proportionally more city services and more expenditures than other areas. Yet they produce far less in taxes.

---

[1] "Our Cities in Crisis," *Senior Scholastic,* 22 November 1968, p. 12.

[2] *Ibid.*

[3] *Ibid,* pp. 15-16, 21-22 (statements only, quoted).

[Crime:] . . . The rise is a nationwide phenomenon, but it gets the most attention in the cities. . . . The simplest answer to the crime problem, some say, is to hire more police, pay them more, train them better. But even this partial solution runs into economic reality: it costs money to hire more men, and most cities are up against the wall financially.

[Congestion:] Getting from here to there can be the most frustrating part of living in a city. Whether you use a car, a bus, or a subway, it is likely to be a slow, utterly nerve-racking trip at rush hour—the time when most people need to go from here to there. . . .

[Pollution:] The opportunity to breathe fresh air and find fresh water has become rare in urban areas. Forecasts of green algae soon to cover the Great Lakes, eye-smarting smog which now inundates parts of the Rocky Mountains, and crude oil slicks which ruined California coastlines, are all related to urbanization.

How Did Nineteenth Century Americans View Cities?

The argument over the virtues and vices of American cities is not a new one. "I view great cities as pestilential to the morals, the health, and the liberties of man," wrote Thomas Jefferson.[4] And he had a point. American towns in Jefferson's time, and for decades after, exhibited the miseries of mankind. In the nineteenth century, epidemics of cholera and other "filth diseases" grew steadily in cities partly because of poor sanitation systems. Refuse thrown on the streets fed roaming swine in New York City as late as 1867.

Stories about the evils of the city filled the printed page during this period. Writers such as Herman Melville, Nathaniel Hawthorne, Henry Thoreau, Henry James and Stephen Crane, described cities as evil and corrupting. Agricultural periodicals told how the city caused the depravity of young farm boys and girls. And, by the late decades of the century, notable Protestant writers, like the Reverend Josiah Strong, warned of impending urban disaster due to the unchecked growth of Roman Catholicism, socialism and political corruption.

On the other hand, Charles N. Glaab contended that there was also a great deal of pro-urban writing during this time.[5]

---

[4]Samuel E. Forman, ed., *The Life and Writings of Thomas Jefferson* (Indianapolis: The Bowen-Merril Co., 1900), p. 154.

[5]Charles N. Glaab, "The Historian and the American Urban Tradition," *Wisconsin Magazine of History* 47 (1963), pp. 20-21.

There is a substantial body of nineteenth century writing which argues not that the city itself is evil but that the American city, with its extremes of wealth and poverty, its materialism, and its exploitation, represented a denial of Christian principles. . . . Theorists of all cities have conceived of noble cities. Even the Bible had "coupled the forms of earthly splendor with the more spiritual excellency of a New Jerusalem."

. . . If Americans were God's chosen people–and this was a vital part of nineteenth century assertions of doctrines of progress–the prophetic vision could include a spiritual capital. "While the beginning of things was a garden in the paradise of Eden," said the Reverend James Cooper, . . . "the end of things, as prophesized in the Book of Revelation is a city, magnificent and populous, the New Jerusalem."

When Did Urbanization Begin in America?

In the beginning of our history there was no controversy over cities because there were no cities. The American continent north of Mexico in 1500 contained only sparsely distributed Indian tribes. With a few qualified exceptions, no tribal settlements formed what we call "cities."

Then the Europeans came. They cleared the forests, settled and cultivated the land and recreated European society as best they could. That life included cities. Since the thirteen colonies originated on the Atlantic coast, the six colonial cities which had emerged by the American Revolution were all coastal trade centers. Although small by modern standards, Philadelphia, with its 28,000 inhabitants, was the largest city in British America and the third largest city in the British Empire.

Despite this urban development, the overwhelming number of Americans remained rural during the century after independence. When the new nation began under the Federal Constitution of 1787, only five percent of the people lived in towns and cities over 2,500 in population During the next three decades that percentage remained fairly stable.

How Did the Frontier Contribute to Urbanization?

Urbanization not only developed along the Atlantic seaboard, it took place on the western frontier. The omission of frontier urbanization from novels, films and, until recently, written history should in no way hide the important contribution of the West to the building of cities. Richard C. Wade described the significance of the frontier on urbanization.[6]

The towns were the spearheads of the American frontier. Planted as forts or trading posts far in advance of the line of settlement, they held the West for the approaching population. . . .

. . . .

The West's young cities owed their initial success to commerce. All sprang from it, and their growth in the early years of the century stemmed from its expansion. . . .

. . . .

As these commercial centers grew, some inhabitants turned to manufacturing. . . .

. . . .

The intensive search for new adventures brought rivalries and conflict. Though the commerce of the whole West lay untouched before them, the cities quarreled over its division. . . .

. . . This drive for power and primacy, sustained by merchants and articulated by editors, was one of the most consistent and striking characteristics of the early history of Western cities.

. . . .

Though the young towns drew upon the experience of all the major Atlantic cities, the special source of municipal wisdom was Philadelphia. Many Western urbanites had lived or visited there; . . . it was the model metropolis.

. . . .

Though town and country developed along different paths, clashes were still infrequent. . . . Rural regions supplied the cities with raw materials for their mills and packing houses and offered an expanding market to their shops and factories. In turn, urban centers by bringing the fruits of civilization across the mountains . . . speeded up the transformation of the West from a gloomy wilderness to a richly diversified region. . . .

Bayrd Still discussed the close relationship between the farmer and the town builder in the developing West.[7]

. . . On many a frontier the town builder was as conspicuous as the farmer pioneer; the western city, through the efforts of its founders to extend its

---

[6]Richard C. Wade, "Urban Life in Western America, 1790-1830, *American Historical Review,* Vol. LXIV (1958), pp. 14, 16, 19, 21, 30.

[7]Bayrd Still, "Patterns of Mid-Nineteenth Century Urbanization in the Middle West," *Mississippi Valley Historical Review,* Vol. XXVIII (1941), pp. 187-188.

economic hinterland, actually facilitated the agrarian development of the West. . . .

The migrants who poured into the Mississippi Valley in the middle of the nineteenth century built cities as well as cultivated farms. By the seventies, when the American people were first becoming conscious of the drift of population to the city, the Middle West showed a spectacular urban growth. . . .

What Was the Relationship Between Urbanization and Industrialization?

Beginning about 1820 and during the remainder of the nineteenth century, the rate of American urbanization accelerated. The nation had only 61 cities in 1820, but forty years later that number had increased to 392, and by 1900 the United States contained 1,737 cities. Thus, urban population rose from seven percent at the beginning of this period to forty percent at the end.

Simply put, the reason for this dynamic change in America was industrialization, according to Charles N. Glaab and A. Theodore Brown.[8]

. . . . From 1820 on, technological and economic transformations had contributed to a high rate of urbanization in the United States. The continuance of this urban trend in the years after 1860 led to an ever increasing concentration of Americans in cities of all sizes and engendered the view on the part of many social critics that the "rise of the city" was a fundamental problem facing American society. . . . Urbanization did not proceed at an even pace during the fifty years. Movement to the city naturally accelerated in times of prosperity and fell off in times of depression when economic opportunities in the city diminished. . . . But throughout the period the urban trend was unmistakable; the United States was clearly becoming a nation of cities and city dwellers.

. . . .

As cities grew, their natures and functions in many cases changed. At the beginning of the nineteenth century, the sizable cities of the United States were strung out along the coast; they were ports and . . . faced the sea and the maritime trade which had nurtured them. By the time of the Civil War, however, this could no longer be said. Maritime trade, indeed, was still directly or indirectly an important element of the life of the cities, but new cities had appeared deep in the continental interior and the older ones, the great

---

[8]Charles N. Glaab and A. Theodore Brown, *A History of Urban America* (New York: The Macmillan Co., 1967), pp. 107-108, 27.

seaports, had engaged in great metropolitan rivalries with one another to secure as much as possible of the commerce which came from the interior. Manufacturing had begun to influence the shape of many of the cities. . . .

Why Did Urbanization Accelerate During the Late Nineteenth Century?

The number and size of cities swelled dramatically for several decades after the Civil War to provide the basis of our modern urban network. Blake McKelvey offered an explanation for this urban expansion.[9]

The historic process of America's urbanization acquired new momentum and a significantly different emphasis following the Civil War. As the improved transport facilities reached farther inland, rival trading centers sprang up to serve each frontier. The discovery and exploitation of rich mineral deposits and other natural resources, increasing the national output manyfold, added tremendously to the flow of commerce in which many cities shared and over which the national metropolis on the Hudson continued to exercise a loose domination. But New York's former pre-eminence, based on the strategic location of its great port, was lessened as the rise of new factory towns transformed America, during the second half of the century, into an industrial nation. This process, which relegated exports and imports to a secondary position, created new demands for technological improvements and for organizational services. As competing cities and metropolitan centers endeavored to perform these functions, new trade patterns developed, and new civic and cultural patterns as well.

How Did the South Fit Into the Urban Pattern?

Because the South lagged behind the rest of the nation in industrialization, it made a meager contribution to American urbanization. T. Lynn Smith explained the slow industrial development in the South.[10]

The Census of 1790 showed that Charlestown . . . was the fourth city in the nation. . . . By 1810 the Louisiana Purchase land added New Orleans to

[9]Blake McKelvey, *The Urbanization of America, 1860-1915* (New Brunswick, N.J.: Rutgers University Press, 1963), p. 17.

[10]Rupert B. Vance and Nicolas J. Rath, eds., *The Urban South* (Chapel Hill: University of North Carolina Press, 1954), pp. 25-26.

southern cities, giving the region another large center which ranked just below Charlestown, sixth in size in the nation. . . .

Thirty years later, important urban centers were still conspicuously absent in the South. New Orleans . . . in 1840 stood in a class by itself and ranked fourth in the nation. . . .

On the eve of the Civil War (1860), New Orleans with 168,675 inhabitants was still the only metropolis in the South, although Louisville had begun to come to the fore. No other southern city had passed the 25,000 mark. . . .

It is doubtful that the twenty years of war and reconstruction greatly retarded the development of urban centers in the South. . . . [Nevertheless] as the twentieth century opened, the South contained only six of the nation's 50 large cities, . . . [and by] 1920 was held to seven only. . . .

It is clear that southerners did not create and move into cities as readily as did northerners and westerners. But why did not the immense foreign immigration of the nineteenth century swell southern urban populations? Maldwyn Allen Jones offered an answer to this question.[11]

That the southern states attracted such a small proportion of immigrants was not due, as contemporaries sometimes thought, to the European's moral aversion to slavery. . . . [The South] could offer neither the employment opportunities nor the facilities for obtaining land that were available in the free states [before the Civil War]. . . .

. . . .

Most of the southern states . . . joined in the [post-Civil War] . . . scramble for immigrants. The South had practically no unsold land to dispose of, but it wanted cheap foreign labor to replace its allegedly inefficient Negroes. . . . The truth was that the absence of free land and—until the twentieth century—of large-scale industry deflected the current of immigration elsewhere.

What Price Did Americans Pay for Such Rapid City Building?

Along with the overall high rate of nineteenth century urbanization came numerous problems. Blake McKelvey described some of them.[12]

The cities had also paid sacrifices for their surging growth. Expanding commercial districts engulfed many old residential wards, while factories and

---

[11]Maldwyn Allen Jones, *American Immigration* (Chicago: University of Chicago Press, 1960), pp. 120-121, 188.

[12]McKelvey, *op. cit.,* pp. 231-232.

freight lines segmented established communities and invaded suburban retreats. The inrush of newcomers from abroad had transformed many once-friendly neighborhoods into heterogeneous slums whose densely packed inhabitants often dwelt as indifferent or hostile strangers under the same roof. It was, many felt, a transition period, and the great majority, imbued with a boundless optimism, looked hopefully to the future. Yet the number who rebelled or inadvertently fell out of step was increasing, as the mounting crime ratios disclosed; and recurrent dislocations of the economy left vast hordes destitute.

What is more, problems such as those expressed above were difficult to rectify because of city corruption. Constance McLaughlin Green elaborated on urban corruption.[13]

Corruption in municipal government had sprung up like a toadstool wherever community leadership faltered. . . . Incompetents and scalawags moved into public office. If accumulating civic needs brought about appeals to state legislatures for special commissions to handle such problems as building and managing city waterworks or taking charge of police departments, the usual result was a division of authority, the resignation of honest officials, and a breakdown in civic morale that strengthened boss rule. Once bosses were in the saddle they cracked the whip over underlings. . . .

Bosses' financial support came chiefly from . . . traction and gas companies for franchises and from the underworld of gamblers, prostitutes, and operators of the unlicensed liquor establishments known as "blind pigs." Political support, on the other hand, rested quite as much upon the gratitude slum dwellers and voters a few economic notches above them felt toward the men who gave their wants some consideration. . . . The rank and file of citizens were slow to see that boss rule with its perversion of power hurt the entire community, that it made a mockery of the fundamental concept of a "government of laws, not men." . . .

What Did Urban Citizens Finally Do About These Problems?

Ultimately, in desperation, some urbanites banded together to try to solve their problems. Blake McKelvey commented on their effort.[14]

---

[13]Constance McLaughlin Green, *The Rise of Urban America* (New York: Harper and Row, 1965), pp. 111-112.

[14]McKelvey, *op. cit.*, p. 232.

Alarmed by these miseries, some humanitarian citizens had begun to transform urban charities into welfare agencies; others, blazing with varied degrees of indignation, were demanding political and economic reforms. The sudden upsurge of the progressive movement around 1910 gave cumulative expression in state and national politics to a multitude of grievances dating back several decades in many communities. And since the state legislatures failed to master numerous issues of control, the urban interests, both public and private, turned increasingly to Washington for administrative supervision. Many of the leaders in this movement had served an apprenticeship in local reform campaigns, and their triumphs in the larger arena further revealed the extent to which urban problems had become national issues.

Summary

For generations controversy has raged in America over the advantages and disadvantages of urban life. The rise of cities resulted from colonial trade, frontier expansion and, most important, nineteenth century industrialization. Because of a lack of industry, urbanization in the South was relatively slow. Throughout the United States, however, corruption, and later reform, accompanied urban development. Thus urban problems became national problems.

Selected References:

Charles N. Glaab and A. Theodore Brown, *A History of Urban America* (New York: The Macmillan Co., 1967).*
A survey of urban growth in America.

Blake McKelvey, *The Urbanization of America: 1860-1915* (New Brunswick, N.J.: Rutgers University Press, 1963).
The relationship of urban growth to other phases of American life.

Lewis Mumford, *The City in History* (New York: Harcourt, Brace & World, 1961).
A lengthy synthesis of the city's role in civilization from its origins to its present. Included is a 55-page bibliography.

Jacob Riis, *How the Other Half Lives* (New York: Hill and Wang, 1957 edition).*
Originally published in 1890, this noted study of tenement life in New York showed the need for urban reform.

TERM PROJECTS:

A. Describe life in a tenement about 1900 and compare it to ghetto life today.

B. Describe the major problems of any large city in your state during the Gilded Age.

CHECKUP FOR STUDY

Name: ______________________________

1. Explain the historical implications of the cartoon.

2. Do you consider cities good or bad? Why?

3. Comment: "To avoid Indian attacks, the first white settlers built America's cities high in the mountains."

4. How did cities change in the nineteenth century?

To remove this page: Open the book as wide as possible several times to loosen this page from the binding. Lay the book flat on your desk and gently but firmly pull this page *straight up* and away from the binding from top to bottom.

5. What role did the city play in frontier history?

6. Why did foreign immigrants not flood the South?

7. What problems accompanied the growth of cities?

8. How did citizens try to rectify urban problems?

9.

10.

President McKinley (the tailor) measures Uncle Sam for a new suit to fit the fattening results of his imperial appetite. Anti-imperialists offer him reducing medicine.

Puck, XLVIII, September 5, 1900, pp. 7-8

16 Big Brother Is Eyeing You

IMPERIALISM: The policy of a nation to extend power and domination over one or several others, either directly by use of force or indirectly through influence.

REFERENCE DATES:

1887-1889	U.S. leased Pearl Harbor, Hawaii; U.S. shared in Samoan protectorate
1898	Spanish-American War: Cuba occupied; Hawaii, Puerto Rico, Guam and the Philippines annexed

1899	Filipino Insurrection initiated; Open Door Policy announced; U.S. annexed several Samoan Islands
1900	Boxer Rebellion erupted; "Imperialism" the Presidential election issue
1904	Hay-Bunau-Varilla Treaty ratified; Roosevelt Corollary to the Monroe Doctrine announced
1910	"Dollar Diplomacy" inaugurated in Latin America

Is America Buying Control of the World?

Since World War II, many American companies have expanded their investments abroad, constructing factories, purchasing goods, employing workers and marketing their products. Any serious American traveler in the world today can see the visible results of such enterprise: Eskimo Pies in Lapland, Gillette razor blades in South Africa, A & W Root Beer in Singapore, Avon products in England and Pepsi-Cola in Brazil. Put in monetary terms, U.S. investments abroad have risen from ten billion dollars in 1950 to over fifty billion by the late 1960s. Such investments have caused fears, as *Senior Scholastic* explained.[1]

> While the story of these and other U.S. giants girdling the economic globe is often music to the ears of stockholders, the rustle of U.S. dollars is not always so pleasant for some of the nations on the other end of the U.S. investment "invasion." . . .
>
> . . . .
>
> In some parts of the underdeveloped world the belief is becoming more and more widespread that U.S. investors simply drain the land of its natural resources, exploit local laborers who are willing to work for low wages, and return home with bulging pockets of booty. . . .
>
> In Europe, some governments are presently worrying aloud that the giant U.S. corporations are paring away their freedom to regulate their own economy. A recent best-selling European book *The American Challenge* by French editor Jean-Jacques Servan-Schreiber, prophesies: "In 15 years, the [world's]

---

[1] "U.S. Investments Abroad: Are We 'Buying' the World," *Senior Scholastic,* Vol. XCII, 14 March 1968, p. 12.

third industrial power, after the U.S. and the Soviet Union, could easily be not Europe but American industry in Europe."

Whether American investments abroad are imperialistic in character is a matter of current debate. When and how the United States dramatically expanded its influence overseas is not. The remainder of this Theme will discuss the major thrust of American expansion abroad.

How Did the International Image of America Change by 1900?

By the end of the nineteenth century, the United States had emerged as a world power, rich in people and resources and strong in moral convictions of its righteousness. No country in the world produced as much foodstuffs, iron, coal and steel as did the United States. This nation's banking wealth rivaled England's, its navy equalled Germany's and its population surpassed that of all European nations save Russia. Ernest R. May assessed the dramatic emergence of America as a world power.[2]

> . . . Up to the 1890's . . . European diplomats and political analysts coupled it [the U.S.] with such states as Sweden, the Netherlands, Belgium, and Spain. By the early twentieth century, on the other hand, some of the very same people had begun to say in all seriousness that Europe was in danger from America. The distinguished French historian, Henri Hauser, for example, asserted in a little volume on American imperialism in 1905 that the principal topic of conversation in France was the so-called "American peril." In little more than a decade the United States had moved from among the second-rate powers to a front rank among first-rate powers.

Did a Threat to National Security Contribute to Imperialism?

The United States had not only developed into a strong nation by 1900, it had emerged as an imperialist power. The cause for this change, the annexation of overseas colonies, is still a matter of historical dispute.

The first reason given for imperialism was the necessity to make the nation secure. Naval expansionist Captain Alfred T. Mahan expressed

---

[2]Ernest R. May, *The Reconstruction of American History,* ed., John Higham (New York: Harper and Row, 1962), pp. 181-182.

this reasoning at the time. Despite his arguments, however, neither he nor any noted spokesmen of naval power before 1898 demanded indiscriminate territorial annexation.[3]

> . . . To provide this [national defense], three things are needful: First, protection of the chief harbors by fortifications and coast-defense ships, which gives defensive strength, provides security to the community within, and supplies the bases necessary to all military operations. Secondly, naval force, the arm of offensive power, which alone enables a country to extend its influence outward. Thirdly, it should be an inviolable resolution of our national policy that no European state should henceforth acquire a coaling position within three thousand miles of San Francisco,—a distance which includes the Sandwich [Hawaiian] and Galapagos islands and the coast of Central America. For fuel is the life of modern naval war; it is the food of the ship; without it the modern monsters of the deep die. . . .

How Did Business Interests Contribute to Imperialism?

As important to the reason for imperialism as national defense were economic interests. For decades, historians have argued over whether American businessmen demanded the annexation of colonies to increase their trade. Julius W. Pratt contended that they did not.[4]

> It seems safe to conclude, from the evidence available, that the only important business interests (other than the business of sensational journalism) which clamored for intervention in Cuba were certain of those directly or indirectly concerned in the Cuban sugar industry; that opposed to intervention were the influence of other parties (including at least one prominent sugar planter) whose business would suffer direct injury from war and also the overwhelming preponderance of general business opinion. . . .
>
> . . . .
>
> . . . [However] when Dewey's dramatic victory on the first of May offered a far eastern base from which the threatened markets in China might be defended, . . . [business] had gladly accepted the result, and long before the close of the wonderful year 1898 it was building high hopes upon the supposed opportunities for trade and exploitation in a string of dependencies

[3]Alfred T. Mahan, "The United States Looking Outward," *Atlantic Monthly* 66 (December, 1890), p. 823.

[4]Julius W. Pratt, "American Business and the Spanish–American War," *Hispanic American Historical Review,* Vol. XIV (1934), pp. 178, 200-201.

stretching from the Philippines to Porto Rico. . . . In no section of American opinion had the year wrought a greater transformation than in that of the business men.

More recently, Walter LaFeber argued that businessmen convinced President McKinley to declare war.[5]

. . . The President did not want war; he had been sincere and tireless in his efforts to maintain the peace. By mid-March, however, he was beginning to discover that, although he did not want war, he did want what only a war could provide: the disappearance of the terrible uncertainty in American political and social life, and a solid basis from which to resume the building of the new American commercial empire. . . .

. . . .

Influences other than the yellow press [sensationalism] or congressional belligerence were most important in shaping McKinley's position of April 11. Perhaps most important was the transformation of the opinion of many spokesmen for the business community who had formerly opposed war. . . . This transformation brought important financial spokesmen, especially from the Northeast, into much the same position that had long been occupied by pro-interventionist business groups and journals in the trans-Appalachian area. McKinley's decision to intervene placated many of the same business spokesmen whom he had satisfied . . . by his refusal to declare war.

Did Neo-Manifest Destiny Contribute to Imperialism?

In addition to strategic and economic reasons for imperialism was the Neo-Manifest Destiny. This new version of Manifest Destiny was both a revival and a revision of that which was prominent in the middle of the century. (See Theme 11.) Religious and racial superiority were evident in both. Indiana Republican Albert J. Beveridge reflected this feeling of superiority in his speech "The March of the Flag" in late 1898.[6]

---

[5]Walter LaFeber, *The New American Empire, An Interpretation of American Expansion, 1860-1898* (Ithaca, N.Y.: Cornell University Press, 1963), pp. 400, 403. © 1963 by the American Historical Association. Used by permission of Cornell University Press.

[6]Albert J. Beveridge, "The March of the Flag," speech quoted in *Modern Eloquence,* Vol. IX, ed. Ashley H. Thorndike (New York: Lincoln Scholarship Fund, 1928), pp. 372-373.

It is a noble land that God has given us; a land that can feed and clothe the world. . . . It is a mighty people that He has planted on this soil; a people sprung from the most masterful blood of history. . . . It is a glorious history our God has bestowed upon His chosen people; a history heroic with faith in our mission and our future. . . .

. . . .

Have we no mission to perform, no duty to discharge to our fellowman? . . .

A decade earlier the influential religious leader Josiah Strong wrote in a similar vein.[7]

. . . It seems to me that God, with infinite wisdom and skill, is training the Anglo-Saxon race for an hour sure to come in the world's future. . . . Then this race of unequaled energy, with all the majesty of numbers and the might of wealth behind it—the representative, let us hope, of the largest liberty, the purest Christianity, the highest civilization—having developed peculiarly aggressive traits calculated to impress its institutions upon mankind, will spread itself over the earth. . . .

Richard W. Leopold provided an interpretation of the above statement.[8]

Only after the War with Spain had begun did American religious bodies and periodicals launch a systematic campaign for overseas territory. For some years before, however, they had helped develop a climate of opinion which made that campaign successful. By asserting that injustice and suffering everywhere is the concern of all and by stressing the responsibility of the powerful to lift up the weak, they contributed toward destroying the provincialism of American citizens and toward reminding them of their obligations before God and man. . . .

However, unlike the earlier version of Manifest Destiny, the imperialist binge of the late nineteenth century had social Darwinism to support the religious and philosophical assertions. Richard Leopold elaborated on the rationale for Neo-Manifest Destiny.[9]

---

[7]Josiah Strong, *Our Country* (New York: The Baker and Taylor Co., 1885), pp. 174-175.

[8]Richard W. Leopold, *The Growth of American Foreign Policy, A History* (New York: Alfred A. Knopf, Inc., 1962), pp. 125-126. © Copyright 1962 by Richard W. Leopold. Reprinted by permission of Alfred A. Knopf, Inc.

[9]*Ibid*, p. 126.

. . . By the middle of the 1880's racists and political scientists were also drawing upon the Darwinian hypothesis when they described international relations as a jungle in which the weak were crushed and the virile spread themselves over the globe. It was impossible, they declared, for any nation to remain aloof. To stand still was to fall behind in the march of civilization. . . .

Annexing distant possessions, then, promoted the national interest and insured the nation's survival. But it did more. It benefited backward peoples by raising their standard of living and by teaching them the art of self-government. Here was an ennobling purpose, a civilizing mission that it was the duty—indeed, the destiny—of certain races to undertake.

What Was the Political Reaction to the Creation of an Empire?

By the Treaty of Paris, signed in late 1898, Spain yielded to the United States its colonies in Latin America and Asia. To test public reaction to the acquisition of overseas colonies, politicians debated the issue openly. Bernard A. Weisberger suggested that President McKinley's victory over William Jennings Bryan and the anti-imperialists should not have surprised anyone in the election of 1900.[10]

The anti-imperialist debate provides a final footnote on the story of the years from 1877 to 1900. Many of the most outspoken opponents of annexation come from the ranks of intellectuals and reformers who were past fifty, and had been birthright Republicans. They believed that the republic they had known—of equality under law, self-restraint in appetite, and probity in government—would not survive the creation of an empire, complete with military adventurers and swindling proconsuls. But the republic of which they were dreaming had been disappearing for years; 1896 was its funeral rite.

On the other side were the imperialists, many of them vigorous young men, soon to become Progressives. They had reached maturity when the transcontinental railroad, the trust, the city, and the battleship were already realities instead of threatening novelties. They welcomed the power and challenges of the new society. They believed that an empire abroad could coexist with progress at home, and that strong, efficient, modern government could carry on the paternalistic and moralistic goals of the old Protestant tradition. The kind of nation that they dreamed of had been gestating for a long time and, in a sense, the year 1896 was its birth-year.

---

[10]Bernard A. Weisberger, *The New Industrial State* (New York: John Wiley and Sons, 1969), pp. 136-137.

What Were the Early Effects of American Colonialism?

From the end of the Spanish-American War (1898) to the American entrance into World War I (1917), the United States government engaged in an aggressive policy of expansion in Latin America. By means of purchase, coercion and military intervention, the United States made the Caribbean virtually into an "American lake." A critic of American imperialism, Samuel Guy Inman described the expanse of this empire a quarter century after America fought Spain.[11]

> Run your eyes rapidly down the map and note the countries where the United States is now in practical control. And remember that this control always brings resentment and enmity among the people, though their officials may approve it. Here is the list:—
>
> Cuba, where the United States has a navy base, with marines often found in the interior of the country, with the threat of intervention always held over the Cuban Government. . . .
>
> Haiti, where two thousand United States marines direct and protect the Haitian Government, elected under their supervision; where an American financial adviser exercises absolute control over finances. . . .
>
> Santo Domingo, where for the first time in the history of republics, one republic, without declaring war on another, landed an army, dismissed the president and congress, and for seven years ruled entirely, without even a semblance of national government. . . .
>
> Panama, where, as President Roosevelt said, "I took Panama," since which time it has been under control of the United States. . . .
>
> Nicaragua, where we have maintained one hundred marines since 1912, keeping in control a government which—according to the United States Admiral in charge—is opposed by eighty per cent of the Nicaraguans, but which is favorable to American bankers. . . .
>
> Honduras, where the American minister and two American corporations have long been the controlling powers, and where recently marines have been landed for "protection of American life and property." . . .

Next, Inman listed five Central and South American nations where United States financial interests directed the fiscal policy of each nation. These included Salvador (New York bankers collected customs receipts to insure payment of their loans); Colombia (diplomatic pressure pro-

---

[11]Samuel Guy Inman, "Imperialistic America," *Atlantic Monthly,* Vol. CXXXIV (July, 1924), pp. 107-108. Copyright © by the Atlantic Monthly Company, Boston, Mass. Reprinted with permission.

tected U.S. petroleum concessions); Peru and Ecuador (American advisers influenced national decisions); and Bolivia (a commission of American bankers controlled national finances).

Finally, critic Inman assessed American capitalist influence in three other Latin American nations.[12]

> We must now retrace our steps on the map and look at the third class of countries. These are the ones dominated by North American capitalists, though not having Americans officially appointed to direct their fiscal programme.
>
> They number three as follows:—
>
> Guatemala, where American bankers control the business, American money is the medium of circulation, and the United Fruit Company and other American financial interests have secured control of the railroads, which now become a part of the International Railways of Central America—the largest American-owned railway enterprise outside of the United States.
>
> Costa Rica, where after thirty years' peace, American oil and banana interests recently fomented a revolution against a reform government and at present largely control the economic life of the country and often act as brokers for the government.
>
> Mexico, where Americans own one third of the $2,500,000,000 of the nation's wealth, with seventy-three per cent of the oil lands and much the largest part of the 54,874,557 acres of land owned by foreigners (an area equal to France, Spain, Portugal, and Switzerland), and where American financial representatives are the most important plenipotentiaries received by the Mexican Government.

Eventually, in the 1930's, the United States terminated its occupation in Latin America. However, it never kept its eye off the Caribbean. At present, the United States still retains two colonies, Puerto Rico (conquered in 1898) and the Virgin Islands (purchased in 1916). And it maintains a naval base at Guantanamo, Cuba, and military fortifications in the Canal Zone. It also holds 99-year leases in the Corn Islands of Nicaragua, Guayana, Trinidad, Antigua and Santa Lucia.

How Has American Capitalism Influenced Cuban History?

Of particular note is the relationship of the United States with Cuba. American military and economic influence in Cuba was the most extreme

---

[12]*Ibid*, p. 109.

in all of Latin America. After capturing the island and occupying it for five years, the United States under the terms of the Platt Amendment in 1901 made Cuba an American satellite nation. This arrangement ended in 1934.

During the quarter century which followed this political independence, Cubans lived under a series of right-wing military dictators, the last being Fulgencio Batista (1952-1959). "In the long range perspective of United States policy," Robert F. Smith wrote, "the emphasis has been placed on order, stability, and the protection of American interests. This has meant that the United States has generally opposed sweeping economic reforms and Cuban nationalism. . . ."[13]

Cubans ended American influence in 1959 by supporting Fidel Castro's successful revolution. This movement fed upon the discontent of landless peasants, an insecure middle class and alienated intellectuals. "A strident nationalism that placed the blame for many of Cuba's troubles on the United States foreign policy and on a sugar industry that relied on American capital and markets," Ramón Eduardo Ruiz asserted, "offered Castro the means by which to win popular backing. . . ."[14]

Summary

Referred to as "imperialism," American annexation of colonies and commercial expansion abroad during and after the late nineteenth century resulted from one or several causes. These included a potential threat to the nation's security, a desire to increase personal and national profits, and a belief that national survival required such action. While imperialism did provide the United States with material benefits, it also produced grave political consequences.

Selected References:

Henry F. Graff, ed., *American Imperialism and the Philippine Insurrection* (Boston: Little, Brown & Co., 1969).*

---

[13]Robert F. Smith, *The United States and Cuba: Business and Diplomacy, 1917-1960* (New York: Bookman Associates, 1960), p. 183.

[14]Ramón Eduardo Ruiz, *Cuba: The Making of a Revolution* (Northampton: University of Massachusetts Press, 1968) p. 169.

Testimony of closed-door hearings before the Senate Foreign Relations Committee in 1902.

J. Rogers Hollingsworth, ed., *American Expansion In the Late Nineteenth Century,* American Problems Series (New York: Holt, Rinehart and Winston, 1968).*
Extracts of prominent interpretations of various issues related to the Spanish-American War and expansionism.

Ernest R. May, *Imperial Democracy: The Emergence of America as a Great Power* (New York: Harcourt, Brace & World, 1961).
American foreign policy in the 1890's and its impact on Europe.

George H. Nadel and Perry Curtis, eds., *Imperialism and Colonialism* (New York: The Macmillan Co., 1964).*
A collection of essays which define the terms as applied during the past five centuries.

TERM PROJECTS:

A. Analyze one of the causes of imperialism.
B. If you were a Cuban, how would you have reacted to American influence in your country between 1934 and 1960?

CHECKUP FOR STUDY

Name: ______________________________

1. How do you feel about U.S. economic influence in the world?

2. Why did naval expansionists want colonies?

3. What arguments support the idea that business interests caused war with Spain?

4. What arguments deny that business interests caused war with Spain?

To remove this page: Open the book as wide as possible several times to loosen this page from the binding. Lay the book flat on your desk and gently but firmly pull this page *straight up* and away from the binding from top to bottom.

5. How did religious leaders contribute to imperialism?

6. In a few words, identify an "imperialist" and an "anti-imperialist."

7. How extensive was American business influence in the Caribbean by the mid-1920's?

8. How did conservative American capitalists assist Fidel Castro to power?

9.

10.

"The dead returned to life"

Courtesy of the *Minneapolis Journal*
John D. Hicks, *The American Nation,* Houghton Mifflin, Boston
Second Edition (1949 copyright)

17 What Some Called Progress

REGULATION: Government intervention into the social and economic activities of the nation, state and municipality.

REFERENCE DATES:

1890	Sherman Anti-Trust Act passed
1901	William McKinley assassinated; Theodore Roosevelt succeeded him as President
1906	Hepburn Act, Pure Food and Drug Act and Meat Inspection Act expanded federal regulation

1912	Woodrow Wilson (New Freedom) elected over Theodore Roosevelt (New Nationalism), William Howard Taft (original progressivism), and Eugene V. Debs (socialism)
1914	Clayton Anti-Trust Act and Federal Trade Commission Act strengthened federal regulation
1916	Child Labor Act (declared unconstitutional, 1918) and Adamson Eight-Hour Act extended federal control; Woodrow Wilson reelected over Charles Evans Hughes

WHAT ORGANIZATIONAL PATTERN IS AMERICAN INDUSTRY UNDERGOING?

Today American industry is in the midst of the largest and longest-lasting merger movement in its history. Beginning in 1950, when a couple of hundred companies independently initiated the process of combining with other firms, mergers have continued to grow in number. Over five thousand mergers have taken place in each of the last years of the 1960's.

Those large and diversified corporations which acquired other companies in fields unrelated to their principal operation are what financiers call "conglomerates." For example, Ling-Temco-Vought, whose primary business is aircraft and aerospace, owns companies which produce such unrelated products as sports equipment, meats and pharmaceutical goods. Gilbert Burck has written of this development.[1]

> The great conglomerate movement is generating widespread doubt, apprehension, and even dismay. Aggressive builders, displaying the legendary boldness and imagination of the great American business barons, are falling over one another in their haste to create large multi-market companies [conglomerates]. And in the process many are engaging in practices and confecting situations that someday may land their resplendently varied structures in deep trouble.
>
> These latter-day empire builders are violating no laws and flouting no accounting conventions. [Nevertheless, the Federal Trade Commission has become upset over the entire affair.]

---

[1]Gilbert Burck, "The Merger Movement Rides High," *Fortune,* Vol. LXXIX (1969), p. 79.

How Did American Industry Change During the Gilded Age?

Several periods of industrial combining have preceded the present merger spree. In the 1920's, and twice before that during the Gilded Age (the last three decades of the nineteenth century) notable periods of corporation mergers occurred. Concentrating on the Gilded Age, Alfred D. Chandler, Jr., discussed how industry changed.[2]

Between the depression of the 1870's and the beginning of the twentieth century, American industry underwent a significant transformation. In the 1870's the major industries serviced an agrarian economy. Except for a few companies equipping the rapidly expanding railroad network, the leading industrial firms processed agricultural products and provided farmers with food and clothing. These firms tended to be small, and bought their raw materials and sold their finished goods locally. Where they manufactured for a market more than a few miles away from the factory, they bought and sold through commissioned agents who handled the business of several other similar firms.

By the beginning of the twentieth century, many more companies were making producers' goods, to be used in industry rather than on the farm or by the ultimate consumer. Most of the major industries had become dominated by a few large enterprises. These great industrial corporations no longer purchased and sold through agents, but had their own nation-wide buying and marketing organizations. Many, primarily those in the extractive industries, had come to control their own raw materials. In other words, the business economy had become industrial. Major industries were dominated by a few firms that had become great, vertically integrated, centralized enterprises.

. . . .

. . . [Thus] *the* major innovation in the American economy between the 1880's and the turn of the century was the creation of the great corporations in American industry. This innovation . . . was a response to the growth of a national and increasingly urban market that was created by the building of a national railroad network—the dynamic force in the economy in the quarter century before 1880. After 1900 the newly modified methods of interfirm and intrafirm administration remained relatively unchanged. . . .

What Was Public Reaction to Industrial Corporations?

Accompanying the growth of industrial combinations was the passage in the 1870's of state regulatory laws, commonly called granger laws. After

[2]Alfred D. Chandler, "The Begining of 'Big Business' in American Industry," *Business History Review,* Vol. XXXIII (1959), pp. 4, 31.

their invalidation by the Supreme Court in the mid-1880's, Congress passed the Interstate Commerce Act, which established the Interstate Commerce Commission (ICC). This regulatory body could investigate complaints of unfair business practices on products transported between states, but it could not enforce any of its recommendations.

Three years later, in 1890, Congress passed the Sherman Anti-Trust Act. By definition the industrial combination called a "trust" differed markedly from the modern conglomerate. A trust dominated a single field of enterprise (meat, oil, sugar, etc.) through the exchange of stock and the creation of interlocking directorates. That is, a company handed over its controlling interest to a board of directors, and those directors sat on the boards of most rival companies, too. Thus the directors were able to initiate policies which eliminated competition and created a monopoly while the companies involved gave the appearance of being independent. A conglomerate neither dominates a single field of production nor has interlocking directorates.

Technically, trusts were short-lived, even though the public has continued to use that term when referring to large industrial combinations. In *Addystone Pipe and Steel* v. *United States* (1899), the Supreme Court so weakened the legal structure of the trust that large combinations such as Standard Oil terminated as trusts and reorganized as "holding companies." These new combinations purchased or leased physical facilities of rival companies, and/or acquired fifty-one percent of their stock. By doing so, they circumvented the legal restrictions of the time.

Why Did Congress Pass the Sherman Anti-Trust Act?

It appears that Congress passed the Sherman Anti-Trust Act in 1890 for a variety of reasons. M. A. Adelman described the primary motive behind the passage of this law.[3]

> . . . The debates reflected a strongly conservative and property-oriented outlook; and the Sherman Act was a very conservative law. . . . The law sought merely to curb the trusts—to what extent, was not clear. Any illusions

[3]M. A. Adelman, "Industrial Organization: Public Regulation of Business," review of *The Federal Antitrust Policy: Organization of American Tradition* by Hans Thorelli, in *American Economic Review,* Vol. XLIV (1956), pp. 483-484.

about the Act being a trust-busting instrument, or aimed at the maintenance of competition [are false]. . . . Senators Sherman, Hoar, and Edmunds (who among them fashioned the Act) . . . accepted the presence of the great combinations. . . .

Their primary object . . . [was] to keep big business from annoying small business and curtailing its opportunity for "free" or "fair" competition; but they . . . [were] not concerned with possible control of the market by a few manufacturers.

How Did the Sherman Act Affect Industrial Combinations?

The Sherman Anti-Trust Act in its early years proved ineffective. Between 1890 and 1901 the federal government initiated only eighteen suits under the Act, four of which were against labor unions, and it achieved only five indictments.

Traditionally, judges have received the blame for such ineffective regulation for catering to outdated concepts of unrestricted free enterprise. In Hans Thorelli's view, judges possessed "sublime ignorance of economic realities." He added that much of the blame rested with elected leaders. In reviewing Thorelli's work, Russel B. Nye explained this point.[4]

That the Sherman Act in its early years languished . . . is directly the fault of . . . the three Presidents [Benjamin Harrison, Grover Cleveland and William McKinley] preceding Theodore Roosevelt. . . . [They] were simply not interested in making the law effective. The year 1903, with the establishment of the Anti-Trust Division, the Bureau of Corporations, and the Northern Securities case, thus marked the conclusion, rather than a turning point, in the institutionalization of an economic policy long in forming, and finally translated into law by the Sherman Act.

During the administrations of the next three presidents, federal antitrust suits numbered over two hundred with about fifty percent indictments. Whereas the first three presidents had initiated only eighteen suits, Theodore Roosevelt's administration in nearly eight years sued forty-four trusts, to gain him the title of "trust-buster," a misnomer he disliked; William Howard Taft in the next four years initiated ninety

[4]Russel B. Nye, review of Thorelli, *Federal Antitrust Policy,* in *American Historical Review,* Vol. LXI (1956), pp. 426.

suits; and Woodrow Wilson before 1921 challenged another eighty trusts.

Simultaneously the number of mergers began to decline. Douglass C. North warned students, however, that trust-busting and merger declines are not necessarily related.[5]

> [To explain the decrease of mergers after 1903], some observers have put the stress upon the Sherman Anti-Trust Act, subsequent acts such as the Clayton Act, passed in 1914, and more vigorous prosecutions by the antitrust division of the Department of Justice. Others have pointed to the success of new entrants into the field, who have continuously overturned major firms; and the failure of large firms to hold their position in the economy in the face of competition from new, young upstarts suggests that this has, indeed, been important. Still others point to rapid technological change which continually creates new, superior products to compete successfully with older ones. . . .

How Did Progressivism Arise?

The early failure to regulate big business contributed to expressions of discontent. As people looked about society, they found, among other things, vile abuses of power. From the shamefulness of the cities, through the corruption of the states, to the decadence on the national scene, government had failed to guarantee the public the government's primary purpose of being, impartial justice for all. Instead, government under corporate influence had concentrated on a secondary purpose, the creation of wealth for material improvement.

As a result, critics arose to challenge those in control. Difficulties abounded, however, for few could identify or agree on the primary cause of their dissatisfaction. Athough not mutually exclusive in their demands, groups of critics proposed different ways to solve the nation's ills. Prohibitionists pleaded for government restriction of alcohol production to improve national morality; "single tax" groups demanded Henry George's single tax proposal to curb tax injustice; feminists urged women's suffrage to insure righteousness in politics; Social Gospel adherents pleaded for renewed church responsibility to end urban immorality. While anarchists wished to do away with government, socialists wanted expanded

---

[5]Douglass C. North, *Growth and Welfare in the American Past* (Englewood Cliffs, N. J.: Prentice-Hall, 1966), p. 160.

government, excluding private ownership. Populist farmers in the 1890's agreed with the latter as far as railroads and middlemen were concerned, but obviously they rejected nationalization of farm production.

Eventually some of these groups of critics united, primarily those in urban centers. Gerald N. Grob and George Athan Billias outlined this cohesion.[6]

> Between 1900 and 1917, these uncoordinated efforts at reform were institutionalized in what came to be known as the Progressive movement. Pluralistic rather than unitary, the Progressive movement was actually a series of movements operating at the local, state and national levels of government and society. The movement consisted of a loose coalition of [urban] reformers who sought a variety of goals: political reforms such as the initiative, referendum, recall, and the destruction of urban political machines and corruption; economic reforms such as regulation of public utilities and the curtailment of corporate power; and social reforms such as the Americanization of the immigrant, the amelioration of the lot of the urban poor, and regulation of child and woman labor, as well as many others. . . .

How Did New Nationalism Differ From New Freedom?

In a general sense, by 1912 many reformers took political sides over two major political questions. Should the federal government initiate a program of greater economic regulation? And, should the federal government provide for the social welfare of the people? Theodore Roosevelt and his followers, many of whom were former Republican Party members, founded the Progressive Party to argue in favor of the "New Nationalist" approach to the questions. Democrat Woodrow Wilson offered alternative solutions which he called the "New Freedom." In the following brief excerpts, Roosevelt and Wilson offer their views on these questions.

On the subject of industrial control, Theodore Roosevelt argued in favor of greater public regulation.[7]

---

[6]Gerald N. Grob and George Athan Billias, *Interpretations of American History: Patterns and Perspectives,* Vol. II (New York: The Free Press, 1967), p. 143.

[7]Theodore Roosevelt, *The Works of Theodore Roosevelt,* Vol. XVII (New York: Charles Scribner's Sons, 1926), pp. 265-266.

. . . In the last twenty years an increasing percentage of our people have come to depend on industry for their livelihood, so that to-day the wage-workers in industry rank in importance side by side with the tillers of the soil. As a people we cannot afford to let any group of citizens or any individual citizen live or labor under conditions which are injurious to the common welfare. Industry, therefore, must submit to such public regulation as will make it a means of life and health, not of death or inefficiency. We must protect the crushable elements at the base of our present industrial structure.

Wilson answered his opponent.[8]

. . . You know that Mr. Roosevelt long ago classified trusts for us as good and bad, and he said that he was afraid only of the bad ones. Now he does not desire that there should be any more bad ones, but proposes that they should all be made good by discipline, directly applied by a commission of executive appointment. . . . All that it is proposed to do is to take them under control and regulation.

. . . .

. . . Our purpose is the restoration of freedom. We propose to prevent private monopoly by law, to see to it that the methods by which monopolies have been built up are legally made impossible. We design that the limitations on private enterprise shall be removed, so that the next generation of youngsters, as they come along, will not have to become protégés of benevolent trusts, but will be free to go about making their own lives what they will.

As for social welfare, Roosevelt had stated his position earlier in 1910 at Osawatomie, Kansas.[9]

This New Nationalism regards the executive power as the steward of the public welfare. It demands of the judiciary that it shall be interested primarily in human welfare rather than in property, just as it demands that the representative body shall represent all the people rather than any one class or section of the people.

Wilson opposed public welfare.[10]

---

[8]Woodrow Wilson, *The New Freedom* (Garden City, N.Y.: Doubleday, Page and Co., 1913), pp. 194, 222.

[9]Roosevelt, *op. cit.,* pp. 19-20.

[10]Wilson, *op. cit.,* p. 198.

I do not want to live under a philanthropy. I do not want to be taken care of by the government, either directly, or by any instruments through which the government is acting. I want only to have right and justice prevail, so far as I am concerned. Give me right and justice and I will undertake to take care of myself.

That President Wilson replaced his New Freedom with Roosevelt's New Nationalism during his second year in office—he accepted the Sherman Anti-Trust Act and Federal Trade Commission Act—suggests that Wilson's original concept of regulation was untenable. As for his position on social welfare legislation, although accepting the La Follette Seaman's Act (1915), Child Labor Act (1916) and Adamson Eight-Hour Act (1916) under pressure, Wilson offered the people little in comparison to what the nation needed. Americans would have to wait until the 1930's for that.

How Have Historians Interpreted the Progressive Era?

Debate persists over how to interpret the progressive movement. Those involved in the events of that time, as the generation which followed, saw the progressive movement as a class struggle. Liberal reformers banded together to fight conservative corporations and their allied corrupt politicians. By the 1950's, a new explanation of progressivism appeared. The progressives were middle class leaders, very moral and very conservative, who were fighting to regain a way of life robbed them by the industrial revolution. While their methods may have been liberal at times, passing laws to expand democracy and to regulate business, their goals remained conservative, to preserve free enterprise and to return political power to people like themselves. Their optimism provided them with courage and confidence.

More recently a new interpretation of progressivism has challenged these earlier views. David Eakins explained this newer rendition.[11]

. . . Progressive Era legislation such as the Federal Reserve Act, the Federal Trade Commission Act, the Hepburn Act, the Meat Inspection Act and

---

[11]David Eakins, "Ideology That Shaped Reform," review of *The Corporate Ideal in the Liberal State, 1900-1918,* by James Weinstein, *This World* magazine, *San Francisco Examiner and Chronicle,* April 28, 1968, p. 36.

even the Pure Food and Drug Act was supported and often drafted by businessmen who looked to the government to provide stability and order in a too-competitive industrial society.

It is true, Weinstein cautions, that many of the original demands for reforms came from groups near the bottom of the American social ladder. The more perceptive businessmen responded to these demands (and to their own fear of a growing radicalism if they were not met) by making sure that they would control the various local and Federal reform agencies.

The businessmen became involved in governmental policy-making in order to protect his own short-run interests; that is, his profits. But he also took a longer-range view of his self-interest. He became aware that the creation of a more responsible social order was necessary. . . .

. . . .

These men became liberals out of a recognition of the need for change for their own sakes. Their liberalism was neither "anti-big business" nor was it neutral. It demanded an active, interventionist government that would provide for an efficient, orderly, stable (and hence profitable) corporate society. This was corporate liberalism. Within such a context reforms were not only possible—they were necessary. And within such a context concessions to other interest groups such as labor and farmers were not only possible—they were essential to the creation of the broad support that such a corporate order required.

Summary

Present mergers in American industry are part of a historical trend dating back to the Gilded Age. In that period public reaction to the rise of monopolies led to the creation of state and federal laws to regulate them. Protesting against these industrial combinations and other problems of the time, reformers of many types joined together to form the progressive movement. The political philosophy and accomplishments of that movement have influenced Americans to this day.

Selected References:

Richard Hofstadter, *The Age of Reform: From Bryan to F.D.R.* (New York: Alfred Knopf, 1955).*
A speculative evaluation of reform stressing a "status revolution."

Arthur Link, *Woodrow Wilson and the Progressive Era, 1910-1917* (New York: Harper & Row, 1958).*
Wilsonian progressivism and the end of the movement.

Arthur Mann, *The Progressive Era, Liberal Renaissance or Liberal Failure?* American Problem Studies (New York: Holt, Rinehart and Winston, 1963).*
Selected excerpts on major questions of the age.

George E. Mowry, *The Era of Theodore Roosevelt, 1910-1912* (New York: Harper & Row, 1958).*
A synthesis of early progressivism and the role Roosevelt played in it.

TERM PROJECTS:

A. Describe the works and significance of the "muckrakers."

B. How did various progressive leaders handle the question of immigration restrictions?

CHECKUP FOR STUDY

Name: ______________________________

1. How would Hans Thorelli disagree with the cartoon?

2. What is the difference between a trust and a conglomerate?

3. Why were trusts short-lived?

4. Why was the Sherman Act initially ineffective?

To remove this page: Open the book as wide as possible several times to loosen this page from the binding. Lay the book flat on your desk and gently but firmly pull this page *straight up* and away from the binding from top to bottom.

5. What motivated the passage of the Sherman Act?

6. List the reasons why mergers declined after 1903.

7. Why is it difficult to define the Progressive Era as one of conflict between "good" and "evil"?

8. How did Roosevelt and Wilson differ over social welfare?

9.

10.

The Camouflaged Steed: "I've often heard of the horrors of war, but I never expected to be one."

Cartoon Cavalcade, ed. Thomas Craven, Simon & Schuster, New York, 1943, p. 114; from *Life,* October 18.
T. S. SULLIVANT, L '18

18 Make War Not Love

GREAT WAR: Before 1939, this popular term denoted World War I, itself not the first world-wide conflict, but the largest to that date.

REFERENCE DATES:

1914	General war in Europe began between Central Powers (Germany, Austria-Hungary, Turkey) and the Allies (England, France, Russia)
1915	War zones created; submarine attacks began; *Lusitania* sunk

1917	U.S. declared war on Germany and Austria-Hungary
1918	Wilson announced the 14 Points; Armistice agreed upon
1919	Treaty of Versailles concluded
1920	Senate twice rejected Versailles Treaty; separate peace treaties ratified

How Did President Johnson Modify American Policy in Vietnam?

When Lyndon B. Johnson became President in 1963 after the assassination of President John F. Kennedy, domestic problems appeared uppermost in his mind. Yet within two years foreign policy issues had become far more important.

During his campaign for the presidency in 1964, President Johnson declared that his primary commitment to South Vietnam was to help that country help itself. He indicated as much before the American Bar Association in New York City on August 12, 1964.[1]

> . . . Some say that we should withdraw from South Vietnam. . . . Some others are eager to enlarge the conflict. They call upon us to supply American boys to do the job that Asian boys should do. They ask us to take reckless action which might risk the lives of millions and engulf much of Asia, and certainly threaten the peace of the entire world. Moreover, such action would offer no solution at all to the real problem of Vietnam.

Less than a year later, during a speech at Johns Hopkins University, Johnson modified his earlier stand. He decided to increase the American commitment to the war. The increased involvement of American forces led to widespread public dissatisfaction and perhaps contributed to the President's retirement from office in 1969.[2]

> In recent months attacks on South Vietnam were stepped up. Thus it became necessary to increase our response and make attacks by air. This is

[1]Lyndon Baines Johnson, "Restraint and Law," quoted in *Vital Speeches of the Day*, Vol. XXX (1964), p. 675.

[2]Lyndon Baines Johnson, "United States Vietnam Policy," quoted in *Vital Speeches of the Day*, Vol. XXXI (1965), p. 387.

not a change of purpose. It is a change in what we believe that purpose requires. . . . We will not withdraw, either openly or under the cloak of a meaningless agreement.

What Was the Reaction to the Outbreak of World War I?

One half century earlier, another President announced one policy only to change his mind and follow another. During the early summer of 1914, Americans watched events in Europe with anguish. Some believed that war was outdated; others found relief when war finally came in August. For many, however, there was indifference. America was far removed from the lunacy of the Old World. Thus, President Woodrow Wilson struck a chord close to the hearts of many Americans with his initial statement of policy relating to the conflict.[3]

The effect of the war upon the United States will depend upon what Amercan citizens say and do. Every man who really loves America will act and speak in the true spirit of neutrality, which is the spirit of impartiality and fairness and friendliness to all concerned. The spirit of the Nation in this critical matter will be determined largely by what individuals and society and those gathered in public meetings do and say, upon what newspapers and magazines contain, upon what ministers utter in their pulpits, and men proclaim as their opinions on the street.

The people of the United States are drawn from many nations, and chiefly from the nations now at war. It is natural and inevitable that there should be the utmost variety of sympathy and desire among them with regard to the issues and circumstances of the conflict. Some will wish one nation, others another, to succeed in the momentous struggle. It will be easy to excite passion and difficult to allay it. Those responsible for exciting it will assume a heavy responsibility. . . .

. . . .

I venture, therefore, my fellow countrymen, to speak a solemn word of warning to you against that deepest, most subtle, most essential breach of neutrality which may spring out of partisanship, out of passionately taking sides. The United States must be neutral in fact as well as in name during these days that are to try men's souls. We must be impartial in thought as well as in action, must put a curb upon our sentiments as well as upon every

[3]Woodrow Wilson, *Senate Document 566*, Sixty-third Congress, Second Session (Washington, D.C.: Government Printing Office, 1914), pp. 2-3.

transaction that might be construed as a preference of one party to the struggle before another.

What Reasons Did Wilson Give for Entering the War?

Two and one-half years later, in April, 1917, President Wilson was of a different opinion about American policy. In an address before Congress, the President asked for a Declaration of War.[4]

On the third of February last I officially laid before you the extraordinary announcement of the Imperial German Government that on and after the first day of February it was its purpose to put aside all restraints of law or of humanity and use its submarines to sink every vessel that sought to approach either the ports of Great Britain and Ireland or the western coasts of Europe or any of the ports controlled by the enemies of Germany within the Mediterranean. . . . Vessels of every kind, whatever their flag, their character, their cargo, their destination, their errand, have been ruthlessly sent to the bottom without warning and without thought of help or mercy for those on board, the vessels of friendly neutrals along with those of belligerents. Even hospital ships and ships carrying relief to the sorely bereaved and stricken people of Belgium, though the latter were provided with safe conduct through the proscribed areas by the German Government itself and were distinguished by unmistakable marks of identity, have been sunk with the same reckless lack of compassion or of principle.

. . . .

. . . Neutrality is no longer feasible or desirable where the peace of the world is involved and the freedom of its peoples, and the menace to that peace and freedom lies in the existence of autocratic governments backed by organized force which is controlled wholly by their will, not by the will of their people. We have seen the last of neutrality in such circumstances. We are at the beginning of an age in which it will be insisted that the same standards of conduct and of responsibility for wrong done shall be observed among nations and their governments that are observed among the individual citizens of civilized states.

. . . .

. . . It is a fearful thing to lead this great peaceful people into war, into the most terrible and disastrous of all wars, civilization itself seeming to be in the balance. But the right is more precious than peace, and we shall fight

---

[4]Woodrow Wilson, speech to Congress of April 2, 1917, *Congressional Record,* Sixty-fifth Congress, First Session, 55, pp. 102-104.

for the things which we have always carried nearest our hearts—for democracy, for the right of those who submit to authority to have a voice in their own Governments, for the rights and liberties of small nations, for a universal domination of right by such a concert of free peoples as shall bring peace and safety to all nations and make the world itself at last free. To such a task we can dedicate our lives and our fortunes, everything that we are and everything that we have. . . .

How Did the Public React to the Policy Change?

Despite protests from a vocal minority against America's entrance into World War I, the majority calmly submitted to the involvement. Richard W. Leopold described this resignation.[5]

And so America went to war. There were no crowds in the street shouting "On to Berlin!" as there had been in Paris in August, 1914. There was no violent rage, as there would be in December, 1941. There was no thought of territorial gain, as there had been in some quarters in June, 1812 and May, 1846. There was no expectation of an easy victory, as there had been in April, 1898. The American people had not wanted this war and did not relish it any more than the English people would wish to oppose Hitler over Poland in September, 1939. Both cases were marked by a calm resignation over the seemingly inevitable, by a reluctant conviction that there was no honorable alternative, and by a grim determination to get a dirty job over with as quickly as possible.

Did Submarine Attacks Force America into War?

Since the American Declaration of War, historians have debated the cause of President Wilson's change of policy. At first, the answer seemed simple enough. As Wilson had stated before Congress, Germany had not respected American neutrality by sinking American ships. Supporting this viewpoint, Charles Seymour emphasized the role of the submarine in causing America's entrance into the Great War.[6]

Thus, from the point of view of material interests, there could be no comparison between the damage resulting to Americans from the Allied blockade

[5] Leopold, *op. cit.*, pp. 336-337.

[6] Charles Seymour, "American Neutrality: The Experience of 1914-1917," *Foreign Affairs*, Vol. XIV (1935), p. 30.

and that from the intensive submarine campaign. If the latter were permitted, under protests comparable to those sent to the Allies, the result would be an almost complete blockade of American commerce, since shippers would not dare send cargoes and crew out to destruction. A clear illustration of the effect of the submarine campaign on American commercial, industrial, and agricultural interests was given by the congestion of our ports that followed the threat of submarine attacks in February and March, 1917. Freights were snarled, goods were spoiled, business was menaced with a complete tie-up.

Even so, Wilson might not have taken his firm stand against the submarine if merely property rights had been threatened. He was always careful not to interpret national policy in terms of purely material interests. Despite the difficulties involved, the economic aspects of the diplomatic conflict with Germany might have been adjudicated. But the submarine warfare involved attacks upon American lives, whether sailors on merchant ships or passengers. To Wilson it seemed a war on humanity. Between property interests and human rights there lay a clear distinction. . . .

Accepting the fact of German disregard for American neutral rights, Harry Elmer Barnes argued that Britain was as responsible as Germany in such matters.[7]

The United States could not have been more perfectly set up for neutrality than it was in July and August, 1914. President Woodrow Wilson was a lifelong and deeply conscientious pacifist. His convictions in this matter were not emotional or impressionistic, but had been based upon deep study and prolonged reflection. Moreover, he was married to a woman noted for pacific sentiments and firm convictions on such matters. She strongly backed up her husband in his pacific beliefs and policies. As Secretary of State, we had in William Jennings Bryan the world's outstanding pacifist. . . .

. . . .

England started out in 1914 by making a scrap of paper out of the Declaration of London governing contraband in war-time. Next, we proceeded to allow her to make use of armed belligerent merchantmen as if they were peaceful commercial vessels. England violated our neutral rights far more extensively between 1914 and 1917 than she did before the War of 1812, even to the point of flying the American flag.

---

[7]Harry Elmer Barnes, "The World War of 1914-1918," in *War in the Twentieth Century,* ed. Willard Waller (New York: Random House, 1940), pp. 71, 73, 81-82.

Wilson came to believe, however, that Great Britain was fighting for civilization and that so trivial a thing as international law must not be allowed to stand in her way. . . .

. . . .

The net result . . . was that we entered the World War in April, 1917. We did so, even though there was no clear legal or moral basis for our so doing. If there ever was an instance in which the facts were clearly in accord with a neutrality policy it was in the spring of 1917. We should have fought both Germany and Britain or else neither. But the country went into war, with most of the citizens of the United States feeling that our self-respect and national honor demanded it. No other course seemed open to us.

Did America Fight to Promote and Protect Profits?

Granted that both England and Germany violated American neutrality. Yet, what were those American ships doing in a war zone besides asserting their neutral rights? They were carrying goods for Americans who were profiting from war sales. Charles C. Tansill suggested that profits from selling war materials greatly influenced American foreign policy.[8]

Within a few weeks after the outbreak of the World War it became apparent to competent military observers that victory for either side would largely depend upon the possession of adequate supplies of munitions of war. The nation that labored under the greatest handicap in this regard was Great Britain, whose assistance to France in the early months of the war was sharply limited because of a glaring deficiency in effective artillery and in high explosive shells. Although the production of British factories could be rapidly increased there would remain an alarming shortage of supplies necessary for the conduct of successful warfare. The only means of meeting this situation was through the importation of munitions of war from neutral nations. European neutrals, however, soon placed embargoes upon the shipment of war materials, so the British Government was forced to look to America as the only important neutral that could supply her needs.

In America the rise of "big business" had produced a vast industrial organization that could fill war orders in an amazingly short time, and the very fact that this organization was severely suffering from a widespread business de-

---

[8]Charles C. Tansill, *America Goes to War* (Boston: Little, Brown and Co., 1938), p. 32.

pression meant that these orders would receive special attention. It was not long before immense exports of American munitions were crowding British ports. In 1916 the value of American war supplies to the Allied Governments amounted to more than a billion dollars, and the intimate economic ties thus created served to supplement the sentimental bonds that had long attached America to the side of the Entente Powers.

Was American Security Involved?

Taking issue with the viewpoint that profits drove President Wilson to favor the Allies, Edward H. Buehrig contended that a threat to America's security forced Wilson into war.[9]

The intent to remain neutral, which Wilson set out with in August, 1914, did not long remain uncompromised. Great Britain wielded vast economic power as a consequence of her large merchant marine and control over a great and productive empire. Reinforcing this gigantic economic complex in peacetime, and mobilizing it in wartime for political purposes, was the British Navy. For the United States to yield to this all-pervasive influence was the course of least resistance, and was the more attractive because any other action would have entailed serious economic sacrifice. Yet Wilson might have foregone the rewards of bending before British power had it not been for still another circumstance. For a hundred years Anglo-American relations had progressively improved, until by 1914 the accommodation between the two countries was complete. This state of affairs had for decades been the cornerstone of the security of the Western Hemisphere and was the underlying condition of the unprecedented freedom of action so long enjoyed by the United States. This is understood better today than it was then, but Wilson was not the man to disturb a relationship so significant and so firmly established. By the fall of 1914, therefore, the United States, both by omission and acquiescence, had set a course highly favorable to the British cause.

Did Wilson Have a Choice?

There is another explanation of why the United States entered the Great War. Ernest R. May argued that President Wilson, having exhausted all other alternatives, had no other course but war.[10]

---

[9]Edward Buehrig, "Idealism and Statecraft," *Confluence*, Vol. V (1945), p. 257.

[10]Ernest R. May, in *The Reconstruction of American History*, ed. John Higham (New York: Harper and Row, 1962), p. 192.

All of us saw Wilson's efforts to avoid conflict with the British and to prevent a German U-boat campaign as not only rational but almost inevitable response to problems with which the President had to deal. The trade loss resulting from the Allied blockade was negligible. The gain from Allied war buying, on the other hand, meant the difference between prosperity and depression. Moreover, long before propaganda could have had any effect, Wilson estimated that 90 per cent of the public was pro-Ally. When confronting the first German submarine decree, he had to recognize that it threatened the American economy. He also had to take account of the fact that a significant part of the public already felt outraged against Germany not just because of atrocity stories but also because of such acts as the violation of Belgian neutrality and the bombing of open cities.

[Charles] Seymour and [Arthur] Link and I all stressed the importance of seeing Wilson's actions in perspective against those of the Allies and especially of the Germans. We pointed out that the British deliberately endeavored to keep American goodwill while the German government always discussed submarine operations in terms of war or peace with the United States. We endeavored to show . . . that the American government was not making a series of absolute moral judgments but was choosing among the unsatisfactory alternatives available to it at given moments of time.

Concurring in the above, Arthur Link proposed that, failing to obtain peace as a neutral, Wilson sought lasting peace by making war.[11]

It seemed for a moment that Wilson's bold stroke and secret negotiations [in late 1916] might succeed. The British government, for reasons still unknown, returned a favorable response to Wilson's overtures on January 26 [1917]. The Austro-Hungarian government soon sent secret feelers to the White House. Everything now depended upon the reply from Berlin. Bethmann was so excited by Wilson's secret appeal that he rushed to Pless to plead for a friendly response. It was too late to postpone the submarine campaign, for U-boats were already on the way to their stations. But the Imperial Chancellor did obtain permission to send a statement of moderate peace aims and an appeal to Wilson to persevere in his efforts for peace.

Events immediately afterwards led to an intensification rather than to an end to the war. But they need not have turned out that way. Wilson, to be sure, broke diplomatic relations with Germany on February 3, soon after the announcement of the new submarine campaign. But he was still as dead set against belligerency as ever. He clearly would have accepted a severe

---

[11]Arthur Link, "Woodrow Wilson and Peace Moves," *The Listener,* Vol. LXXXV (1966), p. 870.

intensification of the submarine war, and he yielded to the growing American demand for war only after the Germans began to sink passenger liners and American merchantmen without warning, and only after the bungling Zimmermann telegram, proposing a military alliance between Mexico and Germany, had caused him to lose all faith in German good intentions. But in the end, when he made his final decision, it was the conviction that the War was in its last stages, and American participation would hasten its end, that most powerfully influenced the President to decide for belligerency.

Was Going to War Worthwhile in the Long Run?

Whether the United States had any reason for entering World War I is clearly debatable. George F. Kennan offered one viewpoint worthy of consideration.[12]

> I would like first to say a word about the total result of these two world wars in Europe. These wars were fought at the price of some tens of millions of lives, of untold physical destruction, of the destruction of the balance of forces on the Continent–at the price of rendering western Europe dangerously, perhaps fatefully, vulnerable to Soviet power. Both wars were fought, really, with a view to changing Germany: to correcting her behavior, to making the Germans something different from what they were. Yet, today, if one were offered the chance of having back again the Germany of 1913–a Germany run by conservative but relatively moderate people, no Nazis and no Communists, a vigorous Germany, united and unoccupied, full of energy and confidence, able to play a part again in the balancing-off of Russian power in Europe–well, there would be objections to it from many quarters, and it wouldn't make everybody happy; but in many ways it wouldn't sound so bad, in comparison with our problems of today. Now, think what this means. When you tally up the total score of the two wars, in terms of their ostensible objective, you find that if there has been any gain at all, it is pretty hard to discern.

Summary

The outcome of events in World War I differed from America's original intentions. Initially President Wilson had tried to maintain neutrality,

---

[12]George F. Kennan, *American Diplomacy, 1900-1950* (New York: Mentor Books, 1952 ed.), pp. 50-51.

but in 1917 he relinquished this policy in favor of war. Some historians suggest that Wilson had no other alternative but to fight; others disagree. The debatable causes of this change of policy are attributable to submarine attacks, war profits, a threat to national security and idealistic principles. Whatever the cause, the war had questionable consequences.

Selected References:

Herbert J. Bass, *America's Entry Into World War I, Submarines, Sentiment or Security?,* American Problem Studies (New York: Holt, Rinehart and Winston, 1964).*
Selections and commentary on why America entered the war.

Douglass E. Lee, ed., *The Outbreak of the First World War, Who Was Responsible?,* Problems in European Civilization (Boston: D. C. Heath & Co., revised edition 1963).*
Excerpts of historical opinion which attempt to answer the question.

Arthur S. Link, *Wilson the Diplomatist: A Look at His Major Foreign Policies* (Baltimore: Johns Hopkins Press, 1957).
A summary of the complexity of problems which faced Wilson.

Ralph A. Stone, *Wilson and the League of Nations, Why America's Rejection?,* American Problem Studies (New York: Holt, Rinehart and Winston, 1967).*
Answers to the question from selected sources.

Term Projects:

A. Compare and contrast the issue of neutrality in 1917 with that of 1812.

B. If a Republican had been President from 1914 to 1918, what policy would he have followed? Why?

CHECKUP FOR STUDY

Name: ______________________________

1. How did Americans react to the beginning of the Great War?

2. Why would Americans have natural sympathies with each side fighting?

3. Why did President Wilson believe neutrality was no longer possible?

4. How did submarines affect American "human rights"?

To remove this page: Open the book as wide as possible several times to loosen this page from the binding. Lay the book flat on your desk and gently but firmly pull this page *straight up* and away from the binding from top to bottom.

5. Why should the U.S. have fought England as well as Germany?

6. How did European and American neutrals differ?

7. How could going to war create peace?

8. If you were President Wilson, would you have demanded war in 1917? Why?

9.

10.

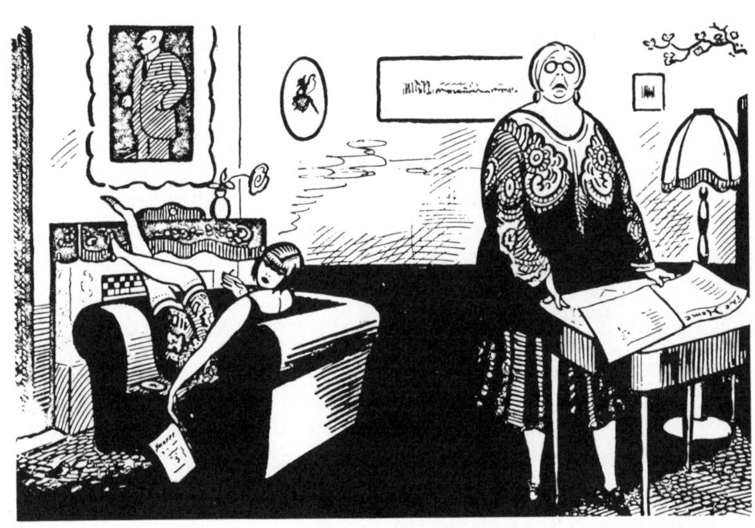

"Mother, when you were a girl, didn't you find it a bore to be a virgin?"

Cartoon Cavalcade, ed. Thomas Craven, Simon & Schuster, New York, 1943, from *Collier's*, 1927
ART YOUNG

19 When Values Clashed

VALUES: Beliefs, customs and institutions which groups hold as true and necessary to their way of life, whether founded upon superstition or reasoning.

REFERENCE DATES:

1919	Women's suffrage passed; inflation, strikes and the Red Scare
1920	Prohibition initiated; Warren G. Harding Red Scare
1923	Harding died in office; Calvin Coolidge became President

1924	Immigration Quota Act; Calvin Coolidge elected over Robert La Follette and John Davis
1927	Lindbergh crossed the Atlantic; Sacco and Vanzetti executed; first "talkie" motion picture
1929	Herbert Hoover inaugurated President; the stock market crash

How Are Rural Values Evident in Modern Urban Life?

Despite the fact that roughly three-quarters of the American people live in urban areas today, and more than fifty percent have inhabited American cities for half a century, many persons exhibit a strong sympathy for values associated with rural and small town life. R. Richard Wohl described this phenomenon.[1]

> It is one of the lasting ironies of American history that a people so eager and energetic in the creation and expansion of their cities—a nation which has so zestfully rushed into an urban existence—should support an elaborate network of ideologies condemning city life. There is a long tradition in the United States . . . which elaborates the farmer's life as the best one for free men in a democratic community. This set of beliefs has been a boon and a philosophical refreshment to a nation in whose earliest years many settled as farmers in the plains and valleys. What is bewildering is that this tradition should be supported and pampered, in this latter day, by city folk who guiltily charge themselves with a hard and inadequate life in the urban community. Advertising men at work in their city offices and following an urban existence, annually celebrate Thanksgiving Day with pictures and slogans of festive farmers—this, in national magazines which today reach largely urban audiences. The tendency is most strikingly seen in the delicate caution of politicians to identify themselves as being rooted in rural origins. . . .

How Did This Rural Sentiment Originate?

This rural sentiment is not new. It is so traditional to American life that Richard Hofstadter called it a myth.[2]

---

[1]R. Richard Wohl, "Urbanism, Urbanity, and the Historian," *The University of Kansas City Review*, Vol. XXII (1955), pp. 54-55.

[2]Richard Hofstadter, *The Age of Reform: From Bryan to F.D.R.* (New York: Alfred A. Knopf, 1955), pp. 23-24.

The United States was born in the country and has moved to the city. From the beginning its political values and ideas were of necessity shaped by country life. The early American politician, the country editor, who wished to address himself to the common man, had to draw upon a rhetoric that would touch the tillers of the soil; and even the spokesman of city people knew that his audience had been in very large part reared upon the farm. . . . For while early American society was an agrarian society, it was fast becoming more commercial, and commercial goals made their way among its agricultural classes almost as rapidly as elsewhere. The more commercial this society became, however, the more reason it found to cling in imagination to the noncommercial agrarian values. The more farming as a self-sufficient way of life was abandoned for farming as a business, the more merit men found in what was being left behind. And the more rapidly the farmers' sons moved into the towns, the more nostalgic the whole culture became about its rural past. The American mind was raised upon a sentimental attachment to rural living and upon a series of notions about rural people and rural life that I have chosen to designate as the agrarian myth. The agrarian myth represents a kind of homage that Americans have paid to the fancied innocence of their origins.

What Prohibits the Stereotyping of the Rural-Urban Conflict?

By the 1920's Americans had reached a point socially where a confrontation of values appeared almost inevitable. Half of the nation's population resided in the cities. Some were new arrivals from rural areas, bringing with them their cultural baggage. Others were the children of rural-born parents who had instilled in them the nineteenth century "agrarian myth."

Contemporaries of the time and historians since have tried to reduce the events of the 1920's to a contest between urban and rural values, or the modern and the outdated, or even worse, good and evil. Representative of this fight were two opponents, since stereotyped, Al Smith and William Jennings Bryan. A New York City Roman Catholic whose father had immigrated to the urban slum from Ireland, Smith opposed Prohibition. Bryan did not. He came from the Nebraska farmlands, was of Anglo-Saxon stock, preached Fundamental Protestantism, and believed in the "agrarian myth."

Despite their differences, both men were Democrats. What is more, at times urbanite Smith acted as provincial as ruralite Bryan, Paul A. Carter pointed out. The real Smith contradicted the stereotyped Smith.

At the time, some New Yorkers believed that their city was culturally isolated from and superior to the rest of America.[3]

In Governor Smith the rejection of the America that was not New York did not go *that* far, but it went far enough that David Burner, in one study of the brown derby campaign of 1928, accused the "Gotham Cockney," as he called Smith, of "an exclusionist provinciality unequalled even during the bids of William Jennings Bryan," Nor was it even a liberal provincialism; Robert Moses later testified that "Smith thought about economics in many ways like a Southern conservative"—or, he might have added, like a mildly progressive Republican such as Herbert Hoover, who *was* born west of the Mississippi. Professor Burner agrees with this estimate by Moses: "On economic issues the Governor was far less adventurous than William Jennings Bryan had been early in the twenties."

Indeed, in a sense the failure of Alfred E. Smith was the failure of William Jennings Bryan, but in reverse; each man was repulsed by the other's most devoted constituents, and each had loyal followers who loved him for the enemies he had made. . . .

Furthermore, Paul A. Carter argued, not all country residents matched the stereotype which "country bumpkins" supposedly projected.[4]

In summation, bigotry and intolerance in the Twenties were not a rural monopoly, and equally a case could be made that humanitarianism and enlightenment—compare the metropolitan Hearst newspapers with the bucolic *Emporia* (Kan.) *Gazette*—were not an urban one. It was as one country boy to another that the *Gazette's* editor, William Allen White, having just finished reading *Main Street* aloud with Mrs. White, wrote to Sinclair Lewis on November 23, 1920, "to tell you what a noble thing you have done" and declared that if he were a millionaire he "would go and bribe the legislature of Kansas to make 'Main Street' compulsory reading in the public schools." The Sage of Emporia seems also to have been on reasonably genial terms with that passionate antiruralist H. L. Mencken—data which do not fit the stereotype either of the city stalking the country or of the country strangling the city. . . .

---

[3]Paul A. Carter, *The Twenties in America* (New York: Thomas Y. Crowell, Inc., 1968), pp. 75-76.

[4]*Ibid,* p. 95.

Why Did the Conflict of Values Erupt?

At the bottom of the conflict between the provincial-minded and the cosmopolitan-minded urban inhabitants lay a frustration. In the view of Richard Hofstadter, Fundamentalists (believers in the literal interpretation of the Bible) attempted to coerce their anti-intellectual views on the enlightened.[5]

The 1920's proved to be the focal decade in the *Kulturkampf* [cultural battle] of American Protestantism. Advertising, radio, the mass magazines, the advance of popular education, threw the old mentality into a direct and unavoidable conflict with the new. The older, rural and small-town America, now fully embattled against the encroachments of modern life, made its most determined stand against cosmopolitanism, Romanism, and the skepticism and moral experimentalism of the intelligentsia. In the Ku Klux Klan movement, the rigid defense of Prohibition, the Scopes evolution trial, and the campaign against Al Smith in 1928, the older America tried vainly to reassert its authority; but its only victory was the defeat of Smith, and even that was tarnished by his success in reshaping the Democratic Party as an urban and cosmopolitan force, a success that laid the groundwork for subsequent Democratic victories.

How Did the Klan Express an Anti-Intellectualism?

The anguished demands for urban conformity to rural standards found expression in a variety of ways during the 1920's. Among them was "the reincarnation" of the Ku Klux Klan and its acts of intolerance toward foreign born, non-Nordic and non-Protestant people. By the mid-1920's it claimed an enrollment of several million members, mainly urban residents. Imperial Wizard Hiram Wesley Evans expressed the KKK view that national uniformity was necessary for national survival.[6]

The Klan, therefore, has now come to speak for the great mass of Americans of the old pioneer stock. . . . To understand the Klan, then, it is nec-

[5]Richard Hofstadter, *Anti-Intellectualism in American Life* (New York: Vintage Books, 1963), p. 123.

[6]Hiram Wesley Evans, "The Klan's Fight for Americanism," *North American Review,* Vol. CCXXIII (1926), pp. 38-39.

essary to understand the character and present mind of the mass of old-stock Americans. The mass, it must be remembered, is distinguished from the intellectually mongrelized "Liberals."

These are, in the first place, a blend of various peoples of the so-called Nordic race, the race which, with all its faults, has given the world almost the whole of modern civilization. . . .

. . . One by one all our traditional moral standards went by the boards, or were so disregarded that they ceased to be binding. The sacredness of our Sabbath, of our homes, of chastity, and finally even of our right to teach our own children in our own schools fundamental facts and truths were torn away from us. Those who maintained the old standards did so only in the face of constant ridicule.

How Did Fundamentalists Restrict Personal Freedom?

National morality was a problem which concerned not only the Ku Klux Klan. Other Fundamentalist-minded Americans wanted to save the nation from the moral disaster which they believed to be imminent. George E. Mowry recounted a few events in this "moral revolution" of the twenties.[7]

The defenders of the old traditions and morals, the agrarian-minded social conservatives and the religious orthodox, did not let this complex series of radical innovations in American society go without an angry and persistent challenge. The spate of movies and books in which sex was free, easy, and explicitly shown was met with such a volume of state and local censorship laws that the film industry decided to establish its own control of morals and manners in self-protection. But what the Hays Office, named after the former Postmaster General Will H. Hays, succeeded in doing with its "two feet on the floor" rules for bedroom scenes was to substitute the suggestive for the explicit. By requiring that virtue must triumph it also divorced the average movie from any connection with life. Book censors also took vigorous action, and in cities like Boston, where the new Catholics and the old Puritans were allied in the effort, even acknowledged literary masterpieces were denied a place in libraries or bookstores.

---

[7]George E. Mowry, *The Urban Nation, 1920-1960* (New York: Hill and Wang, 1965), pp. 28-29.

Some state legislatures and local councils, mostly in the West and South, attempted also to stem the tide of the feminine passion for short dresses and scant bathing suits. But police with yardsticks to measure the required minimum coverage were not unknown, at least in the early years of the decade, on the big city beaches of the Eastern shore. Here and there divorce laws were tightened up, mature hostesses were installed in public dance halls to see that the proximity of the partners did not infringe the local standards of propriety, and occasionally local legislation went so far as that in Norphelt, Arkansas, which prohibited "improper and lascivious sexual intercourse," even among married couples.

Were Fundamentalists the Only Ones Who Tended to Be Shallow?

By the mid-twenties, the nation read in awe of a religious Fundamentalist battle against the encroachments of the scientific age. John T. Scopes, a high school biology teacher, deliberately broke a Tennessee law which prohibited the teaching of evolution in schools. Representing rural America, especially in the South and Middle West, was William Jennings Bryan, three-time losing candidate for president. In opposition was the noted defense lawyer Clarence Darrow, an agnostic and American Civil Liberties Union attorney. Thus began a "duel to the death," as Bryan put it. Little did he realize that the death would be his own, soon after the rural jury convicted Scopes and fined him one hundred dollars. Nevertheless, William E. Leuchtenburg cautioned against a simple interpretation of this event.[8]

. . . Yet the case was not simply a morality play between the good forces of intellectual freedom and the evil spirits of obscurantism. In the Scopes trial, the provincialism of the city was arrayed against the provincialism of the country, the shallowness of Mencken against the shallowness of Bryan, the arrogance of the scientists against the arrogance of the fundamentalists.

The very faith in science, as C. E. Ayres pointed out, had reached the point where it had become "superstition, in another guise." In the 1920's the nation was captivated by radioactivity, even by more mundane matters like calories and vitamins; science, many people believed, was a universal balm that would answer every human need. . . .

---

[8]William E. Leuchtenburg, *The Perils of Prosperity, 1914-1932* (Chicago: University of Chicago Press, 1958), p. 221.

Did Fundamentalism Decline During the Depression?

In the general description of Fundamentalism, historians consider the Scopes Trial as its apex of power. Thereafter that movement declined nationally in importance. Paul A. Carter argued to the contrary.[9]

But many college freshmen in the fifties and sixties were still coming into more than one state university's biological sciences courses armed against Darwinist teachings by systematic Lutheran, Baptist, Christian Reformed, sometimes Roman Catholic or even Orthodox Jewish counterinstruction. . . . Louis Gasper has traced the vicissitudes of both "moderate" and "extremist" Fundamentalism since 1930 in *The Fundamentalist Movement* (1963), and in compiling material for a reappraisal of Fundamentalism during 1964-65, the present writer turned up new specimens in abundance merely by following the public record. The cliché that Fundamentalism somehow "fell apart" after the Scopes Trial–against evidence like the television presence of Billy Graham and others–is attributable mainly to the fact that in the normal course of things academic intellectuals do not meet and converse with many Fundamentalists. . . .

What Misconceptions Have Arisen Over Fundamentalist Actions?

Two prominent misconceptions have arisen as a result of the conflict of values during the twenties. One pertains to the origins of prohibition. Even though Fundamentalists supported its enforcement, James H. Timberlake suggested that they alone did not initiate its passage.[10]

Although today sometimes regarded as a conservative measure, prohibition was actually written into the Constitution as a progressive reform. As an integral part of the Progressive Movement, prohibition drew on the same moral idealism and sought to deal with the same basic problems. . . .

Prohibition did not command universal support, however, for its appeal lay largely with the old-stock, middle class section of the American community. Other progressives, especially those identified with the urban-labor-

---

[9]Carter, *op. cit.*, pp. 78-79.

[10]James H. Timberlake, *Prohibition and the Progressive Movement, 1900-1920* (Cambridge: Harvard University Press, 1963), pp. 1-30.

immigrant elements, disliked the reform and fought it. Although the two groups often cooperated on other measures, they disagreed on the question of prohibition. . . .

The other misconception relates to the continued acceptance of prohibition. In the election of 1928, Herbert Hoover, a dry, beat Al Smith, a wet. That alone is not startling, since the question of continued public support of prohibition was a public issue of the time. For years, however, historians and the public in general believed that Hoover beat Smith over the private issue of religion. Hoover was a Protestant and Smith a Roman Catholic. Only recently, with the election of John F. Kennedy, also a Roman Catholic, have historians begun to reevaluate the issue of religion in the 1928 election. Actually, Walter Lippmann had lucidly seen the shortcoming of Smith after Smith's defeat at the Democratic Convention of 1924.[11]

. . . The Governor's [Smith's] more hasty friends show an intolerance when they believe that Al Smith is the victim of purely religious prejudice. . . . There is an opposition to Smith which is as authentic and, it seems to me, as poignant as his support. It is inspired by the feeling that the clamorous life of the city should not be acknowledged as the American ideal.

The famed Kansas editor, William Allen White, in a letter to Supreme Court Justice Louis D. Brandeis, expressed a similar opinion two months after the 1928 election.[12]

The people were not in a rebellious mood this year, but I think thousands of western progressives balked at Smith, first because he was going too fast; second because he zigzagged on the wrong side of traffic on prohibition; and third because he represented a strange, unfamiliar, and to many narrow minds, an abhorrent tendency in our national life. Partly it was religion that symbolized the distrust. But I think it was chiefly an instinctive feeling for the old rural order and old rural ways, the tremendous impact of a desire for the good opinion of the old lady next door. I think inevitably in this century we shall see another moral censor than she, new moral standards.

---

[11]Walter Lippmann, *Men of Destiny* (New York: The Macmillan Co., 1927), p. 8.

[12]*Selected Letters of William Allen White, 1899-1943,* ed. Walter Johnson (New York: Henry Holt and Co., 1947), p. 290.

But still the old order holds fast in spite of our urban and industrial development. . . .

The modern historian Richard Hofstadter made the point another way.[13]

. . . The prime fallacy in the popular view of the 1928 election lies in noticing only what Smith lost from the religious issue and ignoring what he may have gained. Of course the number of voters who were decisively influenced by the religious issue is something that eludes exact measurement. But it is vital to remember that there are two such imponderables to be considered: not only the number of voters who voted *against* Smith but also the number who voted *for* him because of his religion. Smith's Catholicism, a grave liability in some areas, was a great asset in others. He made about as good a showing as could have been expected from any Democrat that year.

SUMMARY

The conflict of values evident today was also pronounced during the twenties. Rural sentiment and mores clashed with the realities of urban life. Controversies arose over public support of prohibition laws and the acceptance of teaching evolution in public schools. This clash of values, however, was not necessarily responsible for Al Smith's election defeat in 1928. Moreover, to stereotype persons of rural or urban backgrounds as having rural or urban values often proves misleading.

SELECTED REFERENCES:

Paul A. Carter, *The Twenties in America* (New York: Thomas Y. Crowell Co., 1968).*
Guidance on how to interpret a very complex age.

John D. Hicks, *Republican Ascendency, 1921-1933* (New York: Harper & Bros., 1960).*
Standard coverage of the era.

---

[13]Richard Hofstadter, "Could a Protestant Have Beaten Hoover in 1928?" *The Reporter*, Vol. XXII, March 1960, p. 30.

William E. Leuchtenburg, *The Perils of Prosperity, 1914-1932* (Chicago: University of Chicago Press, 1958).*
A survey of the period emphasizing the traditional aspects.

Milton Plesur, *The 1920's, Problems and Paradoxes* (Boston: Allyn and Bacon, 1969).*
Selected readings on various aspects of the decade.

TERM PROJECTS:

A. Compare and contrast the backgrounds of the three Republican presidents during the 1920's.

B. Write a detailed answer to the following question: Did the 1920's produce a renaissance in American art and writing?

CHECKUP FOR STUDY

Name: ______________________________

1. List several values you hold which may have rural roots.

2. Briefly, what is the agrarian myth?

3. Describe Al Smith's provincialism.

4. In your own words define the term "anti-intellectual."

To remove this page: Open the book as wide as possible several times to loosen this page from the binding. Lay the book flat on your desk and gently but firmly pull this page *straight up* and away from the binding from top to bottom.

5. Explain the statement, "national uniformity was necessary for national survival."

6. Comment: "In science lies man's key to survival."

7. Comment: "The death of Bryan was the finale of Fundamentalism."

8. Comment: "The Fundamentalists passed and defended the Eighteenth Amendment."

9.

10.

". . . and Duke, tomorrow you must come up and have lunch with me on the 57th Street breadline."

Denys Wortman, *Mopey Dick and the Duke,* Fairchild Publications, New York, N.Y. 1952, leaf 26

20 When The Bread Ran Out

WELFARE STATE: A system within a democracy whereby the national government provides a great variety of social services for its citizens. These might include public education, crop insurance, low-income housing, veterans benefits and social security programs.

REFERENCE DATES:

1929	Stock market crash precipitated the Great Depression
1933	Franklin D. Roosevelt inaugurated; "One-Hundred Days" initiated New Deal "three R's"

1935	New reforms passed: Social Security Act and "Wagner Act"
1937	"Court packing" issue; recession began
1938	Fair Labor Standards Act and second Agricultural Adjustment Act; Republicans gained in Congress
1940	Depression ended with U.S. defense spending

Is Public Welfare Necessary?

The title of this Theme plays on the subject of the statement, "bread." While the conventional meaning of "bread" is clear, the slang meaning may not be. In this sense, "bread" means "money."

During the 1930's, when Americans faced the worst depression in their history, the bread ran out, both in the conventional and modern slang meanings of the word. Unemployment became so widespread and prolonged after 1929 that people had to line up in front of public or private charity offices to receive their sustenance, sometimes just a loaf of bread. Then, in 1932, the growing number of hungry unemployed people put such a strain on the charities that many closed their doors for lack of funds. Their "bread" had run out.

Not until the advent of the New Deal did the federal government take over the responsibility for direct relief to the destitute. After two years of doing so, the Franklin Roosevelt Administration in 1935 turned over a major portion of that program to the states. From that time to the present, the welfare of indigent people has been primarily a state responsibility.

Criticism of federal welfare programs was not unknown during the depression years. Those opposed to such programs usually disliked the great expense involved and feared deficit spending. Since 1940, when America entered the present age of affluence, criticism has mounted over the continuation of tax-supported welfare programs. *Senior Scholastic* discussed this critical issue.[1]

---

[1]"Welfare: Necessary Investment or Abused Giveaway?" *Senior Scholastic,* Vol. XCIII (October 11, 1968), pp. 6-7, 9-11.

Nobody likes public welfare today. It is under fire from all sides—from those who pay for it, from those who administer it, and from those who receive it. It is the target of critics from left to right in the political arena. Some want to modernize the present system. Some want to abandon it in favor of a new method. Others just want to abandon it. But almost everyone agrees that something is wrong with the way the public welfare system is being run today.

Even the people "on" welfare are grumbling. In major city ghettos, poor people angry at "the Establishment" often find the local welfare office the nearest place to direct their wrath. There is today a growing "welfare rights movement" among the urban poor. . . .

. . . .

What's wrong with the program? A lot, say its critics. The loudest and most frequent attack: the system promotes an unbreakable cycle of dependency, carried down from the generation to generation.

There is a much-quoted story about a British correspondent interviewing a 10-year-old girl in a Chicago slum. He asked what she wanted to do when she grew up. She replied, "Draw." The writer was delighted to discover a budding artist in ghetto surroundings. "What kind of pictures do you like to draw?" he asked. The child then told him she meant "drawing welfare like my mother does."

Many sociologists and other critics believe welfare is helping to create a permanently dependent class of Americans. Many welfare recipients, meanwhile, agree—and also wonder how the cycle can be broken.

. . . .

. . . The whole welfare program, in fact, is increasingly clouded by some deeply entrenched myths and half-truths. Probably the most widely held is the notion of the typical welfare recipient as an idle drifter who prefers living off society to "earning an honest living." Statistics easily topple that notion. The majority of welfare recipients are aged, disabled, or children. Los Angeles officials say that if every *employable* person now on welfare took a job, relief rolls would drop less than two percent in that city.

. . . .

What can be done? Some observers see a way out of the morass only if more money is poured into revitalizing welfare. But they also concede that a change in public attitude would have to come first. . . . The public . . . must be made to believe that society as a whole will benefit from the elimination of poverty.

But the big question remains: Is public assistance the right way to end poverty? Many believe it is. Many others think it is not—and that other ways must be found.

WHO CARED FOR THE POOR BEFORE THE NEW DEAL?

Poverty did not begin with the stock market crash in 1929, of course. America has always had poor people. Josephine C. Brown described their plight.[2]

. . . The system of local poor relief was transplanted root and branch to the Eastern seaboard from Elizabethan England in the ruthless early seventeenth century, and was later carried by pioneer settlers across the continent. This English heritage made poverty a disgrace, branded the poor man as unworthy and shiftless, and attached to relief an indelible stigma.

. . . .

Since the first settlement of this country, colonial, territorial and state poor laws . . . consistently placed responsibility for relief upon local units.

. . . .

During the nineteenth century, farming out [placing paupers in homes which received payment for their care] and indenture [bonded service for several years to repay debts] were gradually superseded in practice by the care of paupers within the walls of alms-houses: generally known as "indoor relief." "Outdoor relief," to the needy in their own homes, was found to be costly. . . .

During this time, Americans began to realize the seriousness of urban poverty, as Robert H. Bremner stated.[3]

It was in the slums of the larger cities that Americans discovered the new poverty that was invading the nation in the wake of industrialization, urban growth, and immigration. Here were new worlds of wretchedness characterized by ways of life foreign to American experience and menacing to conventional standards of decency. . . .

. . . .

While public aid to the poor was neglected, or even regarded with downright hostility, private charity flourished. Those who favored ending public relief outside almshouses and infirmaries argued that private benevolence was adequate to succor the needy who were not completely dependent as to require institutional care. Pauperism and taxation were the twin bugbears of

---

[2]Josephine C. Brown, *Public Relief, 1929–1939* (New York: Henry Holt and Co., 1940), pp. 3-4, 8.

[3]Robert H. Bremner, *From the Depths: The Discovery of Poverty in the United States* (New York: New York University Press, 1956), pp. 4, 50-51.

most nineteenth-century philanthropists. They wished to improve poorhouses, but not to such an extent that people would cease dreading to be sent to them. . . . It seemed to them—that is, to the well-to-do persons who had the leisure and resources to indulge in voluntary charitable work—that what the poor most needed was assistance in developing good character. In their scale of values, good character meant, first and foremost, ability to support oneself.

When Did Social Welfare Begin in America?

The Roosevelt Administration was not the first to provide for interests of a special group. James M. Burns and Jack W. Peltason suggested that such promotion began long before the Great Depression.[4]

In recent years we have heard a great deal about the welfare state. . . . In the first place, governmental promotion is by no means a recent development in the United States. In his first annual address to Congress, President Washington called for a tariff to protect business. In his famous *Report on the Subject of Manufactures* in 1791, Secretary of the Treasury Alexander Hamilton proposed that government help develop business by giving bounties to new enterprises. Henry Clay's American System was a plan in the first part of the last century for federally subsidized roads and waterways, a strengthened banking system, and tariff protection. Parts of these ambitious programs were carried out during the first half of the nineteenth century, and after the Civil War the Republican party bestowed special-interest subsidies on businessmen, farmers, veterans and other groups.

In the second place, almost all groups have at one time or another benefited directly from government aid. During much of the nation's history, business has been the main recipient of help from Washington; today farmers and veterans seem to have preference. . . .

. . . .

. . . For at least 160 years we have had a "welfare state," to some degree. This is certainly true of social services. As far back as colonial times, parishes and counties undertook poor relief, and later on the states set up hospitals, asylums, and other institutions. Nevertheless, until recent years American government—especially the national government—lagged far behind other

[4]James MacGregor Burns and Jack Walter Peltason, *Government by the People: The Dynamics of American National, State, and Local Government* (Englewood Cliffs, N. J.: Prentice-Hall, Inc., fifth edition), pp. 633, 648-649. © 1963. By permission of Prentice-Hall, Inc.

countries in furnishing social services. The situation was paradoxical. On the one hand the federal government gave huge bounties to railroads, farmers, veterans, and other groups. On the other, Washington ignored the dire need of millions of "ill-housed, ill-clad, ill-nourished" Americans.

One reason for this paradox is that America has traditionally been a land of opportunity. The millions of acres of free land, the enormous resources, the technical advances—all helped take care of the people who otherwise might not have made a go of it. Then, too, Americans have traditionally subscribed to a philosophy of rugged individualism and devil take the hindmost. If a man failed to get ahead, people said, it was his own fault. Rather grudgingly the state governments—mainly during the early twentieth century—extended relief to needy groups, especially old people, blind persons, and orphans. But government aid was limited, and private charity was relied on to supply most social services.

Then the nation entered the Great Depression. Unemployment at its peak rose to about twenty-five percent of the total working force. Existing charity agencies could not cope with rising demands for aid. Beginning in 1933, after President Hoover had balked at federal intervention on behalf of the hungry, newly-elected President Roosevelt created a series of federal programs designed to provide relief to the unemployed and stimulate economic recovery. The Federal Emergency Relief Administration (FERA), the Works Progress Administration (WPA) and the Public Works Administration (PWA) offered money, food and work to those in need. Other programs provided assistance and attempted to promote recovery for various special groups, ranging from farmers to urban slum dwellers.

Was the New Deal Era a Breakthrough?

This notable expansion of federal social welfare programs, coupled with direct federal intervention in the economy, has raised the question of whether the New Deal marks a watershed (a dramatic dividing point) in the history of twentieth century America. Historians still debate this issue. Was life in 1940 significantly different from that in 1930? And, if so, did New Deal legislation cause this change? One historian favoring the watershed concept is William E. Leuchtenburg.[5]

---

[5]William E. Leuchtenburg, *Franklin D. Roosevelt and the New Deal, 1932-1940* (New York: Harper and Row, 1963), p. xii.

The Great Depression was one of the turning points of American history. Even at the time, men were aware of a dividing line. In ordinary conversation in the thirties, people would begin by saying "Since '29 . . . ," or "In the days before the crash. . . ." What the Lynds have written about "Middletown" applies to all of America in the 1930s: "The great knife of the depression had cut down impartially through the entire population cleaving open lives and hopes of rich as well as poor. The experience has been more nearly universal than any prolonged recent emotional experience in the city's history; it has approached in its elemental shock the primary experiences of birth and death."

In recent years, historians, writing from the perspective of a quarter of a century, have tended to minimize the significance of the changes wrought by the thirties. They have stressed, quite properly, the continuity between the New Deal reforms and those of other periods, and especially the many debts the New Dealers owed the progressives. They noted, too, that if much was altered in the 1930s, much too remained the same, and the basic values of the nation stayed fairly constant. Yet, in recognizing the strands of continuity, they have too often obscured the extraordinary developments of the decade. The six years from 1933 through 1938 marked a greater upheaval in American institutions than in any similar period in our history, save perhaps for the impact on the South of the Civil War. . . .

Countering this interpretation, Richard S. Kirkendall surveyed recent writings to support the concept of historical continuity.[6]

The recent literature, then, suggests that historians of the New Deal should not neglect continuity and emphasize change alone. Important changes were made, especially in size and power of the federal government and organized labor. Significant preparations for those changes had been made prior to the New Deal, indicating that they constituted only a stage in developments long under way and responses to more than the special conditions of the 1930's. Furthermore, New Dealers as well as anti-New Dealers, uncertain about the course they should follow and clinging to traditions despite the depth of the national crisis, successfully resisted many of the pressures for change in the decade and preserved many major institutions, above all "Big Business" and democracy. In short, both continuity and change, concepts of fundamental importance, need to be employed as major analytical tools by historians of the 1930's as well as other periods. Terms such as revolution and watershed seem to exaggerate the nature of change that took place in the depression decade.

---

[6]Richard S. Kirkendall, "The New Deal As Watershed: The Recent Literature," *Journal of American History,* Vol. LIV (1968), p. 852.

What Does State History Reveal?

To qualify the two opposing interpretations of the New Deal, James T. Patterson urged the consideration of state history during the period.[7]

Few historians would maintain that the New Deal left the states unchanged. States centralized services, applied new taxes, approved progressive labor laws, and increased relief spending. A host of ambitious federal agencies prodded state departments into new services. Without the depression and New Deal, the striking developments in state government of the 1940s and 1950s might not have come so quickly. The over-all picture, however, reveals almost as much continuity as change on the state level from the progressive period (excepting perhaps the 1920s) to the 1960s, and it suggests that historians would do well to revise nationalistic interpretations of the New Deal. The New Deal years witnessed neither federal dictation, a completely cooperative federalism, nor a dramatically new state progressivism. Moreover, many of the changes that did occur, notably in relief administration and taxation, were forced upon the states by the depression and not by the New Deal.

New Dealers must unquestionably accept some responsibility for this limited effect on the states. Some federal officials neglected state affairs; others appointed hostile personnel; still others were unnecessarily fearful of offending entrenched machines. The lack of coordination among various federal agencies was at times distressing. But the most striking feature of federal-state relations during the 1930s was not the failure of New Dealers but the limits in which they had to operate. Time was short, courts hostile, state institutions blocked change, and state parties were often divided, conservative, or concerned with patronage instead of policy. Roosevelt, by working with instead of against the *status quo* in the states, kept federal-state friction to a minimum and concentrated on achieving the national legislation that proved more important in assuring social change in twentieth-century America.

In an investigation at the state level, James F. Wickens illustrated that the New Deal was but one of a series of events which modified life in one state.[8]

. . . Though state responsibility boarded on irresponsibility in caring for the indigent during the late thirties, Colorado did accept the national outline

[7]James T. Patterson, "The New Deal and the States," *American Historical Review*, Vol. LXXIII (1967), p. 84.

[8]James F. Wickens, "Colorado in the New Deal," *Pacific Historical Review* 38 (1969), pp. 290-291.

of welfare measures. As the prominent social worker Mrs. Efay Grigg wrote in 1948, "Colorado has moved out of an era of voluntary and intermittent charity into organized, planned and coordinated programs of public and private services." Besides federal and state involvement with welfare and planning, which still exhibit vitality today, there are a multiplicity of programs begun before World War II which to this day affect the lives of everyone in the state.

Does this mean that events in Colorado history support national interpretations of Richard Hofstadter, Carl Degler and William E. Leuchtenburg, that the New Deal marks a watershed in American history? It does if emphasizing the social history of Colorado. It does not if considering economic history, for, as previously noted, World War II, not the New Deal, stimulated economic change. But what about political philosophy?

The New Deal does not appear to have revolutionized Colorado political thinking. Unlike William E. Leuchtenburg's suggestion that "in eight years, Roosevelt and the New Dealers had almost revolutionized the agenda of American politics," political thought among leaders in Colorado remained much the same as it had been since the progressive movement. Characteristics of that era which Leuchtenburg suggests the New Deal supplanted—progressive sentimentality, "Methodist-parsonage morality," individualism, rigid utopianism and anti-intellectualism—all persisted beyond the Great Depression as the marrow of the Colorado political personality. These attitudes were basic to nineteenth century frontier thinking. By no means did the end of that frontier in 1890 or the beginning of a "new frontier" in 1961 extinguish these beliefs. . . .

Summary

Controversy over federal welfare programs has continued since their initiation in the Great Depression. Critics charge that such programs encourage the development of a welfare state, and worse, of a welfare mentality among recipients. Actually, special interest groups have won government support since the origins of the nation. How much New Deal programs contributed to this development, perhaps changing American life dramatically, is open to speculation.

Selected References:

Joseph Boskin, *Opposition Politics: The Anti-New Deal Tradition* (Beverly Hills: Glencoe Press, 1968).*

A study of opposition to New Deal policies from the Great Depression to the present.

James M. Burns, *Roosevelt, the Lion and the Fox* (New York: Harcourt, Brace & Co., 1956).*
A biography of Roosevelt which analyzes his achievements and failures as President.

Morton Keller, ed., *The New Deal: What Was It?* American Problems Studies (New York: Holt, Rinehart and Winston, 1963).*
Extracts of works which evaluate Roosevelt and the New Deal.

William E. Leuchtenburg, *Franklin D. Roosevelt and the New Deal, 1932-1940* (New York: Harper & Row, 1963).*
A thorough yet short history of the age.

TERM PROJECTS:

A. Write a detailed answer to the following question: What caused the Great Depression?

B. Investigate the following question: How new was the New Deal?

CHECKUP FOR STUDY

Name: ______________________________

1. What does the title of this Theme mean?

2. What were "poor laws"?

3. Why did poverty increase in the late nineteenth century?

4. Why was the federal welfare policy paradoxical?

To remove this page: Open the book as wide as possible several times to loosen this page from the binding. Lay the book flat on your desk and gently but firmly pull this page *straight up* and away from the binding from top to bottom.

5. What is a historical watershed?

6. Comment: "We businessmen have never asked for handouts. Why should the poor?"

7. Do you think the New Deal was a watershed in American history? Why?

8. From your reading in this book and others, list major agencies and laws labeling each as relief, recovery or reform. Denote the time period of their origin as (E) early New Deal and (L) late New Deal, using January 1935 as the dividing time.

9.

10.

"Who, me?"

Cartoon Cavalcade, ed. Thomas Craven, Simon & Schuster, New York, 1943, from *Colliers*, 1943, by permission of the artist, *HOFF*.

21 When the Eagle Replaced the Ostrich

ISOLATIONISM: A foreign policy which intentionally abstains from international commitments such as alliances, leagues and economic sanctions. (Figuratively, an isolationist nation buries its head in the sand like an ostrich.)

REFERENCE DATES:

1931	Japan captured Manchuria
1933	Adolf Hitler became Chancellor of Germany
1935-1937	American Neutrality Acts prohibited foreign involvement; Italy conquered Ethiopia; Japan attacked China

1938	Munich Conference, symbol of appeasement in international relations.
1939	"Cash-and-carry" permitted; German-Soviet non-aggression pact; World War II began
1941	Lend-lease initiated; Atlantic Charter announced; North Atlantic naval warfare; Pearl Harbor attacked

After Vietnam, What Principle Should American Foreign Policy Follow?

When the Vietnam war ends, the United States will have to decide whether to pull out of South Vietnam, maintain bases in nearby countries, or, as some suggest, completely withdraw from Asia. Eugene V. Rostow argued in favor of continued involvement for the sake of national security.[1]

> . . . Why do we not withdraw to the developed countries, as they propose, and abandon the third world to communism, racism, and chaos? We can protect ourselves in our fortress, they argue. And we have problems enough at home.
>
> This is the new version of the old isolationism. It has led us to disaster in the past. If we follow it now, it can only lead us to disaster in the future. . . .
>
> Those who advocate withdrawing into our own continental fortress should ask themselves what sort of country we might be if large parts of the world were united in hostility toward us. A fortress under siege is not a pleasant place to live. A garrison state is an uncongenial environment for freedom. . . .

Unlike Rostow, there are many who are critical of American policy in Asia and demand a complete withdrawal from Vietnam. They have earned the label "neo-isolationists." Theodore C. Sorensen disagreed with that label as well as with the idea that national security necessitates military involvement in Vietnam.[2]

---

[1]Eugene V. Rostow, "National Security or Retreat to Isolation? The Choice in Foreign Policy," *The Department of State Bulletin,* Vol. LVIII (1968), p. 438.
[2]Theodore C. Sorensen, "Who Are the Isolationists?" *Saturday Review,* 11 January 1969, p. 72.

Those who advocate a policy of "no more Vietnams" do not thereby deserve the label of isolationists. They are responsible realists who recognize the practical limitations of our military and diplomatic power. They realize that we have no more right than the Russians or Chinese to impose either our will or our way upon other peoples. They want us to lead by the force of example, not force of arms, by emphasizing multilateral instead of national solutions, and non-military instead of military means. That is not isolationism.

On the other hand, those who developed or now defend these past few years of America's policy in Vietnam—who look upon our role as that of world policeman and who advocate a hard line in the Paris talks today—these are the real isolationists.

Already, escalating the hot war in Vietnam, and the cold war in general, have cost us heavily in terms of international prestige and respect. They have diminished the attention and assistance we have been able to give to the Atlantic alliance, to the Alliance for Progress, and to other key spots around the globe. They have helped to build unnecessary economic barriers between ourselves and the rest of the world.

How Did Isolationism Dominate Foreign Policy After the Great War?

Isolationism was a mainspring of American foreign policy in the nineteenth century. As the United States acquired colonial commitments at the end of that century, however, and under the vigorous foreign policy of Theodore Roosevelt, the isolationist policy weakened. Eventually (as noted in Theme 18) Woodrow Wilson sent troops abroad to fight in World War I "to make the world safe for democracy." After these servicemen returned home, however, they and other Americans became disillusioned, as John E. Wiltz pointed out.[3]

America's leaders, historians agree, had oversold the World War. Instead of presenting American participation as a matter of national interest, distasteful but necessary, they made it a crusade for democracy. At the peace conference and after, however, there seemed to be as much selfish nationalism in the world as before, and if anything less democracy. Americans felt disgusted for having been so foolish as to become party to Europe's war. Despite

[3]John E. Wiltz, *From Isolation to War, 1931–1941* (New York: Thomas Y. Crowell, 1968), p. 7.

Wilson's exalted ideas the war had been a European affair, fought over European problems, for European ends. No American interest, the public concluded, had been at stake. Millions of people agreed with Senator Homer T. Bone (D) of Washington when he declared in 1935 that "the Great War . . . was utter social insanity, and was a crazy war, and we had no business in it at all."

Other Americans were disillusioned by the vindictive peace the visitors had imposed at Paris in 1919. These were people who had thrilled to President Wilson's idea of a "peace without victory" and hailed his Fourteen Points, including Point 14 urging a League of Nations. When they learned that in Paris's superheated atmosphere Wilson had compromised principle and acquiesced in a conqueror's peace, they rejected the League and decided that the United States must live in isolation. . . .

As a result, Wiltz contended, the United States returned to an inward-looking foreign policy.[4]

So it was, in the decades between the two world wars, that Americans determined to isolate themselves from "foreign" embroilments. Reinforced from many sources, this isolationist urge derived essentially from a longing for peace. The 1917-18 crusade for democracy seemed to have turned into a crusade against war. Carried on in the name of humanitarianism, Christianity, and Americanism, the new crusade "caught on," and peace became an obsession for millions of Americans. The word "peace" took on a theological quality; it struck a chord whenever it found its way into a sermon, speech, or prayer. And when President Harding voiced moving sentiments about peace he was not indulging in "bloviation" [hot air], as he was wont to call some of his lesser oratory; Harding and others meant what they said about peace.

Through the decade of the 1920s the isolationist impulse manifested itself in hostility to the League of Nations and refusal to accept responsibility for peace. Otherwise Americans were willing to participate in disarmament conferences, discuss ways to strengthen international law, or enter a treaty to outlaw war. Then came the 1930s and the collapse of the Paris settlement of 1919. Fearing another general war, Americans added a new dimension to their isolationism: if war enveloped other parts of the world the flames must not scorch America. Let the rest of the world destroy itself; America must live. . . .

---

[4]*Ibid*, pp. 16-17.

How Isolationist Was the United States?

That the United States shirked its responsibility of enforcing the peace during the interim between the two wars does not mean that it initiated a hermit-like approach to foreign policy. Though his own definition of isolationism is debatable, William A. Williams wisely cautioned students in the use of the term.[5]

Internationalization through the avoidance of conflict was the key objective. This did not mean a negative foreign policy. Positive action was the basic theme. The transposition of corporatist principles to the area of foreign relations produced a parallel policy. American leadership and intervention would build a world community regulated by agreement among the industrialized nations. The prevention of revolution and the preservation of the sanctity of private property were vital objectives. [Secretary of State Charles Evans] Hughes was very clear when he formulated the idea for Latin America. "We are seeking a *Pax Americana* [American Peace] maintained not by arms but by mutual respect and good will and the tranquillizing processes of reason." There would be, he admitted, "interpositions of a temporary character"—the Secretary did not like the connotations of the word intervention—but only to facilitate the establishment of the United States as the "exemplar of justice."

Extension to the world of this pattern developed in Latin America was more involved. There were five main difficulties, four in the realm of foreign affairs and one in domestic affairs. The internal problem was to establish and integrate a concert of decision between the government and private economic groups. Abroad the objectives were more sharply defined: circumscribe the impact of the Soviet Union, forestall and control potential resistance of colonial areas, pamper and cajole Germany and Japan into acceptance of the basic proposition, and secure from Great Britain practical recognition of the fact that Washington had become the center of Anglo-Saxon collaboration. . . .

How Did American Isolationism Deteriorate?

During much of the 1930's Americans occupied themselves with domestic problems relating primarily to the Great Depression. They wanted to end unemployment and initiate permanent recovery. What of events

---

[5]William A. Williams, "The Legend of Isolation in the 1920's," *Science and Society*, Vol. XVIII (1954), p. 16.

abroad? "Let them solve their own problems," was the attitude. In fact, to insure that no Americans became involved in foreign issues, Congress enacted a series of neutrality acts between 1934 and 1937 to prevent a repetition of events which brought America into the Great War. The nation remained more isolationist than ever.

Then, in the late thirties, American foreign policy began to change with public opinion. Gerald N. Grob and George A. Billias outlined this shift.[6]

> The outbreak of World War II in Europe in 1939 proved to be an important turning point in the development of American foreign policy. Domestic concerns such as the great depression and mass unemployment receded into the background as the fear of war swept over the country. Unlike Woodrow Wilson, Roosevelt refused to ask his countrymen to remain neutral in thought as well as action. "This nation," he told the American people in a fireside chat in September, 1939, "will remain a neutral nation, but I cannot ask that every American remain neutral in thought as well." From the very beginning of hostilities, Roosevelt's hope was to offer as much military aid to the Allies as he could without going to war. Upon presidential urging, Congress repealed the arms embargo that was then in effect because the two year cash-and-carry clause of the neutrality act of 1937 had expired. The fall of France in the spring of 1940 intensified Roosevelt's desire to rebuild America's military forces and to give England all aid short of war. In 1941 the program of military aid to the Allied cause was expanded considerably by the Lend-Lease Act that was passed in March. By the summer of that year, the United States was involved in an undeclared naval war with Germany as American naval forces assumed the responsibility of protecting shipping in the western half of the North Atlantic. The most dramatic gesture of American sympathy for the British cause came in August of 1941, when Roosevelt and Churchill met off the coast of Newfoundland and agreed to a joint statement on mutual war aims. Known as the Atlantic Charter, the document not only spelled out the hopes of the two leaders for a better world, but referred specifically to "the final destruction of the Nazi tyranny" as a war aim.

The paradox of these events is that none erased isolationism completely, not even the naval warfare between American ships and German submarines. Only after Japan attacked the United States at Pearl Harbor did the Roosevelt Administration abandon its fictional neutrality and the public strongly support military involvement.

---

[6]Gerald N. Grob and George Athan Billias, *Interpretations of American History: Patterns and Perspectives,* Vol. II (New York: The Free Press, 1967), p. 384.

How Did Americans Alienate Japan Before 1924?

To understand the complex background leading to the Japanese attack on Pearl Harbor, one must begin a half century earlier. Fred H. Mathews offered a thumbnail sketch of Japanese-American relations.[7]

> Until the 1890's Japan had figured in American eyes as a potential market for products, arena for missionary activity, or exotic contrast to the dull routine of the home culture. . . .
>
> Events soon outmoded these attitudes. In the decade after 1895, Japan proved her worth by western standards in two major wars and sent an increasing flow of emigrant farm workers to Hawaii and California. On the Pacific Coast these Japanese were received with joy by business and farm employers, but they also inherited much of the hostility visited earlier upon the Chinese [whose immigration the United States stopped in 1882]. Hatred toward one common enemy after another was a strong social cement in the constantly new society. The state's isolation before the age of commercial aviation, with the nearest comparable centers of population several days' journey by train, intensified the sense of common peril loneliness on this "White Frontier" against Asia and the new yellow peril. Many Californians were angry that these new heathen were not only well-organized for mutual protection as were the Chinese, but also demanded equality and assimilation with the support of a proud, sensitive home government. So began a quarter-century cycle of events: discrimination in California, useless anger and helpless apology in Washington, outraged protest but more stringent emigration curbs in Tokyo. The spiral ended in 1924 with almost total exclusion of Japanese immigrants.

What Initiated Renewed Hostility Between America and Japan?

During the next fifteen years, Japanese-American hostility subsided somewhat with the exception of two incidents which caused war scares. The first of these was Japan's occupation of Manchuria in 1931. This action disturbed Americans because it had violated the Open Door Policy of protecting Chinese sovereignty. President Hoover condemned Japan, but he refused to cooperate with a League of Nations economic boycott of Japanese trade. Relations improved after President Roosevelt came to power and refrained from further moral statements on the incident.

The second event to cause friction between the two nations occurred

[7]Fred H. Mathews, "White Community and 'Yellow Peril,'" *Mississippi Valley Historical Review,* Vol. L (1964), pp. 612-613.

in 1937 when Japan invaded China. President Roosevelt requested public support of an international quarantine of the area. Soon afterwards Japan deliberately sank the U.S. gunboat *Panay,* afloat on the Yangtze River. Japanese apologies and strong isolationist sentiment prevented any military action against the Tokyo government.

Relations between the two nations deteriorated steadily after that time. During 1939 and 1940 each nation acted hostile toward the other. The United States began to loan China money to fight Japan and reduce its trade with the latter. In turn, Japan joined the Axis Powers, Germany and Italy.

How Did the United States Contribute to War With Japan?

The deterioration of Japanese-American relations eventually lead to war. Paul Schroeder suggested how the United States contributed to this confrontation.[8]

> In judging American policy toward Japan in 1941, it might be well to separate what is still controversial from what is not. There is no longer any real doubt that the war came about over China. . . . Nor is it necessary to speculate any longer as to what could have induced Japan to launch such an incredible attack upon the United States and Great Britain as occurred at Pearl Harbor and in the south Pacific. One need not, as Winston Churchill did in wartime, characterize it as "an irrational act" incompatible "with prudence or even with sanity." The Japanese were realistic about their position throughout; they did not suddenly go insane. The attack was an act of desperation, not madness. Japan fought only when she had her back to the wall as a result of America's diplomatic and economic offensive.
>
> . . . .
>
> . . . [O]ne needs first of all to define the mistake with which American policy is charged. Briefly, it was this. In the attempt to gain everything at once, the United States lost her opportunity to secure immediately her essential requirements in the Far East and to continue to work toward her long-range goals. She succeeded instead only in making inevitable an unnecessary and avoidable war—an outcome which constitutes the ultimate failure of diplomacy. Until July 1941 . . . the United States consistently sought to attain two limited

[8]Paul Schroeder, *The Axis Alliance and Japanese–American Relations, 1941* (Ithaca: Cornell University Press, 1958), pp. 201, 203-204. © 1958 by the American Historical Association. Reprinted by permission of Cornell University Press.

objectives in the Far East, those of splitting the Axis and of stopping Japan's advance southward. Both aims were in accordance with America's broad strategic interests; both were reasonable, attainable goals. Through a combination of favorable circumstance and forceful American action, the United States reached the position where the achievement of these two goals was within sight. At this very moment, on the verge of a major diplomatic victory, the United States abandoned her original goals and concentrated on a third, the liberation of China. This last aim was not in accord with American strategic interests, was not a limited objective, and, most important, was completely incapable of being achieved by peaceful means and doubtful of attainment even by war. Through her single-minded pursuit of this unattainable goal, the United States forfeited the diplomatic victory which she had already virtually won. The unrelenting application of extreme economic pressure on Japan, instead of compelling the evacuation of China, rendered war inevitable, drove Japan back into the arms of Germany for better or for worse, and precipitated the wholesale plunge by Japan into the South Seas. As it ultimately turned out, the United States succeeded in liberating China only at great cost and when it was too late to do the cause of the Nationalist Chinese much real good.

Why Is It Difficult to Pinpoint the Causes of the War?

Unknown even today is the final answer to the question of what caused the Pearl Harbor catastrophe. Interpretations range from absolute American innocence to deliberate plotting by President Roosevelt to cause the attack. Happily enough, both extremes appear doomed to the trash heap of unverified history. What remains are various theses which contain many uncertainties. Wayne S. Cole warned of the difficulty in making such judgments.[9]

. . . The historian can determine that certain events preceded American entry into World War II and he may find circumstantial evidence suggesting possible causal relationships. But he cannot conduct controlled experiments to measure with any degree of certainty the causal significance of antecedent developments and incidents. Furthermore, these various interpretations of individual historians are based upon different opinions concerning the wisdom of possible pre-Pearl Harbor policies as judged in terms of certain criteria, such as world peace and security, American peace and security, economic

[9]Wayne S. Cole, "American Entry into World War II," *Mississippi Valley Historical Review*, Vol. XLIII (1957), p. 616.

order and prosperity, and freedom and democracy. . . . The path to Pearl Harbor was filled with millions of decisions, great and small, each based upon decisions which preceded it. There were countless forks in the road that led to Pearl Harbor. And no historian can know for certain what lay at the end of the paths that were not followed.

Summary

The present controversy over the future of American involvement abroad has roots, some argue, in the disintegration of isolationism which preceded the American entrance into World War II. Accustomed to abstinence from foreign involvements during most of the nineteenth century, Americans in the twentieth century wrestled with the problem of continued isolationism until the disaster at Pearl Harbor. Since that event American foreign policy has stressed international involvement.

Selected References:

Robert A. Divine, *The Reluctant Belligerent: American Entry into World War II* (New York: John Wiley & Sons, 1965).*
A survey of American foreign policy in the 1930's.

Paul S. Holbo, *Isolationism and Interventionism, 1932-1941*, The Berkeley Series in American History (Chicago: Rand McNally & Co., 1967).*
Primary sources which exemplified the end of isolationism.

George M. Waller, ed., *Pearl Harbor, Roosevelt and the Coming of the War,* Problems in American Civilization (Boston: D. C. Heath and Co., 1965 ed.).*
Excerpts of noted works describing the route to attack.

John E. Wiltz, *From Isolation to War, 1931-1941* (New York: Thomas Y. Crowell Co., 1968).*
An introduction to relevant themes and controversy.

Term Projects:

A. What steps would you have taken to avoid war with Japan?

B. Was Pearl Harbor a surprise? Write a detailed answer.

CHECKUP FOR STUDY

Name: ______________________________

1. What does the Theme title mean?

2. In your own words define "neo-isolationism."

3. Why did Americans in the 1920's desire isolationism?

4. Explain the argument that the Americans were not extreme isolationists in the inter-war period.

To remove this page: Open the book as wide as possible several times to loosen this page from the binding. Lay the book flat on your desk and gently but firmly pull this page *straight up* and away from the binding from top to bottom.

5. What events hindered Japanese-American relations in the 1930's?

6. Why did the Japanese feel bitter toward Americans before 1930?

7. Briefly stated, what is the Schroeder thesis?

8. Why is it difficult to explain the cause of Pearl Harbor?

9.

10.

"They certainly don't look like Commies to me."
The New Yorker, XXXVI, August 27, 1960, p. 21

22 The National Obsession

MARXISM: Named after Karl Marx (1818-1883), a form of socialist philosophy which emphasizes public ownership instead of private ownership; the inevitability of class warfare; the necessity of a working class dictatorship; and the eventual "withering away" of government—all as a means of arriving at a classless society.

REFERENCE DATES:

1848	The first Marxian Socialists immigrated to America
1900-1901	Social Democrats formed the Socialist Party
1919-1920	Red Scare initiated; Communist Party created; Palmer Raids authorized

1935-1939	"United Front" approach attracted American intellectuals to Communist Party
1948-1950	Alger Hiss case
1950-1954	McCarthyism at its peak: Internal Security Act, Rosenbergs executed, Oppenheimer case, Army-McCarthy hearings

Is America in Grave Internal Danger?

For several decades Americans have worried about and debated over internal subversion by Communists. This fear has led some Americans to create and join nearly 1,000 radical right-wing organizations, financed by wealthy individuals like Texas oilman H. L. Hunt, tax-free foundations, and large businesses, such as Eversharp, Inc., Schick Safety Razor Company, Technicolor Corporation of America and Dr. Ross Dog and Cat Food Company.

Among the right-wing organizations which have originated since World War II are the John Birch Society, American Nazi Party, Minutemen, Christian Crusade, Christian Anti-Communist Crusade, The 1976 Committee, Young Americans for Freedom, Americans for Constitutional Action, and National Americanism Commission of the American Legion. Their spokesmen, and other right-wing speakers, have bombarded the American public with warnings of imminent danger. Dan Smoot, Paul Harvey, Billy James Hargis, Fred C. Schwarz, Clarence Manion, and Gerald L. K. Smith, to mention a few, have spread this message, but none has been more successful in organizing resistance to the alleged threat than Robert Welch. In his right-winged bible, Welch identified the threat.[1]

> Communism is not a political party, nor a military organization, nor an ideological crusade, nor a rebirth of Russian imperialist ambitions, though it comprises and uses all of these parts and pretenses. Communism, in its unmistakable present reality, is wholly a conspiracy, a gigantic conspiracy to enslave mankind; an increasingly successful conspiracy controlled by determined, cunning and utterly ruthless gangsters, willing to use any means to achieve its end.

---

[1]Robert Welch, *The Blue Book of the John Birch Society* (Belmont, Mass.: John Birch Society, 1961), pp. 30-31.

Less concerned about the communist danger, Senator Stephen Young of Ohio expressed the fears of many American liberals that the greatest threat may be right-wingism itself.[2]

> Although the danger from internal communism has been lessening, the radicals of the right—in Europe they would be called fascists—now pose a dangerous threat in trying to destroy the civil liberties and institutions which are the foundations of freedom. They accuse everyone who disagrees with their brand of "Americanism" of being a Communist or Communist sympathizer. They question the integrity of our Supreme Court. They stir resentment against our participation in the United Nations. They want the income tax repealed.
>
> They try to block all foreign aid programs. They vilify foreign-born and minority-group American citizens. They spread seeds of suspicion in communities throughout the nation.
>
> The great danger today rises from the fact that millions of well-meaning Americans embrace their programs as valid solutions to the deeply complex problems which confront our nation in an age of swift change and social upheaval. . . .

When Did Socialism and Communism Begin in America?

To understand the origins of America's fear of communism is to trace the development of Marxist socialism in America. Donald D. Egbert and Stow Persons explained the difficulty of identifying the nation's first Communists.[3]

> . . . It should first be noted that "socialist" and "socialism," "communist" and "communism," are all words of relatively recent coinage, even though most of the points of view for which they stand go far back in human history. None of them in the modern sense, can be found before the 1820's, and they all originated in either England or France.

Before the mid-nineteenth century, Americans understood "socialism" to mean experiments in communal living. Those groups with a religious basis—for example, Shakers, Perfectionists and Mormons—and those

[2]*Congressional Record*, Eighty-eighth Congress, First Session, p. 15178.

[3]Donald D. Egbert and Stow Persons, *Socialism and American Life*, Vol. I (Princeton, N.J.: Princeton University Press, 1952), p. 3.

with a utopian purpose—Owenites, Fourierists and liberal Communitarians—all fit the definition of socialist. That is, they were nonmilitant middle class efforts at social improvement. Karl Marx and Frederick Engels used the term "Communist" in their 1848 "Communist Manifesto" to denote a militant working-class movement.

What Are the Nineteenth Century Roots of American Communism?

The year 1848 is eventful in American socialist history, as Theodore Draper noted.[4]

> The first Marxian Socialists in the United States were German immigrants who came over after the ill-fated German revolution of 1848. These German immigrants brought with them a degree of trade-union and political consciousness then unknown in the United States. No sooner had they arrived than they set about duplicating their old-world allegiances in their new homeland. But they did not get very far until after the Civil War. The International Workingmen's Association, the so-called First International, founded in London with the help of Karl Marx in 1864, obtained its first American section five years later.

In spite of these early roots, communism did not worry many Americans before the twentieth century. Donald D. Egbert and Stow Persons described the reasons for the lack of concern.[5]

> After the failure of the [European] Revolutions of 1848, the revolutionary form of socialism to which the name communism had become attached was now largely discredited. Gradually the name lost the militantly revolutionary implications which it had acquired on the Continent. At about the same time the word socialism was losing its narrowly sectarian connotations, partly as a result of the failure of the Owenite movement. . . . As socialism thus became a more inclusive term, it tended to assimilate and replace the word communism, so that by the mid-1860's it was widely accepted as the comprehensive name for the whole movement. . . .
>
> For many years thereafter the meaning of these words was to remain stable, until—shortly after World War I—the terms communist and communism were

---

[4]Theodore Draper, *The Roots of American Communism* (New York: The Viking Press, 1957), p. 11.

[5]Egbert and Persons, *op. cit.*, p. 4.

deliberately reestablished in Russia with all the militant and revolutionary connotations which Marx and Engels had given to them back in 1848.

Why Did the Socialist Party Fail?

During the last third of the nineteenth century, American Socialists expended much of their energies fighting among themselves. The conflict centered over the method they would use to turn the United States into a socialist nation. Some wanted to build a powerful trade union organization which could gain control over the economy and force the government into socialism. In his early years Samuel Gompers was one of these trade-unionists. But he quit the Socialists in the 1880's to help create the American Federation of Labor, a non-socialist union. Other Socialists desired direct political action. They tried to win public support for their Socialist-Labor candidates, who, if elected, would socialize America by government action. A smaller faction of anti-capitalists called anarchists believed that any form of concentrated power—as a government—was in itself destructive of equality and social justice. Thus, they desired to overthrow the government by violent means, if necessary.

By the beginning of the twentieth century, the Socialist Party formed. Heading this new political organization was Eugene Victor Debs, often a candidate for President. Only one Socialist ever won a national office, Victor Berger of Wisconsin. He held a seat in Congress for two decades. Many hundreds of other Socialists never got above state and local offices.

The reasons for this failure of the Socialist Party are multiple. Arthur A. Ekirch, Jr., outlined the Party's development.[6]

> Throughout its history the Socialist Party failed to gain the strong backing of organized labor, which had little of the class consciousness of its European fellows. After 1912 it gradually lost its former sizeable Western agrarian support. The immigrant and foreign-language federations, which made up an important part of the membership before the First World War, were expelled or went over to the Communists. Actually, however, this foreign element in the party may have been a source of weakness, repelling native Americans and drawing the Socialist Party farther toward the left. During the Twenties the Socialists were mostly a small band of intellectuals with pacifist and social-democratic sympathies.

---

[6]Arthur A. Ekirch, Jr., "The Mild Radicals," review of *The Socialist Party in America,* by David A. Shannon, in *Saturday Review,* December 1955, pp. 18, 30.

> . . . Then, when the crash of 1929 seemed to fulfill the Socialists' pessimistic analysis of the prospects of capitalism, the New Deal adopted much of their program. New third parties, more flexible in their doctrines and membership and thus better able to negotiate with the two major parties, took over the popular following that the Socialists might have been expected to recruit as a result of the Depression.

Arthur Schlesinger, Jr., gave further reasons for the Socialist Party's failure.[7]

> Mr. Shannon believes that external forces played the greatest part in the failure of American socialism. The lack of class consciousness in American society, the effective performance of capitalism in American economic life, the inbred pragmatism of the American temperament, the efficiency of liberalism as an instrumentality of reform, the grip of the two-party system in American politics—all these factors . . . militated against the success of socialism. "In a manner of speaking, it was American history that defeated the Socialists."

How Did Communism Gain Limited Popularity?

The Socialists were not the only American Marxists to organize and seek political power. As a result of the overthrow of the Russian Czarist government (1917), dissatisfied American Socialists in 1919 broke away from their party to form various left-wing radical groups. Among them was the American Communist Party.

For the next decade internal dissension characterized the American communist movement. Personal rivalries and warring factionalism prohibited any close unity or direction among radicals. Not until 1929, after Lenin had died and Stalin had risen to power, did these conflicts cease. The Stalinization of the American communist movement unified and strengthened it. It even took on a new name: The Communist Party, U.S.A.

This new party won increasing support during the 1930's. Moshe Decter explained this success.[8]

---

[7]Arthur Schlesinger, "A Party's Rise and Fall," review of Shannon's *The Socialist Party,* in *The New York Times Book Review,* 16 October 1955, pp. 7, 41.

[8]Moshe Decter, "The Great Deception," *American Heritage,* Vol. XIII (December, 1961), pp. 77-78.

How, then, could this tiny, isolated, ineffectual sect, completely controlled from Moscow, become the effective manipulator of the ideals and passions of large numbers of non-Communist Americans? The answers are to be found in a strange confluence of historical, political, and psychological factors that began to emerge clearly at the end of the 1920's. It was not the Communist party that changed its nature and so transformed the objective situation. It was the accidental historical conjunction of the right circumstances and the right intellectual climate among the American intelligentsia which the party, unchanged in nature and objective, was able to adjust to and so exploit.

The circumstances: They began with the Great Depression; then the rise of aggressive Nazism abroad and native fascism (Father Coughlin, Huey Long, Fritz Kuhn) at home; the New Deal; the Spanish Civil War; the emergence of the Soviet Union as the ostensible champion of collective security. The intellectual climate can be summed up in one phrase—the cult of Russia.

. . . .

. . . Properly speaking, that cult . . . first became a significant factor during the Depression and reached its height during the Popular Front [a pre-war coalition of communists and noncommunists against fascism] and again during the wartime alliance with Russia.

How Did Some Americans React to the Threat of Communism?

From its very beginning, Bolshevik communism found little public hospitality in the United States. Property-minded Americans viewed the Russian Revolution with displeasure. Seizing upon this national anti-communist climate, super-patriots found communism a useful excuse upon which to blame America's domestic ills. The result was the Red Scare of 1919-1920. On the surface an anti-communist development, the episode was in reality a "ferocious outbreak of nativism" (anti-foreignism), in the opinion of Stanley Coben.[9]

. . . Rather, the Red Scare . . . was brought on largely by a number of severe social and economic dislocations which threatened the national equilibrium. . . . Runaway prices, a brief but sharp stock market crash and business depression throughout Europe, widespread fear of domestic revolt, bomb explosions, and an outpouring of radical literature were distressing enough. These sudden difficulties, moreover, served to exaggerate the disruptive effects already produced by the social and intellectual ravages of the World War and the

---

[9]Stanley Coben, "A Study in Nativism," *Political Science Quarterly,* Vol. LXXIX (1964), p. 59.

preceding reform era, and by the arrival, before the war, of millions of new immigrants. This added stress intensified the hostility of Americans strongly antagonistic to minority groups, and brought new converts to blatant nativism from among those who ordinarily were not overtly hostile toward radicals or recent immigrants.

Citizens who joined the crusade for one hundred per cent Americanism sought, primarily, a unifying force which would halt the apparent disintegration of their culture. The movement, they felt, would eliminate those foreign influences which the one hundred per centers believed were the major cause of their anxiety.

Although anti-foreignism abated after the 1920's, anti-communism did not, as Robert A. Rosenstone suggested.[10]

Common among rightist groups, especially in the twentieth century, has been an anti-Negro, anti-Semitic, anti-foreign and often anti-Catholic ideology. Along with this, ever since the Russian Revolution, all extreme groups on the right have shared a militant anti-communism. For reasons that have never been satisfactorily explained, between the thirties and the late forties the feelings against Negroes, Jews, Catholics and foreigners seem to have receded from the panoply of acknowledged rightist beliefs. At least they were subsumed into an increasingly violent anti-communism. Thus Senator Joseph McCarthy, leader of a rightist crusade in the early fifties, was himself a Catholic, and two of his chief aides (Roy Cohn and David Schine) were Jews. Somehow these once-foreign elements had Americanized themselves, and they were able to join with older-stock Americans in a militant front against what they usually termed "atheistic communism." This is not to say that all anti-Semitic, anti-Catholic, anti-Negro "hate groups" disappeared from the American scene. But those that remain are truly part of a dwindling "lunatic fringe" and far less important in numbers, financial resources and influence than organizations like the John Birch Society, which concentrate solely on the menace of communism.

Thus it was, with the advent of the Cold War in 1945 between Russia and the United States, that communism became increasingly threatening to the right wing. With disclosures that some Communists had gained employment in Washington during the war, the nation became alarmed,

---

[10]Robert A. Rosenstone, *Protest from the Right* (Beverly Hills: Glencoe Press, 1968), Introduction.

even though President Truman quickly removed them. Fear accelerated in 1948 when Whittaker Chambers, an ex-Communist, accused State Department official Alger Hiss of spying. House Un-American Committeeman Richard M. Nixon prosecuted Hiss. Eventually, after two trials, a court convicted Hiss for perjury, not espionage. The time was ripe for Senator Joseph McCarthy of Wisconsin.

What Is the Lesson That McCarthyism Taught?

Charging that the Truman Administration was full of spies, at first 207, but later just "a lot," McCarthy gained widespread support for his anti-communist charges, enough for some to think that he might become President. After the election of Dwight Eisenhower in 1952, however, and McCarthy's ill-fated attempt to purge the U.S. Army of Communists in 1954, he lost power quickly. The public had tired of the "Red issue," but not forever, as John Cogley asserted.[11]

The McCarthy movement demonstrated a deep-rooted distrust of American institutions, even while it lavished verbal praise upon them. It was the McCarthyist position, for instance, that freedom of the press as it was practiced in this country led to innumerable local editions of the *Daily Worker*. It was the McCarthyist position that academic freedom had in fact led to treasonable doctrines being taught at America's greatest universities. It was the McCarthyist position that political freedom had resulted in "twenty years of treason."

But for all this discontent with the actual workings of democracy, there was no forthright attack on democratic methods or democratic institutions. Clearly the U.S. was going to hell in a basket. But the next logical step was never taken. No one suggested that we should change our democratic framework. The McCarthy assault was not abstract but focused on the concrete results of democracy.

Such attacks can always be made and will probably have a certain validity. For it is of the nature of democracy that the wrong-headed will get a hearing with the wise; that the guilty will have the refuge of civil liberties along with the innocent; that the liar will share the platform with the truth-teller. Democracy is a dangerous business, and we should have known this before Senator

[11]John Cogley, "McCarthyism Revisited," *The Commonweal,* Vol. LXII (1951), p. 151.

McCarthy dramatized it. We should have known that we cannot have democracy without constant hazard.

. . . .

The abuse of democratic institutions should have been taken for granted. The price should have been paid willingly. But as long as people think that democracy is "safe" and fool-proof, ripe pickings for the next Senator McCarthy who comes along will remain.

This, it seems to me, is an essential lesson to be learned from the McCarthy experience. . . .

. . . .

Unfortunately, Senator McCarthy was not defeated on principle. The basic issues the controversy raised still remain to be settled. Until they are, either [a] Senator McCarthy or a reasonable facsimile may reappear at any time—and who knows with what success?

Summary

The lack of concern about the threat of Marxism to the United States in the nineteenth century appears surprising when compared to some Americans' obsessive fear of communism today. Apparently the Red Scare and McCarthyism have overshadowed the failure of Marxism to capture the public fancy, either politically or intellectually. The decline of the Socialist Party and the Communist Party, U.S.A. since World War II reflects this failure.

Selected References:

Benjamin R. Epstein and Arnold Foester, *Radical Right: Report on the John Birch Society & Allies* (New York: Random House, 1966).*
An analysis including background, finances and related interests.

Earl Latham, *The Meaning of McCarthyism,* Problems in American Civilization (Boston: D. C. Heath & Co., 1965).*
An explanation of the subject through excerpts from noted works.

Robert A. Rosenstone, *Protest From the Right* (Beverly Hills: Glencoe Press, 1968).*
A collection of documents and source materials introducing the subject.

David A. Shannon, *The Socialist Party of America* (New York: Macmillan Co., 1955).*
A study of twentieth century socialism in the United States.

TERM PROJECTS:

A. Write an essay on the rise of either right-wingism or left-wingism since 1945.

B. Investigate anarchism in nineteenth century America.

CHECKUP FOR STUDY

Name: ______________________________

1. How does the cartoon relate to the Theme topic?

2. Briefly describe pre-Civil War Socialism.

3. Why did the term "communism" change in meaning after 1917?

4. What has divided American socialists?

To remove this page: Open the book as wide as possible several times to loosen this page from the binding. Lay the book flat on your desk and gently but firmly pull this page *straight up* and away from the binding from top to bottom.

5. How could “American history” defeat socialism?

6. How red was the Red Scare?

7. How did McCarthyism differ from the Red Scare?

8. Comment: “McCarthyites show a distrust of American institutions.”

9.

10.

Soul brothers

San Francisco Chronicle, p. 34, Sec. 3,
Wednesday, September 18, 1968

23 The House Dividing

RACISM: The belief that not environment but "race is the primary determinant of human traits and capacities . . . ," as Webster states, and that these racial diversities "produce an inherent superiority of a particular race."

REFERENCE DATES:

1550-1600 White racism emerged in Elizabethan England

1861-1865 White racism intensified with Civil War emancipation

1917-1919 Black migration north, riots and the re-emergence of the Ku Klux Klan

1954-1965	"Non-violent" phase of civil rights movement; segregation legally defeated in Civil Rights Acts of 1964 and 1965
1965-1967	Peak of ghetto riots; "Black Power" emerged a popular slogan
1968	*Report of the National Advisory Commission on Civil Disorders* issued

HAS RACISM DIVIDED THE NATION?

In the first half of the twentieth century, the lure of economic improvement and the displacement of agricultural laborers by technological advances have propelled poor illiterate black people into southern urban slums and northern and western industrial ghettos. Checked, blacks posed few problems to urban whites. Unchecked, when blacks crossed the racial barrier, at a beach, in job competition, by purchasing a home, etc., racial disturbances have frequently occurred.

Continued ghetto poverty and white suburban affluence have led to growing black resentment during the past generation. By the mid-1960's, racial violence erupted on a scale unprecedented in American history. Disturbed by this disruption, in 1967 President Lyndon B. Johnson appointed Illinois Governor Otto Kerner to head a committee to investigate the causes of such strife. Their report concluded that white racism lay behind much of America's civil disorders. "Our nation is moving toward two societies, one black, one white–separate and unequal," the Kerner report prophesied, unless the nation acted quickly and was willing to pay the price for equality.[1]

In its prediction, the Commission report tends to have missed the point if one considers the historical development of racism in America. Regardless of our Pledge of Allegiance, which states, "one nation...indivisible," this country has never had one society. Because of racism, Americans have always co-existed in a dual society, one black and one white. The remainder of this Theme will analyze aspects of this interpretation.

---

[1]*Report of the National Advisory Commission on Civil Disorders* (Washington, D.C., 1968).

Who Is Prejudiced?

To begin with, no one, black or white, is free of prejudice, as Harry Ferguson asserted.[2]

No person who ever lived, including the most venerated of saints, has ever been free of prejudice.

. . . Mohammed was prejudiced against the merchants of Mecca and killed as many of them as he could.

Jesus Christ was prejudiced against the money changers and drove them from the Jerusalem temple.

Prejudice speaks all languages, violates all boundaries, swims all seas and oceans, strolls the boulevards and walks uncharted jungle trails, seeps through keyholes, feels equally at home in palace or hovel and can blanket an entire city or nation like a malignant fog.

But there are two things prejudice cannot do—see and think. For prejudice is blind and incapable of rational reasoning.

How Did White Racism in America Originate?

The fact that all of us have prejudices does not explain why white men have discriminated against those of black skin. In a review of several recent books on racial relations, J. H. Plumb investigated why whites enslaved blacks and perpetuated prejudice against them.[3]

New World slavery raises two very serious questions. Why was it so easily accepted by all Western European nations at a time when slavery had ceased to be socially important? And, secondly, why did abolitionists become socially and politically effective from the last third of the eighteenth century onward? . . . This brings one to Winthrop D. Jordan's outstanding book.[4] . . . Jordan's thesis is straightforward. The Elizabethan Englishmen coming across primitive black men for the first time were repelled. To them black men were

---

[2]Harry Ferguson, "The Ancient Killer That Walks With Man," *San Francisco Sunday Examiner and Chronicle,* 5 May 1968, Section B, p. 6.

[3]J. H. Plumb, "Slavery, Race, and the Poor," *The New York Review of Books,* Vol. XII, March 13, 1969, p. 3. © 1969/1968 by The New York Times Company. Reprinted by permission.

[4]Winthrop D. Jordan, *White over Black: American Attitudes Toward the Negro, 1550-1812* (Chapel Hill: University of North Carolina Press, 1968).

associated with beastliness; their inferiority made them the lowest link in the Great Chain of Being. Blackness stimulated the Englishman's sense of guilt and horror. His Devil was, after all, black, and he always put a high price upon fairness of skin. The primitive societies of West Africa, with their strange and divergent customs, strengthened the Elizabethan's belief in the eternal, God-given inferiority of the Negro—a little higher, maybe, than the apes, but infinitely lower than the white Englishman. . . .

Hence the proper status of Negroes was slavery. Slavery fitted their natures whose outward sign was the blackness of their skin. And it was because they were black that it became easier to justify slavery and maintain it. . . .

. . . Jordan contends, with much quotation from Elizabethan literature and from African travelers' tales, that the sixteenth-century Englishman regarded the Negro as not only savage, heathen, biologically close to the ape, but also as theologically damned; for the Negro was descended from Ham, Noah's disinherited son, who was cursed by having black offspring. What was more, the Englishman's Devil was always portrayed as black, so Negroes were associated with evil and linked ever more firmly to God's curse. . . .

These attitudes toward the Negroes made the enslavement of them by the English both natural and ferocious. . . . From start to finish American slavery had an extensive racial quality: indeed Jordan calls it racial slavery. . . . Negroes were considered born inferiors, born slaves if you will, to a degree that was never applied to many other groups of slaves. The Roman slave was treated just as brutally, at times far more brutally, than the Southern Negro. He certainly possessed no more rights. But, once freed, the world was open to him. He and his family could rise or fall like any other man in the Roman state, so long as he had either ability or money or both. Not so the Negro. The freed Negro entered a caste which was excluded from most of the benefits and all of the power in the society to which it belonged. And the basis of this exclusion was racial. . . .

Historically, racism in America has had a deep connection with poverty, according to J. H. Plumb.[5]

The type of abuse that was hurled at the slave was hurled at the poor: particularly in English society, from which many Southern slave masters were drawn. . . .

. . . [These poor received] bloody whippings, frequent branding, and enforced labor. The early slave codes were very similar to the legislation designed to control the Elizabethan unemployed poor. Again, the poor were, it is now thought, expected neither to go to Church nor to be welcomed there. . . .

---

[5]Plumb, *op. cit.*, p. 4.

Again, miscegenation: the taboos against marrying the poor were formidable; for a woman it usually meant total ostracism. Yet, of course, the young servant women, like slave Negresses, could be and were fair game for their masters. Even the Sambo mentality can be found in the deliberately stupid country yokel or the cockney clown of later centuries. So, too, the belief, as with Negroes, that they were abandoned sexually, given to both promiscuity and over-indulgence. . . .

. . . .

Just as a discussion of slavery without a consideration of the exploitation of other laborers tend to obscure fundamental issues, so too can racism and questions of civil rights obscure the deeper issues. No amount of civil rights can alleviate the Negro's lot, for much of the hatred of the blacks springs from the rich's fear of the poor and dispossessed. The basis of the problem is exploitation: the gross injustice which acquisitive society always inflicts on those who have nothing to offer but their body's labor. . . .

How Did Free Blacks Fare?

Black slaves lived a separate life; in that sense they were of a different caste from whites. But what of free blacks? They numbered nearly one-half million by the Civil War, about one-quarter million of whom lived in the upper South. There they had to possess a certificate of freedom, or risk their return into slavery. Free blacks could not move about easily among the states or exercise many of the constitutional freedoms which white men guarded so jealously. They lived a free but separate existence.

The other quarter million free blacks lived north of the Mason-Dixon line. There, too, they existed separately before the Civil War, as Leon F. Litwack described.[6]

. . . The northern Negro remained largely disfranchised, segregated, and economically oppressed. Discrimination still barred him from most polls, juries, schools, and workshops, as well as from many libraries, theaters, lyceums, museums, public conveyances, and literary societies. Although he himself was responsible for this exclusion, the white man effectively turned it against the Negro. Having excluded the Negro from profitable employments, the whites scorned his idleness and poverty; having taxed him in some states

[6]Leon F. Litwack, *North of Slavery: The Negro in the Free States, 1790-1860* (Chicago: University of Chicago Press, 1961), p. 279.

for the support of public education, they excluded his children from the schools or placed them in separate and inferior institutions and then deplored the ignorance of his race; having excluded him from various lecture halls and libraries, they pointed to his lack of culture and refinement; and, finally, having stripped him of his claims to citizenship and having deprived him of opportunities for political and economic advancement, the whites concluded that the Negro had demonstrated an incapacity for improvement in this country and should be colonized in Africa. Nevertheless, most Negroes remained in the United States and chose to die on American soil, knowing full well that social proscription would follow them to the grave. Symbolic of the Negro's position in the ante-bellum North was the public cemetery, or potter's field, of Cincinnati: whites were buried east to west and Negroes north to south. After all, white supremacy had to be preserved, even among the dead.

Why Did Emancipation Not Bring Equality?

The Union victory in the Civil War provided black people with freedom; it did not give them equality or integrate them into white society. Among the reasons for this failure to unite the nation are three which stand out clearly. First, most abolitionists demanded an end to slavery, but like other Americans few wanted integration. As Leon F. Litwack has observed: "Abraham Lincoln, in his vigorous support of both white supremacy and denial of equal rights for Negroes, simply gave expression to almost universal American convictions."[7] One of those few who did favor equal rights was William Lloyd Garrison, according to a review by C. Vann Woodward.[8]

> . . . His big thing was that abolitionism was a *radical* and not a reform movement, that slavery, and the racial dogmas that justified it so thoroughly, permeated American society and government, North as well as South, that the eradication of the institution and its ideological defenses—and the racism of the latter was as important to him as slavery—was a root-and-branch operation. On that he never equivocated.
>
> Garrison's abolitionist opponents were reformers, not radicals. . . . They believed that American society, government, and institutions were fundamentally sound and that once the alien institution of slavery was removed, all would be well. . . .

---

[7]*Ibid*, p. vii.

[8]C. Vann Woodward, "White Racism and Black 'Emancipation'," *The New York Review of Books,* 29 February 1969, p. 5.

Second, emancipation was a military measure, not one based upon a consensus of sympathy for the slave. C. Vann Woodward argued that the results were not beneficial.[9]

Convincing evidence supports the conclusion that the outbreak of the Civil War actually "increased the virulence of midwestern racism." For the war opened the prospect of an inundation of the North by fugitive or liberated Negroes. . . .

. . . .

The backlash to emancipation was frightening. Republicans suffered a disastrous defeat at the polls in the fall of 1862. . . .

. . . .

. . . [Thus] "in most places Negroes remained fundamentally as before —victims of discrimination, . . . of social ostracism, and of economic subordination."

Third, as Reconstruction fever subsided, enthusiasm for solving the freedman's problems waned, as Kenneth M. Stampp explained.[10]

. . . When radical Republicans used federal power to interfere in these matters, the majority of southern white men formed a resistance movement to fight the radical-dominated state governments until they were overthrown, after which southern whites established a caste system in defiance of federal statutes and constitutional amendments. For many decades thereafter the federal government simply admitted defeat and acquiesced; but the South refused to forget or forgive those years of humiliation when Negroes came close to winning equality. In southern mythology, then, reconstruction was a horrid nightmare.

As for the majority of northern white men, it is hard to tell how deeply they were concerned about the welfare of the American Negro after the abolition of slavery. If one were to judge from the way they treated the small number of free Negroes who resided in the northern states, one might conclude that they were, at best, indifferent to the problem—and that a considerable number of them shared the racial attitudes of the South and preferred to keep Negroes in a subordinate caste. For a time after the Civil War the radical Republicans, who were always a minority group, persuaded the northern electorate that the ultimate purpose of southern white men was to rob the North of the fruits of victory and to re-establish slavery and that federal

---

[9]*Ibid*, pp. 8-9.

[10]Kenneth M. Stampp, *The Era of Reconstruction, 1865-1877* (New York: Vintage Books, 1965), pp. 14-15. Copyright © 1965 by Kenneth M. Stampp. Reprinted by permission of Alfred A. Knopf, Inc.

intervention was therefore essential. In this manner radicals won approval of, or acquiescence in, their program to give civil rights and the ballot to southern Negroes. Popular support for the radical program waned rapidly, however, and by the middle of the 1870's it had all but vanished. In 1875 a Republican politician confessed that northern voters were tired of the "worn-out cry of 'southern outrages'," and they wished that "the 'nigger' the 'everlasting nigger' were in . . . Africa."

How Have Whites Treated Blacks Since Reconstruction?

The end of Reconstruction in 1877 was not the beginning of a new day in racial relations among blacks and whites. For approximately one century, from that time to the present, the bulk of black people have lived in a separate society within the boundaries of the United States. As C. Vann Woodward has lamented, "it seems harder than ever to locate precisely that legendary 'interlude of virtue' when Americans renounced their racism and rededicated themselves to their ideals of equality. The present seems depressingly continuous with the past."[11]

Black people have lived a life of social isolation, North, South and West. Segregated by Jim Crow laws, economics and prejudice, his has been a life of poverty and fear. Sometimes fanatical white racists have used lynchings to keep him in line. By 1951, of the nearly 5,000 reported lynchings in the nation since Reconstruction, about two-thirds of the victims were blacks. Though most such acts took place in the South—Mississippi and Georgia provided around 500 each—Illinois and Ohio, for example, lynched more blacks than whites.[12]

Why Has Black Power Gained Support?

In recent years increasing numbers of black people have moved toward a more militant resistance to white racism. Christopher Lasch suggested the causes of this movement.[13]

---

[11]Woodward, *op. cit.*, p. 11.

[12]*Negro Year Book* (New York: William H. Wise, 1952), p. 273.

[13]Christopher Lasch, "The Trouble With Black Power," *The New York Review of Books,* Vol. X, February 29, 1968, pp. 4-5.

Whatever else "Black Power" means, the slogan itself indicates that the movement for racial equality has entered a new phase. . . . "Black Power" articulates, at the very least, a new sense of urgency, if not a sense of impending crisis. Together with last summer's riots, it challenges the belief, until recently widespread, that the United States is making substantial progress toward racial justice. . . .

. . . "We shall overcome" no longer expresses the spirit of the struggle. Race war seems a more likely prospect. . . . In the form in which it existed until 1963 or 1964, the civil rights movement is dead: this is not a conjecture but a historical fact. . . .

. . . Why has "Black Power" displaced "freedom" as the rallying-point of Negro militancy?

There are several reasons for this change. The most obvious is that the apparent victories of the civil rights coalition have not brought about any discernible changes in the lives of most Negroes, at least not in the North. . . . Even the most superficial accounts of the summer's riots see the connection between hopes raised by civil rights agitation and the Negroes' disappointing realization that this agitation, whatever its apparent successes, has nevertheless failed to relieve the tangible miseries of ghetto life.

. . . .

. . . [Furthermore,] American history seems to show that a group cannot achieve "integration"—that is, equality—without first developing institutions which express and create a sense of its own distinctiveness. That is why black nationalism, which attempts to fill the cultural vacuum of the ghetto, has had a continuing attraction for Negroes, and why, even during the period of its eclipse in the Thirties, Forties, and Fifties, nationalism won converts among the most despised and degraded elements of the Negro community. . . .

Is Black Nationalism Another Term for Black Racism?

To critics of black nationalism, the movement possesses racist overtones. Self-imposed segregation, assertions of black superiority, the rejection of established white social values, all reek of racial hatred resulting from decades of inequality. To answer such charges, Christopher Lasch echoed the feelings of black separatists.[14]

. . . Those who see in the Black Muslims no more than "the hate that hate produced" mistake the character of this movement. . . . The Muslim style of

[14] *Ibid*, p. 5.

life . . . "has definitely provided an escape from degradation for lower-class Negroes." If anyone doubts this, he should consider the Muslims' well-documented success in redeeming, where others have failed, drug pushers, addicts, pimps, criminals of every type, the dregs of the slums. . . .

. . . Without necessarily abandoning the myth of the Negroes as a chosen people, the new-style nationalists have secularized this myth by identifying the American Negroes . . . with the contemporary struggle against colonialism in the third world. . . . Many of the younger nationalists propose to fight it out here in America, by revolutionary means if necessary, and to establish—what? a black America? an America in which black people can survive as a separate "nation"? an integrated America?

Summary

While the Kerner Report suggests that the nation is on the verge of dividing racially, a survey of race relations throughout American history indicates that the nation has never been racially united. Ever since the arrival of the first "Negar" into the English colonies in North America, white racism has been the prevailing characteristic of black-white relations. Emancipation failed to terminate the racist attitude. Recently "Black Power" has reflected a more militant reaction of black people to racism.

Selected References:

John Hope Franklin, *From Slavery to Freedom, A History of Negro Americans* (New York: Alfred A. Knopf, 1967 ed.).
A scholarly account ranging from life in Africa to the present racial crisis.

Alan P. Grimes, *Equality in America: Religion, Race, and the Urban Majority* (New York: Oxford University Press, 1964).*
Three interpretive essays on prejudice interweaving history and sociology.

United States Presidential Commission on Civil Disorders, *Report of the National Advisory Commission on Civil Disorders* (Washington, D.C.: Government Printing Office, 1968).*
The Kerner report, for better or for worse, provides many insights into the ugliness which is America.

Harvey Wish, ed., *The Negro Since Emancipation* (Englewood Cliffs, N.J.: Prentice-Hall, 1964).*
Biographies of and excerpts from the writings of noted Negroes beginning with Frederick Douglass and concluding with Elijah Muhammed.

TERM PROJECTS:

A. Read the Kerner Report and reviews of it. Then write a critical analysis of civil disorders in the United States today.

B. Discuss the contributions of any one American black person who lived after Reconstruction and before World War II.

CHECKUP FOR STUDY

Name: ______________________________

1. Why did Englishmen enslave Africans?

2. How did English poverty affect American slaves?

3. Comment: "Once a fugitive slave entered the North, equality awaited him."

4. What is the difference between a "radical" and a "reforming" abolitionist?

To remove this page: Open the book as wide as possible several times to loosen this page from the binding. Lay the book flat on your desk and gently but firmly pull this page *straight up* and away from the binding from top to bottom.

5. With so few free blacks in the North, why did northerners oppose emancipation?

6. How did northerners permit southerners to check freedmen after Reconstruction?

7. Why is the present "depressingly continuous with the past"?

8. Define "Black Power" in your own words.

9.

10.

EVOLUTION
From the Infinite Variety of Nature to the Universal Pudd'nhead

24 What A Character!

NATIONAL CHARACTER: That which distinguishes one nationality from another, as a German from a Frenchman, or a native of China from a person of Japanese origin.

SELECTED POPULATION STATISTICS OF THE UNITED STATES

(Compiled from U.S. Bureau of the Census Reports)

Selected Years	*Total Population*	*Particular Group*	*Group Population*	*Per Cent*
1600	---	Indians	750,000 est.	100
1690	210,000	Negroes	17,000	8.1
1790	3,900,000	English-blooded	2,380,000	61
1860	31,500,000	Negroes	4,440,000	14.1

Selected Years	*Total Population*	*Particular Group*	*Group Population*	*Per Cent*
1880	50,200,000	Reservation Indians	256,000	0.5
		People under 25 years	14,721,000	29.2
1900	76,300,000	Foreign Born	10,341,000	13.6
1970	205,000,000 est.	People under 25 years	95,000,000 est.	46
		Negroes	22,800,000 est.	11
		Indians	600,000 est.	0.3
		Foreign Born	10,250,000 est.	5

Why Investigate the American Character?

Most modern Americans are the descendants of immigrants from various backgrounds. Yet, today, citizens of the United States think of themselves as "Americans." Is there any cultural meaning to this term? What traits distinguish an American from a person of another nationality? Are there any such traits?

Writers have argued over these questions for generations and their interpretations vary widely. Their disagreement should not discourage one from examining the subject. Michael McGiffert pointed out the reasons why the investigation should continue.[1]

. . . To say that Americans are different–which collectively they are, though the implications need not be invidious–is not to say that they are radically different–which is not necessarily so. The task of investigation is to check the proposition of exceptionalism by examining the nature and extent of supposed characterological differences.

Critics of the concept of national character sometimes object that excessive attention to the peculiarities of nations is pernicious because it impedes the realization of an international or supranational community of mankind. It is contended that "men are more alike" and that the differences which divide the nations ought to be de-emphasized in the interest of world order and concord. Such remonstrances, however well intended, appear to be misdirected: national differences will not be wished away by refusal to examine them, let alone by denying that they exist. On the contrary, quite aside from national strategies of survival, the general interests of humanity are better served by candid assessment of differences to the end that erroneous stereotypes may be corrected and avenues of international communication may be

[1]Michael McGiffert, ed., *The Character of Americans: A Book of Readings* (Homewood, Ill.: The Dorsey Press, 1964) p. ix. Reprinted with permission.

improved. Furthermore, the investigation of national character is not restricted to the elements of contrast; correctly conceived, although the inquiry may sometimes be warped to the purposes of chauvinism and propaganda, it is concerned as much with the transnational congruities of character as with culturally conditioned differences. This fact furnishes an additional argument for comparative studies of national character.

In this Theme we shall explore several perceptible traits which Americans exhibit and which may, or may not, be characteristic of them. These include a homogenized population, a sense of equality, a pronounced mobility and a marked abundance.

Are Americans Unique Cultural Beings?

The search for an American identity can begin with the question of uniqueness. Do Americans have a separate cultural basis? One of the earliest examinations of the subject came in 1792 from Hector St. John de Crèvecoeur. Born in France and a long-standing resident of New York (though he referred to himself as a Pennsylvanian), Crèvecoeur saw the American as a new entity.[2]

> . . . What then is the American, this new man? He is either a European, or the descendant of a European, hence that strange mixture of blood, which you will find in no other country. I could point out to you a family whose grandfather was an Englishman, whose wife was Dutch, whose son married a French woman, and whose present four sons have now four wives of different nations. *He* is an American, who leaving behind him all his ancient prejudices and manners, receives new ones from the new mode of life he has embraced, the new government he obeys, and the new rank he holds. He becomes an American by being received in the broad lap of our great *Alma Mater*. Here individuals of all nations are melted into a new race of men, whose labours and posterity will one day cause great changes in the world. Americans are the western pilgrims, who are carrying along with them that great mass of arts, sciences, vigour, and industry which began long since in the east; they will finish the great circle. The Americans were once scattered all over Europe; here they are incorporated into one of the finest systems of population which has ever appeared, and which will hereafter become distinct by the power of the different climates they inhabit.

---

[2]Hector St. John de Crèvecœur, *Letters from an American Farmer* (New York: E. P. Dutton and Co., 1912), pp. 43-44.

Modern writers refer to the concept which Crèvecoeur suggested as the "melting pot" theory, a term dating back to the early years of this century. Philip Gleason discussed the popularity of this concept among people in many walks of life.[3]

> . . . References to the melting pot appears not only in formal studies of ethnic adjustment in the United States, but the expression is also used by foreign observers and it crops up frequently in the press as well. A Chicago newspaper, for example, editorially commented the selection of Miss Hawaii to represent the United States in the 1962 Miss Universe contest because she was the "typical child" of "a true American-style 'melting-pot.' " . . . Television and the advertising industry also make use of the symbol. . . . An advertisement for a recent book on cities asks: "Cities and suburbs–melting pots or trouble spots?"

The validity of using the term "melting pot" in characterizing an American is highly debatable. Philip Gleason also presented the viewpoint of those who challenge the theory.[4]

> Perhaps the most serious distortion of understanding that the melting pot symbolism entailed was the notion of uniformity of product. That which comes out of a melting pot we think of as uniform in color, consistency, texture and other qualities; the repeated use of melting pot symbolism reinforced, if it did not generate, the expectation that the result of ethnic interaction should also be absolutely uniform. It is this emphasis on uniformity which more than anything else has caused liberals to condemn the melting pot "theory."

At any rate, Americans melt mainly within their own racial, religious or ethnic groups. Italian Roman Catholics will marry German Roman Catholics, but few tend to mary German Protestants or Jews. Chinese-Americans frequently marry Chinese-Americans rather than the descendants of Japanese, Koreans or Filipinos.

Does Equality Identify an American?

If Americans appear to be a conglomeration of various cultural groups rather than one separate entity, perhaps these people have a common

---

[3]Philip Gleason, "The Melting Pot: Symbol of Fusion or Confusion?" *American Quarterly,* Vol. XVI (1964), pp. 20-21.

[4]*Ibid*, p. 44.

bond which identifies them. The young French aristocrat, Alexis de Tocqueville, after a nine-month tour of America (1831-32) during the Jacksonian age, offered an answer to the problem of identity.[5]

> Amongst the novel objects that attracted my attention during my stay in the United States, nothing struck me more forcibly than the general equality of conditions. I readily discovered the prodigious influence which this primary fact exercises on the whole course of society, by giving a certain direction to public opinion, and a certain tenor to the laws; by imparting new maxims to the governing powers, and peculiar habits to the governed. I speedily perceived that the influence of this fact extends far beyond the political character and the laws of the country, and that it has no less empire over civil society than over the Government; it creates opinions, engenders sentiments, suggests the ordinary practices of life, and modifies whatever it does not produce. The more I advanced in the study of American society, the more I perceived that the equality of conditions is the fundamental fact from which all others seem to be derived, and the central point at which all my observations constantly terminated.

If we are to believe Marcus Cunliffe, the equality of conditions is a basically unchanged quality of the American character.[6]

> . . . The American character seems to have been formed in essence within a generation of George Washington's accession to the presidency. How else are we to account for the remarkable freshness, even for the present day, of Alexis de Tocqueville's *Democracy in America,* which was based on a visit to the United States in 1831-32? "National character" is a hazy expression. But for our approximate purposes we may think of it as an assemblage of beliefs and patterns of behavior which are widely recognized, inside and outside the country in question, as being more common among its citizens than among those of other nations. If this clumsy description is acceptable, then we may go on to suggest that Tocqueville's diagnosis of American attitudes . . . could be applied with surprising relevance to the America of 1870 or even 1950.

In considering equality as typically American, one should use caution. Alan P. Grimes qualified the concept of equality.[7]

---

[5]Alexis de Tocqueville, *Democracy in America,* Vol. I, trans. Henry Reeve, fourth edition (New York: J. and H. G. Langley, 1841), p. 1.

[6]Marcus Cunliffe, *The Nation Takes Shape: 1789-1837* (Chicago: University of Chicago Press, 1959), pp. 186-187.

[7]Alan P. Grimes, *Equality in America: Religion, Race, and the Urban Majority* (New York: Oxford University Press, 1964), pp. vii-viii.

Equality, like freedom, involves a relationship. If every man seeks to be free, every freedom-seeking man becomes in some way an obstacle in the path of someone else's freedom. . . . As much of the history of the eighteenth and nineteenth centuries demonstrated, democracy in America led to an unequal division of freedom, granting superior freedom to the majority who were Protestant in religion and white in race. In time, such an unequal distribution of freedom was challenged.

. . . Equality, as an ethical standard, recognizes the diversity of men and acknowledges differentiation while rejecting invidious discrimination; it does not, its proponents argue, level men to the lowest common denominator, but elevates them to the highest common dignity. The principle of equality, considered in this light, does not declare that all men are in fact equal; it does declare that allegations of religious and racial superiority cannot be proven, and, therefore, in the interest of public peace men ought to treat each other in these affairs as though they were equal.

How Has Mobility Molded the National Character?

One aspect of life that may have contributed to the possible equality of Americans is their mobility. Since the end of slavery Americans have had few restrictions to prevent them from moving. In comparison to persons in many other countries, Americans are more prone to move. Everett S. Lee wrote of the significance of mobility on the American character.[8]

. . . The point is that migration has been a force of greatest moment in American civilization, and that from the magnitude and character of migration within this country certain consequences logically follow. . . . It is therefore not maintained, paraphrasing [Frederick Jackson] Turner, that migration explains American civilization. It certainly does not, but that it was and is a major force in the development of American civilization and in the shaping of American character hardly anyone will deny. . . .

In America we can say that migration is a part of our way of life. We are all but a few generations removed from our immigrant ancestors, whether they landed at Plymouth Rock or Ellis Island. Within our country, migration is of such scale as to astound foreign observers. In recent years one in each five persons moved from one house to another in each twelve-month period,

---

[8]Everett S. Lee, "The Turner Thesis Reexamined," (*American Quarterly*, Vol. XIII, 1961), pp. 78-79, 83. Copyright, 1961, Trustees of the University of Pennsylvania.

one in fourteen migrated from one county to another, and one in thirty from one state to another. These are crude figures for both sexes and all ages. At the age of maximum migration, 20-24, one in six males moved from one county to another, and one in ten shifted state of residence. Over twenty per cent of the native population lives outside the state of birth, but again this is a weighted average for all ages and makes the incidence of interstate migration seem smaller than it is since at ages fifty and thereafter nearly two out of five native Americans have set up residence outside the state of birth. Migration of this order has been the rule rather than the exception in American history and . . . the present high level of interstate migration has existed since at least 1850.

. . . We are indeed a nation of migrants and we always have been.

. . . .

. . . Migration has been phenomenally successful for Americans. The immigrant from abroad did find superior economic opportunities and if they were fleeing oppression they found freedom. Within our country the major flows of migration have been from areas of lower to higher economic returns. . . . The natural interpretation by the migrant is that migration has been a good thing; having done it once he is willing to do it again if another area looks more attractive. This attitude he imparts to his children and to nonmigrants with whom he comes in contact. . . .

. . . It is maintained, however, that from a psychological and sociological, as well as from an economic, point of view, migration is one of the most important factors in American civilization. There are few characteristics which are shared by so many Americans as migrant status and spatial movement. . . .

What Influence Has Abundance Played?

A final point to consider in the examination of the American character is the importance of national abundance. In 1954 David M. Potter completed his notable book *People of Plenty: Abundance and the American Character*. The message is thought provoking, as the review by Gary MacEoin suggested.[9]

. . . Abundance is partly a physical and partly a cultural manifestation. The physical assets of this country existed when men first set foot here

---

[9]Gary MacEoin, "Abundance and Outlook," *Commonweal,* Vol. LXI (1954), p. 74.

countless centuries ago, but they have been converted into abundance only in the past two hundred years. Other countries have comparable assets but none has ever created an economy of abundance.

We have in consequence a social conditioning different from that of all other peoples, past and present. . . . Even the infant has a unique set of experiences. His parents are younger than those of other "advanced" societies. His mother's milk is substituted or supplemented by other foods. He sleeps in a separate room. He is kept warm without being wrapped in heavy clothes. Diaper services make possible the postponement of toilet training. At an early age he is launched on the tremendous competitive race which is the corollary of the American freedom to advance, a race which will continue all through life, since social pressures of a society in which consumption is the main goal tend to identify a full life with the ability to consume spectacularly.

In another review, Karl W. Deutsch pointed out other consequences of American abundance.[10]

This abundance has strengthened some of our tendencies toward generosity and gentleness. On the other hand, in conjunction with social mobility and intense competition, it has enhanced some of our feelings of insecurity, and our anxieties for status and prestige which psychologists have noted. In the growth of our cities, it made millions turn from the frontier long before free land was exhausted. In connection with the mass market, abundance has given rise to mass advertising, which sees man at bottom only as a consumer, and must try to teach him so to see himself.

While economic abundance has made American democracy appear natural to Americans, "to other peoples, our democracy has seemed infinitely desirable but unattainable. But, if the realities of the relationship between democracy and abundance had been understood by people of other countries or . . . by those Americans who were seeking to impart our message, our democracy would have seemed more desirable, and our abundance more attainable. Both . . . would have had the effect of strengthening the moral influence of the United States."

What Must Precede a Description of National Character?

In a review of Potter's thesis, and in a sense as a critique of the entire field of study in national character, C. Wright Mills proposed that scholars

[10]Karl W. Deutsch, "A People of Plenty in a World of Want," *Yale Review,* Vol. XLIV (1954), pp. 293-294.

approach the subject in the future from an entirely different viewpoint than that which they had pursued.[11]

. . . At least two . . . mechanisms seem to be at work in the formation of something that can be called national character.

First, as a social structure a nation consists of the roles men enact in the several major institutional areas that compose it—in the political economy and the military order, in families and churches and educational plants. Different types of men are selected for these roles and, in turn, their continuous enactment of these roles drapes their social characters. To the extent that there will, in due course, tend to be some unity of character.

A second approach is through certain types of Representative Men who are displayed in public communications before the national public as the very models of aspiration. There is The Japanese Samura or The British Gentleman or The German Junker. People tend to identify themselves with these splendidly typical figures, to try to be like them, to form their own self-images in the terms provided by such public images. To the extent that such models are nationally diffused something that might be called national character tends to prevail. The "formlessness" of "The American" and of America as a civilization is due in large part to the fact that no truly Representative Men of this sort prevail.

The weakness of most attempts to delineate a national character is that they pick out a single cause and they assume that there is a character type. Crèvecoeur asking "What then is the American, this new man?" ought to be answered: There is no one man, The American. This is not to say that we must descend into a sort of romantic pluralism, in which we can only grasp each individual as an utterly unique being. That too is literary nonsense.

At any given time it is possible—and indeed necessary to understanding—to construct types of men and women who *are* typical of the social structure of the United States or of its several major institutions. The first step in an adequate study of "national character" is the discernment of these types and their careful description. . . .

SUMMARY

Some social scientists believe that they can accurately identify national characteristics. Assuming that they are right, their studies of Americans reveal, among others, four general characteristics. These include cultural

---

[11]C. Wright Mills, "Bounteous New Man," *Saturday Review*, July 16, 1955, p. 19.

intermixing, social equality, population mobility and abundance. There are arguments both supporting and rejecting these characteristics as distinctive of Americans. In any case, one must be careful when generalizing about national characteristics.

SELECTED REFERENCES:

Orrin E. Klapp, *Heroes, Villains and Fools: The Changing American Character* (Englewood Cliffs, N.J.: Prentice-Hall, 1962).*
The American character revealed through a sociological analysis. Major social types in the American society serve as models.

Michael McGiffert, ed., *The Character of Americans: A Book of Readings* (Homewood, Ill.: The Dorsey Press, 1964).*
A wide sampling of scholarship which attempts to discover "what the American is, has been, and may become."

Melvin Steinfield, *Cracks in the Melting Pot: Readings in Racism and Discrimination in American History* (Beverly Hills: Glencoe Press, 1970).*
Contemporary writings and modern accounts of events and attitudes throughout American history. Covers experiences of numerous racial and ethnic groups.

Alexis de Tocqueville, *Democracy in America,* ed. Richard D. Heffner (New York: The New American Library of World Literature, 1956).*
One of the most perceptive examinations of Americans which a foreigner has written. Stress is on political equality.

TERM PROJECTS:

A. As an editor, make a critical analysis of Tocqueville's *Democracy in America,* explaining why you feel it is inaccurate on certain points.

B. Investigate the contributions of various racial and ethnic groups to the American way of life in fields such as food, clothing, transportation, household furnishings, arts, etc.

CHECKUP FOR STUDY

Name: ______________________________

1. Briefly define national character.

2. List some reasons why the study of national character is important.

3. To what theory does Crèvecoeur subscribe?

4. How would Grimes differ with de Tocqueville?

To remove this page: Open the book as wide as possible several times to loosen this page from the binding. Lay the book flat on your desk and gently but firmly pull this page *straight up* and away from the binding from top to bottom.

5. By Everett S. Lee's definition, are you a typical American? Why?

6. How is an American baby different from most other babies?

7. What do you find surprising in the "Selected Population Statistics" at the beginning of this Theme?

8. Explain how the cartoon illustrates the Theme topic.

9.

10.

Index

A

B

C

D

J

K

L

M

P

Q

R

S

T

U

V

W